Understanding the
Literature of World War I

To Stoney and Sparrow, with deep love, affection, and admiration.

Understanding the Literature of World War I

A STUDENT CASEBOOK TO ISSUES, SOURCES, AND HISTORICAL DOCUMENTS

James H. Meredith

14 Jan 05

The Greenwood Press
"Literature in Context" Series
Claudia Durst Johnson, Series Editor

GREENWOOD PRESS
Westport, Connecticut • London

Library of Congress Cataloging-in-Publication Data

Meredith, James H., 1955–
    Understanding the literature of World War I : a student casebook to issues, sources, and historical documents / James H. Meredith.
        p. cm.—(The Greenwood Press "Literature in context" series, ISSN 1074-598X)
    Includes bibliographical references and index.
        ISBN 0–313–31200–1 (alk. paper)
1. American literature—20th century—History and criticism—Handbooks, manuals, etc.
2. World War, 1914–1918—Literature and the war—Handbooks, manuals, etc. 3. English
literature—20th century—History and criticism—Handbooks, manuals, etc. I. Title. II.
Series.
PS228.W37M47 2004
810.9'358—dc22   2004017892

British Library Cataloguing in Publication Data is available.

Library of Congress Catalog Card Number: 2004017892
ISBN: 0–313–31200–1
ISSN: 1074–598X

First published in 2004

Greenwood Press, 88 Post Road West, Westport, CT 06881
An imprint of Greenwood Publishing Group, Inc.
www.greenwood.com

Printed in the United States of America

The paper used in this book complies with the
Permanent Paper Standard issued by the National
Information Standards Organization (Z39.48–1984).

10 9 8 7 6 5 4 3 2 1

To my wife Kathi, again; to my father James, who got me interested in military history; to my children Katie Melba and Christopher John, who give me hope for the future; and to the boys, Romeo and Henry, who stood guard at my desk throughout the project.

Contents

Acknowledgments

I'd like to thank the Dean of the Faculty and the Director of Research at the United States Air Force Academy for their inestimable help throughout this project. I could not have personally visited such places as the Imperial War Museum and the National Archive II without their consistent support. Also, I'd like to thank Colonel Tom Bowie, Lieutenant Colonel Pete Swartz, and Professor Richard Lemp, who were Department Heads during this project, for the invaluable support they all gave me. Also, I'd like to thank Jae Olson and Mary Fordham for all the administrative work they have done for me over the last several years. They have made my work a lot easier. Finally, I'd like to thank *War Literature & the Arts: A Journal of the Humanities* (http://www.wla journal.com/) for giving me a start in the war literature profession. It is an extraordinary publication.

Every reasonable effort has been made to trace the owners of copyright materials in this book, but in some instances this has proven impossible. The author and publisher will be glad to receive information leading to more complete acknowledgement in subsequent printings of the book and in the meantime extend their apologies for any omissions.

Introduction

The English teacher in me wants to write an extensive introduction about what I learned about the war while preparing this book, but the military professional in me stops me from doing so. A small part of me still regrets that I have decided, then, to save the words for those who were really there and bore witness to this historic catastrophe. I would love to say more.

Before you begin an extensive study of World War I, watch the PBS television series *The Great War and the Shaping of the 20th Century.* For me, it was a life-changing experience. Second, go to the Western Front; enough of it still remains. Go to the cemeteries and see the rows upon rows of graves. It is stunning. If that is not possible, then go to one of the many Web sites on the Internet about the Western Front. Finally, go to the Imperial War Museum in London and the National Archives in College Park, Maryland, and read the first-hand accounts of the war. If you cannot do that then get on the Internet and go to the World War I Document Archive (http://www.lib.byu.edu/~rdh/wwi/1914.html) and read their holdings. The experience is mesmerizing. Finally, join the Great War Society and browse their fabulous Internet site, "World War I: Trenches on the Web" (http://www.worldwar1.com/). In other words, get personally involved in the war.

It has been my pleasure to teach at the United States Air Force Academy since 1984. During that time, I have taught some of America's best young men and women. Over the last three years particularly, I have concentrated on World War I as the primary focus of my teaching, and my students have responded enthusiastically. There is so much outstanding literature and film about World War I that there should never be a dull moment in the classroom, and there wasn't. One aspect of the war that they understood emphatically was that while the weapons of war have gotten far more sophisticated in the intervening years, military service, whether it involves combat or not, has not fundamentally changed at all. Although only a very few cadets have had military service prior to their appointment to the Academy, they all could easily empathize with the soldiers going "over the top," which was a term first used in World War I when soldiers charged out of their trenches and into battle. Yes, my students could feel the experience in their bones, already.

The primary purpose of this casebook, of course, is to provide a fundamental context to the understanding of the literature of World War I, which I can safely say is not an easy matter. That said, let me explain the features of this book that should uniquely prepare a teacher or reader for a serious reading of World War I literature. First of all, this book is a product of years of study not only about World War I but war literature as well, which means that after you finish reading it you should have a solid comprehension of the genre. Second, while the book's format provides a chronology to get a broader perspective, the only way to gain an appreciation of the war is to read the words of those who participated in it, which this book offers abundantly. Despite the fact that this was the first war on a global scale, there was something strangely claustrophobic and intimate about the experience.

There are only a handful of World War I combatants left today, yet the words of those who experienced this great war still seem strangely familiar. As this book demonstrates, the reason for this familiarity is that their language largely created our contemporary world. I have read hundreds, if not thousands, of books on World War I, and I found that while the earlier books provided details about the direct experience of the war, they also lacked a sufficient context; the author clearly took for granted that his reader at the time had been reading the newspaper. Over the years, however, as more and more books have been written about the war, there is more context but less immediate description of the war.

This book, therefore, tries to balance context and narrative in a way that the reader develops both knowledge and familiarity at the same time. Chapter 1 is primarily a study of the language of the combatants and how it is demonstratively different from the words of those who played a noncombatant role in the war. It is by far the longest chapter because quite frankly it is the most important. The soldier not only played the most fundamental role in the war, he also suffered the most trauma as well. Other work in this chapter includes the contributions of the political leaders and diplomats, the bunglers, who started this great conflict.

Subsequent chapters examine several other experiences of the war as well. Chapter 2 analyzes some of the traumas of the home front—the place where mothers and fathers of the soldiers had to find a way to cope with their trauma.

Chapter 3 examines the emergence of modern war poetry, which tends to be ironic, realistic, and skeptical. Chapter 4 explores the advance of strategic technologies that brought the war to the home front and to a certain degree made everyone a combatant. Chapter 5 looks at the aftermath of the war.

Documents include war diaries and memoirs, official government communiqués, treaties, and reports. Topics for written or oral communication and suggestions for further reading end each chapter.

It is my fundamental belief that World War I did not truly end until the fall of the Berlin Wall in the late 1980s. Not only did World War I traumatize everyone, one way or the other in 1914–1918, the war continues to affect us today. When I began this project in 2000, the threat of chemical warfare was seemingly as obsolete as the Model T Ford, but by 2004, the potential for gas warfare had become a major reason for a new war in Iraq. At least talk of weapons of mass destruction had returned. The lessons of World War I have proven difficult for the civilized world to unlearn.

World War I Chronology

28 June 1914	Archduke Ferdinand of Austria is assassinated in Sarajevo. A diplomatic crisis between Serbia and Austria-Hungary spins out of control and draws Germany and Russia into the dispute. Russian mobilization for war incites a mobilization response from Germany. France and England pledge support for Russia.
1 August 1914	Germany declares war on Russia. World War I begins when Germany initiates the Schleiffen Plan and invades Belgium on 4 August. France prepares for war by implementing Plan XVII and fights engagements in Alsace and Lorraine, the Battles of the Frontiers. England prepares to send the British Expeditionary Force to the continent. The French use tear-gas grenades against the German army, the first use of chemicals in the war. On 12 August, the British begin the North Sea blockade of Germany. The Battle of Tannenberg begins on 26 August.
5 September 1914	The 1st Battle of the Marne begins and by 9 September, the German army starts to retreat back across the Marne River and begins to entrench. The "Race to the Sea" begins.
18 October 1914	The 1st Battle of Ypres, Belgium, which will be a constant battlefield until the end of the war.
25 December 1914	The Christmas Truce.
4 February 1915	Germany announces submarine blockade and begins sinking ships bound for England and France.

10 March 1915	British attack the German position at Neuve Chapelle.
22 April 1915	The 2nd major battle at Ypres begins, and the Germans use chlorine against the British line, the first use of poisonous gas in the war. On 25 April, British and Commonwealth (ANZAC) soldiers make their first landing on the Gallipoli Peninsula.
7 May 1915	The *Luisitania* is sunk off the Irish coast by a German submarine. On 23 May, Italy, once a potential German ally, declares war on Austria-Hungary, its traditional enemy.
8 December 1915	The British begin evacuating soldiers from the Gallipoli Peninsula, which is finally completed by 9 January 1916. On 19 December, Sir Douglas Haig takes over command of the British Expeditionary Force from Sir John French. The Germans blow phosgene gas against the British Front at Ypres.
21 February 1916	The German offensive against Verdun begins and lasts until the end of December 1916.
31 May 1916	The only major naval engagement of the war, the Battle of Jutland, begins.
1 July 1916	General Haig's first major offensive begins at the Somme. It is the worst day in the military history of Great Britain.
1 February 1917	Germany's unrestricted submarine warfare renews and begins the indiscriminate sinking of ships in the Atlantic that will eventually draw the United States in the war against them.
24 February 1917	The Zimmerman Telegraph is delivered to United States authorities by the British government.
2 April 1917	Woodrow Wilson addresses Congress and declares war against Germany.
26 May 1917	The first combat troops from the United States arrive in France and begin organizing for the arrival of the entire American Expeditionary Force. General Pershing would not arrive until 13 June 1917. On 27 May, 30,000 French soldiers stage a mutiny at Chemin des Dames.
31 July 1917	The battle for Passchendaele (3rd Battle of Ypres) begins.

24 October 1917	The Italians begin a massive and chaotic retreat at Caporetto after the combined forces of Germany and Austria manage a successful breakthrough.
8 November 1917	The Bolshevik revolt begins against the Russian Provisional Government.
8 January 1918	U.S. President Wilson delivers Fourteen Points speech to Congress.
3 March 1918	Treaty of Brest-Litovsk signed. On 21 March, Germany begins Operation Michael against British forces at the Somme.
26 June 1918	Soldiers from the U.S. Marine Brigade and the U.S. 7th Infantry Regiment finally defeat German forces at Belleau Wood.
July 1918	The outbreak of Spanish influenza reaches epidemic levels.
8 August 1918	The beginning of the end begins as Allied forces initiate the Amiens offensive and German forces start retreating toward the Hindenburg Line.
28 September 1918	British forces assault German line at Ypres (4th Battle of Ypres begins)
31 October 1918	Turkey stops fighting. Austria will sign an armistice on 3 November.
11 November 1918	The armistice with Germany begins on the 11th hour. All guns along the Western Front go silent for the first time since August 1914.
18 January 1919	The Paris Peace Conference begins with U.S. President Woodrow Wilson personally present for negotiations.
28 June 1919	The formal signing of the Treaty of Versailles, which marks the official end of the war with Germany.

NOTE

Sources for this chronology include James Hannah, ed., *The Great War Reader* (College Station: Texas A & M), xxix–xxxvi; "Timeline," FirstWorldWar.com, http://firstworldwar.com/timeline/index.htm; and Martin Gilbert, *The First World War: A Complete History.*

1 _____

War at the Front:

An Analysis of Ernest Hemingway's *A Farewell to Arms* (1929), Erich Maria Remarque's *All Quiet on the Western Front* (1929), and Robert Graves's *Good-bye to All That* (1929)

LITERARY ANALYSIS

A Farewell to Arms (1929)

> And now to arms, all of us! I have seen weeping among those who cannot go first. Everyone's turn will come. There will not be a child of our land who will not have a part in the enormous struggle. To die is nothing. We must win. And for that we need all men's power. The weakest will have his share of glory. There come times, in the live of peoples, when there passes over them a tempest of heroic action.
>
> Georges Clemenceau

In Ernest Hemingway's classic World War I novel, *A Farewell to Arms,* protagonist Frederic Henry bitterly comments about abstract "patriotic" words, such as those expressed in the "call to arms" speech above:

> I was always embarrassed by the words, sacred, glorious, and sacrifice and the expression in vain. We had heard them, sometimes standing in the rain almost out of earshot, so that only the shouted words came through, and had read them, on proclamations that were slapped up by billposters over other proclamations, now for a long time, and I had seen nothing sacred, and the things that were glorious had no glory and the sacrifices were like the stockyards at Chicago if nothing was done with the meat except to bury it. There were many words that

you could not stand to hear and finally only the names of places had dignity. Certain numbers were the same way and certain dates and these with the names of the places were all you could say and have them mean anything. Abstract words such as glory, honor, courage, or hallow were obscene beside the concrete names of villages, the numbers of roads, the names of rivers, the numbers of regiments and dates.[1]

Henry represents the sentiment of a whole generation of World War I combatants who disdained these words by politicians and other leaders, particularly by those who had not fought at the front. The words that the combatants favored were those that only they could have uniquely known, the particular language of the battlefield and the argot of soldiers—the name of a specific hill in the middle of the action or a creek that they all had to cross in no-man's land. This was the special language of Great War soldiers, which separated those who had been at the front from those who had not. Moreover, real soldiers do not trust speeches for any reason, primarily because they can get you killed.

For these reasons, Hemingway's *A Farewell to Arms* is an ideal beginning for this study of World War I. In a perfect confluence of form and meaning, this novel not only critiques the abstract rhetoric of diplomats and political leaders, the same ones who started the Great War, but it also praises the private language of the individual, those who were just trying to survive. This complex differentiation of language, particularly about war, underscores a generational attitude toward the postwar, modern world. This generation primarily felt betrayed, combatants and noncombatants alike, by politicians and civilian society. In his estimable *Ernest Hemingway and the Expatriate Modernist Movement,* critic Kirk Curnutt observes that

> Of the many displacements experienced by Hemingway's generation, none affected them as intensely as "the Great War," as World War I was called before the rise of Adolf Hitler guaranteed its gruesome sequel.... Perhaps the greatest casualty was the idea that war was a noble endeavor fought for patriotism, the honor and glory of sacrifice, and the valiant defense of one's principles and convictions.[2]

Although Hemingway was wounded on the Italian Front in 1918, where he served as a Red Cross volunteer driving ambulances, he did not serve long enough in the trenches—six days—to develop the sentiments of a disillusioned veteran all by himself; he had to cultivate them from the literary and intellectual environment that was prevalent after the war. As just stated, Hemingway was wounded only on his sixth day at the front, where he was working in a canteen, distributing refreshments to the Italian troops at Fossalta di Piave, on 8 July 1918.[3] He never spent long periods of time at the front, and he never directly faced combat, but he was wounded, which does give him some credibility. While Hemingway's wounding and subsequent infatuation with Agnes von Kurowsky do form an autobiographical basis for the bitterness in *A Farewell to Arms,* they are not entirely the basis of the facts. Agnes von Kurowsky was the nurse who had helped Hemingway literally back on his feet, and as is common among wounded soldiers, he fell deeply in love with her. However, von Kurowsky did not reciprocate, and Hemingway's heart was broken. He felt betrayed by love, and he projected these feelings into the sense of generational betrayal of the war veteran. Yet no matter what has been said about him, Hemingway was not a used-up veteran of the war—a veteran, yes, but not a trauma case.

With Hemingway, it is important to make a distinction between what is fact and what is fiction because many readers have confused his experiences with those of his characters. As Michael Reynolds demonstrates in *Hemingway's First War: The Making of* A Farewell to Arms, and James Nagel later amends and clarifies in his own study of Hemingway's World War I experiences, *Hemingway in Love and War: The Lost Diary of Agnes von Kurowsky* (with Henry Villard), *A Farewell to Arms* is more historical fiction than it is autobiographical. Hemingway went to great pains in researching the historical facts of this novel because of his relative lack of combat experience. In fact, Hemingway was not even in Europe when the Italians suffered their humiliating retreat at Caporetto in 1917, which he so accurately conveys in the novel. The reason Hemingway was so successful in writing about the war was that he had read about the Italian debacle in history books. Hard-bitten war veterans, who base their war writings on personal experience, do not usually develop love as a major parallel theme, as Hemingway does in this novel. Hemingway was able to craft his novel by thorough research, by projection of other emotions based on other experiences, and, more important, by an intense concentration on language and style. In the end, the story itself is not as compelling as how the story is told.

By using the language of loss, Hemingway is able to project the disjointedness of the postwar, modern period. The novel is about both the public language of war and the private language of loss. While *A Farewell to Arms* portrays the tragedies of World War I with realistic detail—indiscriminate killing and destruction—the novel is really a romance about the loss of love, the death of a lover, and the diminution of humanity. Yes, it is a love story.

Frederick Henry narrates this novel, this love story, retrospectively in the first person. At the time of narrating the story, it has been several years since the death of Catherine Barkley, who dies giving birth to Henry's stillborn child. It is a double blow. In describing the experience, he philosophizes about the tragic way of the world: "The world breaks everyone and afterward many are strong at the broken places. But those that will not break it kills. It kills the very good and the very gentle and the very brave impartially. If you are none of these you can be sure it will kill you too but there will be no special hurry" (249). It is no wonder that Henry, like many other veterans of war, began thinking that the world was out to "break" them because it *was*. This was the first *world* war in which most of the casualties were killed or wounded by artillery that was fired from an unknown source—from somewhere out there in the world. Henry himself was wounded by a mortar round. As such, it doesn't take much imagination to think that the world was out to destroy you. The "world" eventually becomes a euphemism not only for aggressive bad luck but also for a paranoid sense that unknown forces are out to get you. Henry articulates and personalizes this universal paranoia. More importantly, Henry has survivor's guilt. This novel has all the traditional characteristics of a wartime boy-meets-girl-boy-loses-girl story, except for one major difference: instead of the happy-ever-after ending, one of the lovers dies. Moreover, instead of it being the man in uniform, the would-be warrior, it is the nurse, the would-be caregiver. It is a harsh twist of fate. In war, one would expect the soldier to die but not the nurse, the one who brings healing to the wounded. Such modern incongruities are the foundation of Henry's utter despair and paranoia about a world that has been turned upside down by a massive war.

Because he has survived the war and is still alive while Catherine is now dead, he feels a complex mixture of sorrow and guilt, which permeates the whole novel. However, while Henry's complex feelings may be private, he has no problem sharing them with the world because he realizes that his problems are not unlike everyone else's. The whole world shares in his sense of loss and paranoia. The whole world seems to have survivor's guilt. The novel's atmospherics, thus, are pervasively gloomy; rain pours down constantly and everywhere because there is no good place to go, or at least that is the way Henry remembers it: "It stormed all that day. The wind drove down the rain and everywhere there was standing water and mud. The plaster of the broken houses was gray and wet. Late in the afternoon the rain stopped and from out number two post I saw the bare wet autumn country with clouds over the tops of the hills and the straw screening over the roads wet and dripping" (185). Rain serves as an external metaphor, an objective correlative, for Henry's inner despair at the loss of Catherine and at the loss of a civilized world. Moreover, rain and mud were a constant refrain of the real war as well.

Therefore, loss of a traditional sense of both a private and public world in the modern era is at the thematic heart of a novel primarily concerned about broken hearts. In a world where happy endings are not possible, the conclusion of *A Farewell to Arms* is famous for the sadness it evokes:

But after I had got them out and shut the door and turned off the light it was-
n't any good. It was like saying good-by to a statue. After a while I went out and
left the hospital and walked back to the hotel in the rain. (331–332)

Emotionally broken and alone in a shattered world, Henry walks home—to
a rented room in a hotel—in the cold rain, having just said farewell to the embrace—to the arms—of a lover he could never hope to replace. He has deserted from the army that previously gave his life a semblance of order, and
now he has lost the love that fulfilled him and gave his life temporal meaning
in an otherwise meaningless world. The war turned life upside down, as is exemplified in the language of Frederic Henry, modernity's Everyman. Old-
fashioned values of the older Victorian generation, such as propriety (after all,
Catherine Barkley does have a child out of wedlock), have been cast away by
the new, lost generation. Modernity does not provide any comfort or guides
to help the "lost generation" find their way—they are all left alone to walk
home in the rain.

All Quiet on the Western Front (1929)

Unlike the famous Hemingway, relatively little is known about Remarque
except that he wrote *All Quiet on the Western Front,* which is probably the most
well-known modern war novel in the world. During World War I, Remarque
was drafted and served in the German army at the age of 18, and his service
was distinguished as much as it was difficult. He was wounded on several occasions and Remarque used his combat experiences to write his war novel,
which is full of realistic detail. The Nazis banned Remarque's famous war novel
in 1933, but he had already left Germany for Switzerland in 1932. Although
he became a U.S. naturalized citizen in 1947, he eventually settled back in
Switzerland, living his remaining days in Porto Ronco on Lake Maggiore.[4] Remarque's novel is a universal standard in high school and college classes because not only is the story so basic in the details of the trenches but also because
it is so genuinely told that it communicates in any language. It is a simple story
about a complex experience.

The narrator in the novel is Private Paul Bäumer, who is serving in the German army. Remarque's novel is also told in the first person, not retrospectively,
but as the action is actually happening, which makes for very engaging reading and further explains its universal appeal. Yet the immediate, first-person
narrative in the end creates an ironic twist because the reader discovers Bäumer
does not survive the war. With his death, the story cannot later be told in ret-
rospection. This novel is not only another example of the impossibility of
happy endings in the modern world but of modern incongruities as well. There

is no explanation as to how this narrative (which imitates the immediacy of a war diary) got into print since the narrator (and therefore the diary's writer) is killed in the novel's conclusion. The effect of this ending is as depressing as the end of the Hemingway's novel, underscoring the universal despair of the postwar world.

Despite the problems the death of the narrator presents, the immediacy of this type of first-person narration is compelling and offers an intimate look into the absurd horrors of the war and how language is transformed to cope with modern reality:

> The terror of the front sinks deep down when we turn our back upon it; we make grim, coarse jests about it, when a man dies, then we say he has nipped off his turd, and so we speak of everything, that keeps us from going mad; as long as we take it that way we maintain our own resistance.
>
> But we do not forget. It's all rot that they put in the war-news about the good humor of the troops, how they are arranging dances almost before they are out of the front-line. We don't act like that because we are in a good humor: we are in a good humor because otherwise we should go to pieces. Even so we cannot hold out much longer; our humor becomes more bitter every month.[5]

The bitterness in this passage echoes much of *A Farewell to Arms,* especially the idea that the public message of government is at odds with the private reality of the soldiers. The "war-news" reports the good humor of the front-line soldiers when the truth is that the humor of the soldiers could only be called bitter at best. The soldiers make euphemistic fun of death by relating the experience to the movement of bowels, and thereby making death seem ordinary. Rough humor is how they managed the constant anxiety of death, which has become as routine as eating, drinking, and going to the bathroom, a soldier's constant concern.

The one aspect of normal life that Paul and his comrades miss the most on the front lines is the company of women. Unlike Henry, who after all was not a front-line soldier, Bäumer could not possibly have had a serious relationship with a woman because there were hardly any females around to have had one with. For example, Bäumer and a comrade come across an old poster that had once advertised a production that was held some time ago, and they are fascinated by what is on the poster:

> We can hardly credit that such things still exist. A girl in a light summer dress, with a red patent-leather belt about her hips! She is standing with one hand on a railing with the other she holds a straw hat. She wears white stockings and white shoes, fine buckle shoes with high heels.... She is a lovely girl with a del-

icate nose, red lips, and slender legs, wonderfully clean and well cared for, she
certainly baths twice a day and never has any dirt under her nails....

The girl on the poster is a wonder to us. We have quite forgotten that there
are such things, and even now we hardly believe our eyes. We have seen nothing like it for years, nothing like it for happiness, beauty, and joy. That is peacetime, that is as it should be; we feel excited. (141)

Pictures, even faded ones, of women now have replaced real women in the
minds of these soldiers. Technology, in the form of mass media, had now made
it possible to spread propaganda to millions of people to manipulate their feelings about the enemy. As *All Quiet on the Western Front* demonstrates, that
same technology of mass media had also made it possible to disseminate pictures of women that would "excite" young men who had not seen a real woman
for quite some time. It is no wonder a great many individuals felt dehuman-
ized after the war. One could not be sure that they were not being controlled
by the "world," the unknowable source of mass manipulation.

Deprived of the normal comforts of home, faced with the constant fear of
death and loss, Bäumer has become a different person than what he was before
the war. While he is on leave during a rare trip back home, Bäumer recollects
his former life as a student. In his room, which is full of books, Bäumer finds
that he cannot now read these books with the pleasure that he once did. He cries
out, "Words, Words, Words—they do not reach me" (173). As Henry had de-
cried in *A Farewell to Arms,* the value of the old words, the words that were in
common use before the war, were all now being questioned. The words that
Bäumer tries to read in these books cannot reach him now because they have
lost meaning to him as a combat soldier, and he will never be able to recover the
old meaning again. The old words have lost their "currency," their value. It was
no wonder then that the soldiers who fought in the war, and had been literary
men before the conflict, found so much difficulty in the old words. This was the
language that got the world in trouble in the first place. The war totally repudi-
ated the old language of the immediate past and was fearful of a new one.

Good-bye to All That (1929)

Whereas *A Farewell to Arms* and *All Quiet on the Western Front* are works of
fiction, Robert Graves's *Good-bye to All That* is a memoir. That being said, there
are far more similarities among the respective forms of these three books than
there are differences. All three works are angry about the war and the modern
condition. Patrick J. Quinn, in *The Great War and the Missing Muse,* writes
that "Graves wrote *Good-bye to All That* as a parting shot to all those people
who had cluttered up his life with hypocrisy and cant, who had forced him to

be an honorable schoolboy, a loyal Welch Fusilier, and a respectable husband."[6] One could easily say that Graves, too, was mad at the world.

While memoirs are generally considered works of nonfiction, Graves employs hyperbole to such an extent that even his closest friend, Siegfried Sassoon, accused him of making up some of this material. Quinn reports that after reading an advance copy of the book, "Sassoon burst into the offices of Jonathan Cape, Graves's publisher, and threatened to take 'drastic legal action' unless Cape agreed to cancel certain pages."[7] While both Graves's and Sassoon's memoirs could be considered fictionalized autobiography, these two writers, who were former close associates, could not have had more dissimilar sensibilities, literary intentions, or personalities, which was essentially the problem between them now. In the postwar world, the veracity of language—whether it told the truth or not—was of extreme concern to someone like Sassoon, who mind you was almost court-martialed for speaking his mind during the war. To the literary soldiers of war, who had been victims of false words of the old, true words were worth fighting for in the modern world. Integrity of language was a major concern to these modernists, primarily because they knew all too well how easily the whole world could be manipulated—be blown up—by language.

Paul Fussell has called Graves's hyperbolic autobiography the "stagiest" of all the war memoirs. In *The Great War and Modern Memory,* Fussell writes that

> In considering *Good-bye to All That,* it is well to clear up immediately the question of its relation to "fact." J. M. Chen is not the only critic to err badly by speaking of the book as harshly actual" and by saying, "It is the work of a man who is not trying to create an effect." Rather than calling it "a direct and factual autobiography," Cohen would have done better to apply to it the term he attaches to Graves's Claudius novels. They are, he says, "comedies of evil." Those who mistake *Good-bye to All That* for a documentary autobiography (Cohen praises its "accurate documentation") should find instructive Graves' essay "P.S. to "Good-bye to All That," published two years after the book appeared.[8]

In "P.S. to 'Good-bye to All That,'" Graves admits that he wrote the book for money (which he did) and that he included all the makings of popular memoir at the time, even if he had to stretch the truth to make it sound authentic.

All of these comments about *Good-bye to All That* are essentially pointless, however, because the book is too well written, too entertaining, and too informative about the war for the "veracity" issue to truly matter in the long run. To a certain degree, all memoirs are a fiction, and to the more literary-minded reader today, the point is moot. Now, almost 90 years since the war began, the distinctions between fiction and autobiography have narrowed to the extent that it just doesn't matter. Both literary genres convey far larger truths than can be measured by any standard of verisimilitude or notions of what the facts are. The experience of war requires many different literary styles and linguistic connotations to tell its horrible truth. However, looking back, it is easy to see how other combat veterans could have been so concerned about the veracity of language, particularly since so many soldiers had felt betrayed by the "false" language of the past. The language of the new, modern world had to tell the truth in order to avoid another catastrophe like the Great War again.

Like *A Farewell to Arms* and *All Quiet on the Western Front, Good-bye to All That* is also good reading because it tells a fascinating story with a fine sense of irony. Take for example this description of Graves's reading the history of his Royal Welch Fusiliers:

> I caught the sense of Regimental tradition a day or two after my arrival at the Depot. In a cupboard at the Mess, I came across a big leather-bound ledger and pulled it out to read. It proved to be the Daily Order Book of the First Battalion in the trenches before Sevastopol [during the Crimea War], and I opened it at the page giving orders for an attack on the Redan Redoubt. Such and such a company was desired to supply volunteers for the storming party under Lieutenant So-and-so.... The attack failed, for among subsequent entries were orders for the burial of the dead, thanks from headquarters for the gallantry vainly displayed, and a notice that the effects of Lieutenant So-and-so, who had led the storming party, would be sold at public auction in the trenches the next day.[9]

Similar to Bäumer's situation in *All Quiet on the Western Front,* humor is how Graves tries to cope with the horrors of his war experience (even poor Lieutenant So-and-so's). How else could you psychologically cope with having your death announced in your hometown paper and then having to send a retraction in yourself? (It actually happened to Graves.) Irony is how you cope with having your pay cut off because you were supposed to be dead: "The only inconvenience that this death caused was that Cox's Bank stopped my pay, and I had difficulty in persuading it to honor my cheques" (227). He must have felt lucky that, like Lieutenant So-and-so's, his personal effects had not also been sold at public auction.

In order to tell the "truth" about the horrors of war, these three writers, Hemingway, Remarque, and Graves, who experienced differing levels of war at the front, all had to develop a new language in order to tell their "true" war story. The old words had lost their value in the modern, postwar world and new meanings had to be reconstructed out of the linguistic rubble.

HISTORICAL CONTEXT

Both fiction and fact serve to tell a true story. In the case of World War I, there are plenty of primary materials available to tell the tragic story of destruction and loss on a scale never before imagined, that is until 1914. The following is a collection of words by political operatives (terrorists), diplomats, and political figures that tell a story of how this great calamity began. After reading these documents, it will not be hard to discern why so many of the writers and intellectuals in the postwar world became so distrustful of the old words and of the old world. This historical context provides an important framework for the fiction that was just discussed in that many of the locations, themes, places on the map, numbers of regiments, fears, traumas, and experiences (the words Frederic Henry found so important) are echoed in the concrete words of the actual men who were caught up in this tragic drama called the Great War.

THE DIPLOMATIC WAR

The Assassination of Archduke Ferdinand

The seeds of conflict were planted long before the summer of 1914. In 1389, Turkish soldiers defeated Serbian forces at Kosovo, the southern mountainous region of modern Yugoslavia. This humiliation forms the basis of Serbian identity and national pride to this day. On 28 June 1914—exactly 525 years since the Serbs experienced this, their worst military defeat—Archduke Franz Ferdinand, nephew of Emperor Franz Joseph of Austria and heir-apparent of the Austro-Hungarian Empire, paid a state visit to Sarajevo. The archduke's visit to the region on the anniversary of the Serb's most important day was ill timed and incensed radical Serbians, especially the *Narodna Odbrana,* or Black Hand terrorists. So the radicals were out in force on the streets of Sarajevo, hoping to assassinate the man who would one day be the Austrian emperor. After official ceremonies welcoming the archduke to the city were completed, Franz Ferdinand then asked that he be driven to the local hospital to visit the members of his bodyguard who had been wounded in a bomb explosion that had occurred earlier in the day during an assassination attempt by the Black Hand.[10] During the drive to the hospital, Ferdinand's driver took a wrong road and when he started to turn around, Gavrilo Princip stepped up to the slowed vehicle and fired two shots at its passengers, killing the archduke and his wife. Both husband and wife bled to death before they could be gotten to the hospital.

Borijove Jevtic was another conspirator who was also arrested with Princip after the successful assassination. The following is his statement about the incident that set off the Great War. As one would expect from someone who may have had motives other than telling the factual truth, Jevtic's version of the actual shooting is somewhat at odds with the official version.

FROM THE JEVTIC ACCOUNT OF THE ASSASSINATION OF ARCHDUKE FRANZ FERDINAND, 28 JUNE 1914

World War I Document Archive,
http://www.lib.byu.edu/~rdh/wwi/1914/ferddead.html

A tiny clipping from a newspaper, mailed without comment from a secret band of terrorists in Zagreb, capital of Croatia, to their comrades in Belgrade, was the torch that set the world afire with war in 1914. That bit of paper wrecked old, proud empires. It gave birth to new, free nations.

I was one of the members of the terrorist band in Belgrade that received it.

The little clipping declared that the Austrian Archduke Francis Ferdinand would visit Sarajevo, the capital of Bosnia, June 28, to direct army maneuvers in the neighboring mountains.

It reached our meeting place, the cafe called *Zeatna Moruna,* one night the latter part of April 1914. To understand how great a sensation that little piece of paper caused among us when it was passed from hand to hand almost in silence, and how greatly it inflamed our hearts, it is necessary to explain just why the *Narodna Odbrana* existed, the kind of men that were in it, and the significance of that date, June 28, on which the Archduke dared to enter Sarajevo.

As every one knows, the old Austro-Hungarian Empire was built by conquest and intrigues, by sales and treacheries. Men of the upper classes were ardent patriots. They were dissimilar in everything except hatred of the oppressor.

Such were the men into whose hands friends in Bosnia sent the tiny bit of newsprint that April night in Belgrade. At a small table in a very humble cafe, beneath a flickering gas jet we sat and read it. There was no advice or admonition sent with it. Only four letters and two numerals were sufficient to make us unanimous, without discussion, as to what we should do about it.

In Sarajevo all the twenty-two conspirators were in their allotted positions, armed and ready. They were distributed five hundred yards apart over the whole route along which the Archduke must travel from the railroad station to the town hall.

When Francis Ferdinand and his retinue drove from the station they were allowed to pass the first two conspirators. The motorcars were driving too fast to make an attempt feasible and in the crowd were many Serbians; throwing a grenade would have killed many innocent people.

When the car passed Gabrinovic, the compositor, he threw his grenade. It hit the side of the car, but Francis Ferdinand with presence of mind threw himself back and was uninjured. Several officers riding in his attendance were injured.

The cars sped to the Town Hall and the rest of the conspirators did not interfere with them. After the reception in the Town Hall General Potiorek, the Austrian Commander, pleaded with Francis Ferdinand to leave the city, as it was seething with rebellion. The Archduke was persuaded to drive the shortest way out of the city and to go quickly.

The road to the maneuvers was shaped like the letter V, making a sharp turn at the bridge over the River Nilgacka. Francis Ferdinand's car could go fast enough until it reached this spot but here it was forced to slow down for the turn. Here Princip had taken his stand.

As the car came abreast he stepped forward from the curb, drew his automatic pistol from his coat and fired two shots. The first struck the wife of the Archduke, the Archduchess Sofia, in the abdomen. She was an expectant mother. She died instantly.

The second bullet struck the Archduke close to the heart.

He uttered only one word, "Sofia," a call to his stricken wife. Then his head fell back and he collapsed. He died almost instantly.

The officers seized Princip. They beat him over the head with the flat of their swords. They knocked him down, they kicked him, scraped the skin from his neck with the edges of their swords, tortured him, all but killed him.

The next day they put chains on Princip's feet, which he wore till his death. . . .

I was placed in the cell next to Princip's, and when Princip was taken out to walk in the prison yard I was taken along as his companion . . . .

Awakened in the middle of the night and told that he was to be carried off to another prison, Princip made an appeal to the prison governor:

"There is no need to carry me to another prison. My life is already ebbing away. I suggest that you nail me to a cross and burn me alive. My flaming body will be a torch to light my people on their path to freedom."

The Blank Check

After the assassination of the heir-apparent to the Austro-Hungarian Empire, diplomatic communications began in earnest between Emperor Franz Joseph and his strong German ally, Wilhelm II. Germany essentially gave Austria a "blank check" in handling its diplomatic response to Serbia. Russia, the traditional ally of the Serbian people, then got drawn into the diplomatic war of words. The following diplomatic communiqué between Austria-Hungary and Germany inaugurated a tragic narrative of human blundering on a grand scale. The first communiqué is from German Chancellor von Bethmann-Hollweg to Count Tschirschly, the German ambassador to Austria, which unwittingly gave what Austria-Hungary viewed as a blank check in its negotiations with the Serbs.

FROM THE "BLANK CHECK" COMMUNIQUÉ, 6 JULY 1914

World War I Document Archive, http://www.
lib.byu.edu/~rdh/wwi/1914/blankche.html

Berlin, July 6, 1914

Confidential. For Your Excellency's personal information and guidance

The Austro-Hungarian Ambassador yesterday delivered to the Emperor a confidential personal letter from the Emperor Francis Joseph, which depicts the present situation from the Austro-Hungarian point of view, and describes the measures that Vienna has in view. A copy is now being forwarded to Your Excellency.

I replied to Count Szagyeny today on behalf of His Majesty that His Majesty sends his thanks to the Emperor Francis Joseph for his letter and would soon answer it personally. In the meantime His Majesty desires to say that he is not blind to the danger that threatens Austria-Hungary and thus the Triple Alliance as a result of the Russian and Serbian Pan-Slavic agitation. Even though His Majesty is known to feel no unqualified confidence in Bulgaria and her ruler, and naturally inclines more toward our old ally Rumania and her Hohenzollern prince, yet he quite understands that the Emperor Francis Joseph, in view of the attitude of Rumania and of the danger of a new Balkan alliance aimed directly at the Danube

Monarchy, is anxious to bring about an understanding between Bulgaria and the Triple alliance. His Majesty will, furthermore, make an effort at Bucharest, according to the wishes of the Emperor Francis Joseph, to influence King Carol to the fulfillment of the duties of his alliance, to the renunciation of Serbia, and to the suppression of the Rumanian agitations directed against Austria-Hungary.

Finally, as far as concerns Serbia, His Majesty, of course, cannot interfere in the dispute now going on between Austria-Hungary and that country, as it is a matter not within his competence. The Emperor Francis Joseph may, however, rest assured that His Majesty will faithfully stand by Austria-Hungary, as is required by the obligations of his alliance and of his ancient friendship.

Bethmann-Hollweg

The Austro-Hungarian Ultimatum to Serbia

The next telegram is to Baron von Giesl, the chief Austrian diplomat at Belgrade, from Count Berchtold, the Austro-Hungarian minister for foreign affairs. This telegram outlines Austria-Hungary's extraordinary demands to the Serbs.

FROM THE AUSTRO-HUNGARIAN ULTIMATUM TO SERBIA, 23 JULY 1914

World War I Document Archive, http://www.lib.byu.edu/~rdh/wwi/ 1914/austro-hungarian-ultimatum.html

Vienna, July 22, 1914

Your Excellency will present the following note to the Royal Government on the afternoon of Thursday, July 23: On the 31st of March, 1909, the Royal Serbian Minister at the Court of Vienna made, in the name of his Government, the following declaration to the Imperial and Royal Government:

Serbia recognizes that her rights were not affected by the state of affairs created in Bosnia, and states that she will accordingly accommodate herself to the decisions to be reached by the Powers in connection with Article 25 of the Treaty of Berlin. Serbia, in accepting the advice of the Great Powers, binds herself to desist from the attitude of protest and opposition which she has assumed with regard to the annexation since October last, and she furthermore binds herself to alter the tendency of her present policy toward Austria-Hungary, and to live on the footing of friendly and neighborly relations with the latter in the future.

Now the history of the past few years, and particularly the painful events of the 28th of June, have proved the existence of a subversive movement in Serbia, whose object it is to separate certain portions of its territory from the Austro-Hungarian Monarchy. This movement, which came into being under the very eyes of the Serbian Government, subsequently found expression outside of the territory of the Kingdom in acts of terrorism, in a number of attempts at assassination, and in murders.

. . . . .

It is clear from the statements and confessions of the criminal authors of the assassination of the 28th of June, that the murder at Sarajevo was conceived at Belgrade, that the murderers received the weapons and the bombs with which they were equipped from Serbian officers and officials who belonged to the *Narodna Odbrana*, and, finally, that the dispatch of the criminals and of their weapons to Bosnia was arranged and effected under the conduct of Serbian frontier authorities.

The results brought out by the inquiry no longer permit the Imperial and Royal Government to maintain the attitude of patient tolerance which it has observed for years toward those agitations which center at Belgrade and are spread thence into the territories of the Monarchy. Instead, these results impose upon the Imperial and Royal Government the obligation to put an end to those intrigues, which constitute a standing menace to the peace of the Monarchy.

In order to attain this end, the Imperial and Royal Government finds itself compelled to demand that the Serbian Government give official assurance that it will condemn the propaganda directed against Austria-Hungary, that is to say, the whole body of the efforts whose ultimate object it is to separate from the Monarchy territories that belong to it; and that it will obligate itself to suppress with all the means at its command this criminal and terroristic propaganda. In order to give these assurances a character of solemnity, the Royal Serbian Government will publish on the first page of its official organ of July 26/13, the following declaration:

> The Royal Serbian Government condemns the propaganda directed against Austria-Hungary, that is to say, the whole body of the efforts whose ultimate object it is to separate from the Austro-Hungarian Monarchy territories that belong to it, and it most sincerely regrets the dreadful consequences of these criminal transactions.
>
> The Royal Serbian Government regrets that Serbian officers and officials should have taken part in the above-mentioned propaganda and thus have endangered the friendly and neighborly relations, to the cultivation of which the Royal Government had most solemnly pledged itself by its declarations of March 31, 1909.
>
> The Royal Government, which disapproves and repels every idea and every attempt to interfere in the destinies of the population of whatever portion of Austria-Hungary, regards it as its duty most expressly to call attention of the officers, officials, and the whole population of the kingdom to the fact that for the future it will proceed with the utmost rigor against any persons who shall become guilty of any such activities, activities to prevent and to suppress which, the Government will bend every effort.

This declaration shall be brought to the attention of the Royal army simultaneously by an order of the day from His Majesty the King, and by publication in the official organ of the army.

The Royal Serbian Government will furthermore pledge itself:

1. to suppress every publication which shall incite to hatred and contempt of the Monarchy, and the general tendency of which shall be directed against the territorial integrity of the latter;

2. to proceed at once to the dissolution of the *Narodna Odbrana* to confiscate all of its means of propaganda, and in the same manner to proceed against the other unions and associations in Serbia which occupy themselves with propaganda against Austria-Hungary; the Royal Government will take such measures as are necessary to make sure that the dissolved associations may not continue their activities under other names or in other forms;

3. to eliminate without delay from public instruction in Serbia everything, whether connected with the teaching corps or with the methods of teaching, that serves or may serve to nourish the propaganda against Austria-Hungary;

4. to remove from the military and administrative service in general all officers and officials who have been guilty of carrying on the propaganda against Austria-Hungary, whose names the Imperial and Royal Government reserves the right to make known to the Royal Government when communicating the material evidence now in its possession;

5. to agree to the cooperation in Serbia of the organs of the Imperial and Royal Government in the suppression of the subversive movement directed against the integrity of the Monarchy;

6. to institute a judicial inquiry against every participant in the conspiracy of the 28th of June who may be found in Serbian territory; the organs of the Imperial and Royal Government delegated for this purpose will take part in the proceedings held for this purpose;

7. to undertake with all haste the arrest of Major Voislav Tankosic and of one Milan Ciganovitch, a Serbian official, who have been compromised by the results of the inquiry;

8. by efficient measures to prevent the participation of Serbian authorities in the smuggling of weapons and explosives across the frontier; to dismiss from the service and to punish severely those members of the Frontier Service at Schabats and Losnitza who assisted the authors of the crime of Sarajevo to cross the frontier;

9. to make explanations to the Imperial and Royal Government concerning the unjustifiable utterances of high Serbian functionaries in Serbia and abroad, who, without regard for their official position, have not hesitated to express themselves in a manner hostile toward Austria-Hungary since the assassination of the twenty-eighth of June;

10. to inform the Imperial and Royal Government without delay of the execution of the measures comprised in the foregoing points.

The Imperial and Royal Government awaits the reply of the Royal Government by Saturday, the 25th instant, at 6 p.m., at the latest.

. . . . .

Austria-Hungary Declares War on Serbia

Both the German and Austro-Hungarian governments wanted Serbia to pay dearly for the crime committed by a few criminals. The official government of Serbia had nothing to do with the assassination. Yet the emperors of both Germany and Austria-Hungary hated the Serbian people, which is clearly reflected in the attitudes of their respective diplomatic and military staffs. Convinced that Russia would never intervene against them and that mighty Germany would support them if they did, the Austro-Hungarians demanded of the Serbian government more than any sovereignty could ever accede to.

Because little Serbia did not want a war with its much larger neighbor, the government willingly agreed to all but one of Austria's 10 demands. Serbia had no choice but to refuse the last one, which demanded direct Austro-Hungarian participation in the judicial process of trying the Black Hand operatives. Austria-Hungary's demands to Serbia, however, were an all-or-nothing proposition. Despite having almost all of their demands acceded to, Austria-Hungary felt that they had no choice but to declare war against the Serbs. It was a matter of honor.[11]

FROM THE AUSTRO-HUNGARIAN DECLARATION OF WAR ON SERBIA, 28 JULY 1914

World War I Document Archive, http://www.lib.byu.edu
/~rdh/wwi/1914/a-hdecwar.html[12]

At 11:10 A.M. on July 28, 1914, Count Leopold von Berchtold, the Austro-Hungarian Minister for Foreign Affairs, sent the following telegram from Vienna to M. N. Pashitch, Serbian Prime Minister and Minister for Foreign Affairs. This declaration of war was received at Nish at 12:30 P.M.

Vienna, July 28, 1914
The Royal Serbian Government not having answered in a satisfactory manner the note of July 23, 1914, presented by the Austro-Hungarian Minister at Belgrade, the Imperial and Royal Government are themselves compelled to see to the safeguarding of their rights and interests, and, with this object, to have recourse to force of arms. Austria-Hungary consequently considers herself henceforward in state of war with Serbia.

Count Berchtold

The Russian Bear Responds and Germany Declares War on Russia

Russia now perceived that they, too, had no choice but to defend their "honor" and to come to the aid of their unfortunate Serbian allies. Therefore, on

July 29, Russia mobilized a significant segment of its sizable population, which is also the same day that Austria fired on Belgrade with riverboats, the war's first act of armed belligerence. Russia's mobilization was not only seen by Germany as an act of war against their Austrian ally, against them as well. War plans were thus hurriedly prepared. Despite the personal warmth that was expressed between these two royal cousins, Nicholas and Wilhelm, Russia and Germany raced toward war, largely due, however, to forces beyond the control of these two sovereigns. The leading generals of both countries, fearing the other side was gaining an advantage over the other, set in motion their respective machineries of war to the point of no return. When the Germans responded to Russia's partial mobilization with a partial mobilization of their own, the Russian general staff then escalated with a full mobilization. Manpower was Russia's only means to counter German military superiority in weaponry and discipline. Germany's Great General Staff, fearing the enormous size differential between themselves and the Russian forces, countered with a larger mobilization and urged their Austro-Hungarian counterparts to do the same. After sending Russia an ultimatum to cease all military preparations, which was subsequently rejected, Germany felt "honor bound" to declare war on Russia.

FROM THE GERMAN DECLARATION OF WAR ON RUSSIA, 1 AUGUST 1914

World War I Document Archive, http//www.
lib.byu.edu/~rdh/wwi/1914/germandecruss.html

The Imperial German Government has used every effort since the beginning of the crisis to bring about a peaceful settlement. In compliance with a wish expressed to him by His Majesty the Emperor of Russia, the German Emperor had undertaken, in concert with Great Britain, the part of mediator between the Cabinets of Vienna and St. Petersburg; but Russia, without waiting for any result, proceeded to a general mobilization of her forces both on land and sea. In consequence of this threatening step, which was not justified by any military proceedings on the part of Germany, the German Empire was faced by a grave and imminent danger. If the German Government had failed to guard against this peril, they would have compromised the safety and the very existence of Germany. The German Government were, therefore, obliged to make representations to the Government of His Majesty the Emperor of All the Russians and to insist upon a cessation of the aforesaid military acts. Russia having refused to comply with this demand, and having shown by this refusal that her action was directed against Germany, I have the honor, on the instructions of my Government, to inform your Excellency as follows:

His Majesty the Emperor, my august Sovereign, in the name of the German Empire, accepts the challenge, and considers himself at war with Russia.

Germany Invades Belgium

In the meantime, France, an ally of Russia, had also been preparing for war against Germany, their traditional nemesis. France's political leadership was finding that it had little difficulty getting the masses worked up to fight the Germans: the memories of France's humiliating defeat by the Prussians 40 years earlier was still too fresh in the minds of most Frenchmen. It was the Prussian victory over the French in 1870–1871 (the Franco-Prussian War) that not only led to the unification of the modern German state, but advanced militarism as a fundamental element of Teutonic foreign policy. During the 1870–1871 conflict between Napoleon III and Otto von Bismarck, France was easily defeated and abjectly humiliated. As a result, the French government was forced to give up the fertile regions of Alsace and Lorraine.

Also as a consequence of France's humiliating defeat, the French Socialist Party, which advocated the worldwide unification of workers and the diminishment of the military in their culture, rose to national influence. A French nationalist assassinated the one man who could have saved France from stumbling into the 1914 conflict, Socialist Jean Juarès, on 31 July 1914.[13]

Germany's rise to military preeminence was fueled by the fragile ego of Kaiser Wilhelm II, whose infamous withered arm caused him to overcompensate as a blustering militarist. As the presumed ideal Germanic man, Wilhelm had to prove that he and his country possessed superior martial strengths. By 1899, the Kaiser—who desperately wanted Germany to have the strongest European military—and his Great General Staff circumvented the civilian governmental authorities and basically put Germany on a war economy; preparing for war thus became a major preoccupation for the leadership of the German army. More importantly, the Great General Staff began drawing up plans for war.

In 1905, Field Marshal Alfred von Schleiffen, Chief of the Great General Staff, devised a plan that he thought would allow Germany to prevail in a simultaneous war against both Russia in the east and France in the west. According to John Keegan, the Schleiffen Plan has to be "the most important government document written in any country in the first decade of the Twentieth Century; it might be argued that it was to prove the most important official document of the last hundred years, for what it caused to ensure on the field of battle, the hopes it inspired, the hopes it dashed, were to have consequences that persist to this day."[14] In order for Germany to win this two-front war against numerically superior forces, the conflict would have to be swift and decisive. The epitome of German efficiency, the Schleiffen Plan basically put the German army on a strict timetable, so that they could defeat two enemies on two fronts during the same war—one of the most difficult strategic situations any military could ever face. Despite his confidence in German military prowess, Schleiffen was realistic enough to realize that they were unlikely to defeat two armies simultaneously, so Schleiffen contrived to defeat France first, since it was closer, and, then, to turn all of Germany's might against the other remaining enemy—Russia. Although that was the basic plan, there were other complications. It was a well-known fact that France's eastern frontier with Germany was well fortified; therefore, the Schleiffen Plan instead called for his forces to sweep through Belgium, despite its longstanding neutrality. Schleiffen calculated that this diversion would not be too big of a challenge, since neutral Belgium, which had only gained independence from the Netherlands in 1839, possessed only a limited military. Belgium relied on the good will of the other European nations to respect its neutrality. The Germans had no intention of respecting this neutrality, however. The following excerpt is a "request" for free passage through Belgium to invade France. To excuse its intended violation of neutrality, the Germans cynically claimed that France was about to invade Belgium. Of course, Belgium refused Germany's request, which is the subject of the succeeding telegram from the Belgium minister for foreign affairs to the German minister in Brussels.

In the early morning on 4 August 1914, the German army invaded Belgium.

FROM THE GERMAN REQUEST FOR FREE PASSAGE THROUGH BELGIUM, 2 AUGUST 1914

World War I Document Archive,
http://www.lib.byu.edu/~rdh/wwi/1914/germpassbelg.html

August 2, 1914
   (Very Confidential)
RELIABLE information has been received by the German Government to the effect that French forces intend to march on the line of the Meuse by Givet and Namur. This information leaves no doubt as to the intention of France to march through Belgian territory against Germany.

The German Government cannot but fear that Belgium, in spite of the utmost goodwill, will be unable, without assistance, to repel so considerable a French invasion with sufficient prospect of success to afford an adequate guarantee against danger to Germany. It is essential for the self-defense of Germany that she should anticipate any such hostile attack. The German Government would, however, feel the deepest regret if Belgium regarded as an act of hostility against herself the fact that the measures of Germany's opponents force Germany, for her own protection, to enter Belgian territory.

In order to exclude any possibility of misunderstanding, the German Government makes the following declaration:

1. Germany has in view no act of hostility against Belgium. In the event of Belgium being prepared in the coming war to maintain an attitude of friendly neutrality towards Germany, the German Government bind themselves, at the conclusion of peace, to guarantee the possessions and independence of the Belgian Kingdom in full.

2. Germany undertakes, under the above-mentioned condition, to evacuate Belgian territory on the conclusion of peace.

3. If Belgium adopts a friendly attitude, Germany is prepared, in cooperation with the Belgian authorities, to purchase all necessaries for her troops against a cash payment, and to pay an indemnity for any damage that may have been caused by German troops.

4. Should Belgium oppose the German troops, and in particular should she throw difficulties in the way of their march by a resistance of the fortresses on the Meuse, or by destroying railways, roads, tunnels, or other similar works, Germany will, to her regret, be compelled to consider Belgium as an enemy.

In this event, Germany can undertake no obligations towards Belgium, but the eventual adjustment of the relations between the two States must be left to the decision of arms.

The German Government, however, entertains the distinct hope that this eventuality will not occur, and that the Belgian Government will know how to take the necessary measures to prevent the occurrence of incidents such as those mentioned. In this case the friendly ties that bind the two neighboring States will grow stronger and more enduring.

FROM THE BELGIAN REFUSAL OF FREE PASSAGE, 3 AUGUST 1914

World War I Document Archive,
http://www.lib.byu.edu/~rdh/wwi/1914/belgsayno.html

This note has made a deep and painful impression upon the Belgian Government. The intentions attributed to France by Germany are in contradiction to the formal declarations made to us on August 1, in the name of the French Government. Moreover, if, contrary to our expectation, Belgian neutrality should be violated by France, Belgium intends to fulfill her international obligations and the Belgian army would offer the most vigorous resistance to the invader. The treaties of 1839, confirmed by the treaties of 1870 vouch for the independence and neutrality of Belgium under the guarantee of the Powers, and notably of the Government of His Majesty the King of Prussia.

Belgium has always been faithful to her international obligations, she has carried out her duties in a spirit of loyal impartiality, and she has left nothing undone to maintain and enforce respect for her neutrality.

The attack upon her independence with which the German Government threaten her constitutes a flagrant violation of international law. No strategic interest justifies such a violation of law.

The Belgian Government, if they were to accept the proposals submitted to them, would sacrifice the honor of the nation and betray their duty towards Europe.

Conscious of the part which Belgium has played for more than eighty years in the civilization of the world, they refuse to believe that the independence of Belgium can only be preserved at the price of the violation of her neutrality.

If this hope is disappointed the Belgian Government are firmly resolved to repel, by all the means in their power, every attack upon their rights.

Belgium's King Albert I

There was at least one European leader who demonstrated heroism and nobility under pressure during this time, and that was Belgium's King Albert I. In Barbara W. Tuchman's Pulitzer Prize–winning history about the beginning of World War I, *The Guns of August,* she describes the actions of King Albert in response to Germany's aggression:

> In Brussels one hour after the invasion began, King Albert, in unadorned field uniform, rode to meet his Parliament. At a brisk trot the little procession came down the Rue Royale led by an open carriage in which were the Queen and her three children, followed by two more carriages and, bringing up the rear, the King alone on horseback.... Wave on wave of cheers reached out to the King as if the people in one universal emotion were trying to say he was the symbol of their country and of their will to uphold its independence....
>
> Inside the hall, after members, visitors, and the Queen and court were seated, the King came in alone, tossed his cap and gloves onto the lectern in a businesslike gesture and began to speak in a voice faintly unsteady.[15]

The following is an excerpt from that speech.

FROM KING ALBERT I'S SPEECH TO THE BELGIAN PARLIAMENT, 4 AUGUST 1914

World War I Document Archive,
http//www.lib.byu.edu/~rdh/wwi/1914/alberto.html

In the name of the nation, I give it a brotherly greeting. Everywhere in Flanders and Wallonia, in the towns and in the countryside, one single feeling binds all hearts together: the sense of patriotism. One single vision fills all minds: that of our independence endangered. One single duty imposes itself upon our wills: the duty of stubborn resistance.

In these solemn circumstances two virtues are indispensable: a calm but unshaken courage, and the close union of all Belgians.

Both virtues have already asserted themselves, in a brilliant fashion, before the eyes of a nation full of enthusiasm.

The irreproachable mobilization of our army, the multitude of voluntary enlistments, the devotion of the civil population, the abnegation of our soldiers' families, have revealed in an unquestionable manner the reassuring courage that inspires the Belgian people.

It is the moment for action.

I have called you together, gentlemen, in order to enable the Legislative Chambers to associate themselves with the impulse of the people in one and the same sentiment of sacrifice.

You will understand, gentlemen, how to take all those immediate measures which the situation requires, in respect both of the war and of public order.

No one in this country will fail in his duty.

If the foreigner, in defiance of that neutrality whose demands we have always scrupulously observed, violates our territory, he will find all the Belgians gathered about their sovereign, who will never betray his constitutional oath, and their Government, invested with the absolute confidence of the entire nation.

I have faith in our destinies; a country that is defending itself conquers the respect of all; such a country does not perish!

France Prepares for War

Despite the plan, Germany's "invasion" of Belgium did not go as well as the Great General Staff had anticipated, but war rarely goes as scheduled. Although the fortifications at Liège and Namur proved to be defenseless against giant-sized 420-mm Krupp howitzers, the citizenry of Belgium themselves, however, proved to be more resilient. Emboldened by their leader King Albert, the Belgian people began a campaign of guerilla resistance against the German forces marching through their country. Perceiving the situation as a fight to the death, German soldiers responded in kind, and the so-called rape of Belgium began. Keegan reports that the "worst of all the outrages began on 25 August at Louvain. This little university town was a treasure store of Flemish Gothic and Renaissance architecture. At the end of three days of incendiarism and looting, the library of 230,000 books had been burnt out and 1,100 other buildings destroyed."[16] Although the German army committed serious atrocities, it was nothing to the level that was being reported by propagandists at the time (nor would it match the horrors inflicted by the Nazis in the next war). The propagandists in the Entente countries (France, Britain, and Russia) soon began portraying the German soldiers as barbarians, as the dreaded Hun.

At the beginning of the war in 1914, France was ill prepared for an attack, especially by a German invasion from the north through Belgium. Yet like Germany, France, too, had been making plans for war. Since 1871, French military strategists had been fixated on the German threat to the east—through the frontiers of Alsace and Lorraine. In 1898, France devised military Plan XIV, which began a series of plans to organize a defense against Germany along the eastern frontier. (French war plans were numbered sequentially in Roman numerals.) By war's eve, Plan XVII, which required the commander of the French army to attack the German army in the Lorraine region between the two countries, was in place. By not only ignoring the German threat from the north through Belgium but by also placing the entire French army in between two German forces, Plan XVII unwittingly played right into the hands of the Schleiffen Plan. With the bulk of the French army on the eastern frontier facing a minimum of holding forces and a larger German force bearing down from the north, the French soldiers would thus be pulverized by a hammer and anvil.

The French Conscription Law of 1905, which significantly increased the number of available reserves in case of war, had bolstered the confidence of France's military leadership that their country was prepared. Also bolstering France's military confidence was improved relations between the French and British military staffs, including contingencies for a British Expeditionary Force if Germany would ever violate Belgian neutrality. The one strategic area of concern for France remained its alliance with Russia, whose military leadership and forces were as notoriously unprofessional as they were unreliable, two characteristics that in the end would plague the alliance until Russia collapsed and removed itself from the war effort. Despite these serious reservations about Russian military capabilities, France declared war on Germany, which was already invading Belgium.

In the late summer of 1914, prominent French journalist and politician Georges Clemenceau (1841–1929) was concerned that France was not prepared for war. Clemenceau (who had been the country's premier from 1906–1909 and would serve again in that position during the darkest days of the war) attempted to inspire his fellow countrymen to join arms against the Germans. The following excerpt from Clemenceau's call to arms exemplifies the abstract language and enflamed rhetoric used by politicians that later proved to be such an object of disdain for disaffected writers in the postwar period.

FROM CLEMENCEAU'S CALL TO ARMS, 5 AUGUST 1914

World War I Document Archive,
http://www.lib.byu.edu/~rdh/wwi/1914/clemenso.html

William II has willed it. The cannon must speak. The German Ambassador has decided to depart, tired of waiting in Paris for acts of violence which do not occur. Do you know the official reasons for his departure? It is that a French aviator is alleged to have thrown bombs on Nuremberg. In courteous language M. Viviani replied that this was an untruth, although it was only too true that a German troop had come into our territory and killed a French soldier; and the Ambassador, finding nothing to say, slipped away only to return a few minutes later to repair a slight omission. He had forgotten to deliver to the Minister a declaration of war. One cannot think of everything at once...

England, be it said to her honor, did not hesitate. Germany has had many friends, even in important places in the British Government, and she has not recoiled before any method of impressing public opinion in the United Kingdom. Nevertheless, the statesmen of England, and the English people themselves, have too clear a vision of their own interests, coinciding at every point with those of European civilization, for them to entertain the thought of taking miserable refuge in a waiting policy. This whole nation is composed of men who possess peculiarly that superior quality of knowing their own wills and of acting when once they have spoken. They do not give themselves up to enthusiasms, as sometime happens to us, but they advance carefully step by step and they are easier to kill than to drive back. Moreover it was impossible for them to do, in so little time, more than they have done in the time since all dissimulation disappeared from Germany's intentions.

·····

Italy has issued her formal declaration of neutrality. By the way in which French opinion received it, our brothers beyond Piedmont can see that the absurd quarrels of governments insufficiently authoritative have left no trace in our hearts. They have often told us that the Triple Alliance could not act together, in whatever concerned the Italians, unless we were the aggressors and that they refused to believe that such would ever be the case, since our policy was wholly defensive. They have shown that they were wholly sincere. We cannot but be thankful to them for it.

·····

Against what is this revolt of all, this rebellion of human conscience, this insurrection of ideas? Against a Teutonism delirious in megalomania, ambitious to realize what Alexander, Caesar, Napoleon could not accomplish: to impose upon a world that desires to be free the supremacy of steel. It is not a thing for our age; men have too much suffered from it. The modern idea is the right of all, and victory for us could not mean oppression, even for those who fought against us, since Germany has valiantly conquered, like so many other states, her rightful place in the world, and since, if we are fighting the arrogance of tyranny, it is not in order to embrace it in our turn.

And now to arms, all of us! I have seen weeping among those who cannot go first. Everyone's turn will come. There will not be a child of our land who will not have a part in the enormous struggle. To die is nothing. We must win. And for that we need all men's power. The weakest will have his share of glory. There come times, in the live of peoples, when there passes over them a tempest of heroic action.

The United States Declares Neutrality
and the Triple Entente's "No Separate Peace"

In August 1914, European diplomats and politicians who had utterly lost the peace were now trying to rally their respective countries for war. Britain declared war on Germany because of its violation of Belgian neutrality and was preparing to send the British Expeditionary Force to the continent to aid France. Russia, France, and Britain formed the Triple Entente alliance against Germany and Austria-Hungary. The United States, separated from the brewing European conflict by the Atlantic Ocean, was determined to stay out of a war it considered not theirs to fight. The following excerpt is from a speech by Woodrow Wilson given to Congress that reconfirms his intention to remain neutral in the developing war in Europe. Following Wilson's speech is an excerpt from a declaration by the Triple Entente that none of the member countries would unilaterally negotiate peace with Germany. The three signers of this document were the foreign ministers of their respective nations: Paul Cambon of France, Count Benckendorff of Russia, and Edward Grey of Great Britain.

FROM PRESIDENT WILSON'S DECLARATION OF
NEUTRALITY, 19 AUGUST 1914

World War I Document Archive,
http://www.lib.byu.edu/~rdh/wwi/1914/wilsonneut.html[17]

The effect of the war upon the United States will depend upon what American citizens say and do. Every man who really loves America will act and speak in the true spirit of neutrality, which is the spirit of impartiality and fairness and friendliness to all concerned. The spirit of the nation in this critical matter will be determined largely by what individuals and society and those gathered in public meetings do and say, upon what newspapers and magazines contain, upon what ministers utter in their pulpits, and men proclaim as their opinions upon the street.

The people of the United States are drawn from many nations, and chiefly from the nations now at war. It is natural and inevitable that there should be the utmost variety of sympathy and desire among them with regard to the issues and circumstances of the conflict. Some will wish one nation, others another, to succeed in the momentous struggle. It will be easy to excite passion and difficult to allay it. Those responsible for exciting it will assume a heavy responsibility, responsibility for no less a thing than that the people of the United States, whose love of their country and whose loyalty to its government should unite them as Americans all, bound in honor and affection to think first of her and her interests, may be divided in camps of hostile opinion, hot against each other, involved in the war itself in impulse and opinion if not in action.

. . . . .

I venture, therefore, my fellow countrymen, to speak a solemn word of warning to you against that deepest, most subtle, most essential breach of neutrality that may spring out of partisanship, out of passionately taking sides. The United States must be neutral in fact, as well as in name, during these days that are to try men's souls. We must be impartial in thought, as well as in action, must put a curb upon our sentiments, as well as upon every transaction that might be construed as a preference of one party to the struggle before another.

FROM THE TRIPLE ENTENTE DECLARATION ON NO SEPARATE PEACE, 4 SEPTEMBER 1914

World War I Document Archive,
http://www.lib.byu.edu/~rdh/wwi/1914/tripentente.html

DECLARATION

M. Delcasse, Minister for Foreign Affairs, to the French Ambassadors and Ministers abroad

Paris, September 4, 1914

The following declaration has this morning been signed at the Foreign Office at London: "The undersigned duly authorized thereto by their respective Governments hereby declare as follows:

"The British, French, and Russian Governments mutually engage not to conclude peace separately during the present war. The three Governments agree that when terms of peace come to be discussed, no one of the Allies will demand terms of peace without the previous agreement of each of the other Allies."

(Signed)

Paul Cambon

Count Benckendorff

Edward Grey

This declaration will be published today.

Delcasse

THE SOLDIER'S WAR

The End of the Beginning and France's Marshal Joffre at the Marne

Back in August 1914, the honor of every nation seemed worth sacrificing the lives of their citizenry. Many felt that a little war would be a good thing. It would clear the air. Like some eighteenth-century duel between two aristocrats over some personal sight of honor, no one then seemed capable of backing down. However, no one at that time could ever have imagined the carnage that was about to happen during the next four years. In 1914, the number of casualties the politicians were even contemplating absorbing had been significantly surpassed in the first few months alone. During the first months of World War I, casualties already had reached the level never before seen in any of the previous European wars combined. Keegan tallies the bill:

> The French army, with a mobilized strength of two million, had suffered by far the worst. Its losses in September, killed, wounded, missing and prisoners, exceeded 200,000, in October 80,000 and in November 70,000; the August losses, never officially revealed, may have exceeded 160,000. Fatalities reached the extraordinary total of 306,000, representing a tenfold increase in normal mortality among those aged between twenty-five and twenty-nine. Among those in their thirties, the death toll exceeded 80,000. All deaths had fallen on a male population of twenty million and more particularly on the ten million of military age.[18]

The French, who did not keep official casualty figures until 1917, three years into the war, to this day do not know precisely how much this war cost them. In the end, the Central Powers would lose 3.5 million men and the Allied Powers 5.1 million—an average of 5,600 men a day during the war.[19]

Tuchman observes that the

> failure of Plan 17 [XVII] was as fatal as the failure of the Schleiffen Plan, and together they produced deadlock on the Western Front.... The deadlock, fixed by the failure of the first month, determined the future course of the war and, as a result, the terms of the peace, the shape of the interwar period, and the Second Round [World War II]...."
>
> After the Marne the war grew and spread until it drew in the nations of both hemispheres and entangled them in a pattern of world conflict, no peace treaty could dissolve.... There was no looking back, Joffre told the soldiers on the eve. Afterward there was no turning back. The nations were caught in a trap, a trap made during the first thirty days out of battles that failed to be decisive, a trap from which there was, and has been, no exit.[20]

The 1st Battle of the Marne was fought in the early days of September 1914, which, according to the Schliefflen Plan, corresponded exactly to when the decisive battle of the war was supposed to be fought—on the 35th or 40th day of the German invasion.[21] The German army had overrun Belgium and penetrated France to within 30 miles of Paris and was looking indomitable. On the other hand, the Allies could not have looked worse. The British Expeditionary Force had just retreated from a sharp engagement at Mons, Belgium, and was now moved to a position in the rear of the Allied armies. Marshal Joseph Joffre, the French commander, had started moving his forces to meet the German advance on August 25, having finally realized that the great mass of the German army was not going to come across the eastern frontier but rather from the north through Belgium. With the Germans within striking distance of the French capital, the British Expeditionary Forces and the French army were learning almost too late how to form an effective coalitional fighting force. However, the German army, commanded by Helmuth von Moltke (the son of the general who had defeated France in the 1870–1871 war), resembled a fragmented, coalitional army as well. Despite their reputation of soldierly discipline, their officers also demonstrated as much quirkiness as their British and French counterparts. In the end, the British and French were not only successful in stopping the German advance at the Marne River but were able to push the invaders back toward Germany as well. Hew Strachan, in *The First World War: To Arms,* observes that

> strategically and operationally the Marne was a truly decisive battle in the Napoleonic sense. It was exactly the sort of battle which generals in 1914 had been educated to expect. The French had "fixed" the Germans in the east and maneuvered to strike against them in the west; the Germans' initial victories had been valueless because they had neither fixed nor destroyed their opponents, but left them free to maneuver and to fight again. The immediate consequences were political. France and the French army were saved: without that the Entente would have had no base for continuing operations in western Europe. Italy was confirmed in its decision to be neutral, in the unwisdom of honoring its commitment to the Triple Alliance. The longer-term effects were strategic. Germany had failed to secure the quick victory on which its war plan rested. From now on it was committed to war on two fronts. With hindsight, some would say that Germany had already lost the war.[22]

The following excerpt is from an official report by General Joseph Jacques-Césaire Joffre (1852–1931), the commander of French forces during the opening stages of the war. Joffre provided steady leadership in the 1st Battle of the Marne (1914) but was eventually replaced by General Robert George Nivelle in 1916 after French forces suffered horrible losses at Verdun. To prepare his troops for the 1st Marne battle, Joffre gave these ultimate instructions: "The hour has come to advance at all costs and to die where you stand rather than give way."

This heroic language reflects a nineteenth-century view of battle: of cavalry charges and drawn swords.

FROM MARSHAL JOFFRE'S REPORT ON THE MARNE, AUGUST–SEPTEMBER 1914

World War I Document Archive,
http://www.lib.byu.edu/~rdh/wwi/1914/joffre.html

The first month of the campaign began with successes and finished with defeats for the French troops. Under what circumstances did these come about? Our plan of concentration had foreseen the possibility of two principal actions, one on the right between the Vosges and the Moselle, the other on the left to the north of Verdun-Toul line, this double possibility involving the eventual variation of our transport. On August 2nd, owing to the Germans passing through Belgium, our concentration was substantially modified by Marshal Joffre in order that our principal effort might be directed to the north.

From the first week in August it was apparent that the length of time required for the British army to begin to move would delay our action in connection with it. This delay is one of the reasons that explain our failures at the end of August.

Awaiting the moment when the operations in the north could begin, and to prepare for it by retaining in Alsace the greatest possible number of German forces, the Commander-in-Chief ordered our troops to occupy Mulhouse, to cut the bridges of the Rhine at Huningue and below, and then to flank the attack of our troops, operating in Lorraine.

The purpose of the operations in Alsace was to retain a large part of the enemy's force far from the northern theater of operations. Our offensive in Lorraine was to pursue the same purpose still more directly by holding before it the German army corps operating to the south of Metz.

This offensive began brilliantly on August 14th. On the 19th we had reached the region of Saarburg and that of the Etangs (lakes), and we held Dieuze, Morhange, Delme and Chateau Salins.

On the 20th our success was stopped. The cause is to be found in the strong organization of the region, in the power of the enemy's artillery, operating over ground which had been minutely surveyed, and, finally, in the default of certain units.

On the 22nd, in spite of the splendid behavior of several of our army corps, notably that of Nancy, our troops were brought back on the Grand Couronné, while on the 23rd and 24th the Germans concentrated re-enforcements—three army corps, at least—in the region of Luneville and forced us to retire to the south.

This retreat, however, was only momentary. On the 25th, after two vigorous counter-attacks, one from south to north and the other from west to east the enemy had to fall back. From that time a sort of balance was established on this terrain between the Germans and ourselves. Maintained for fifteen days, it was afterward, as will be seen, modified to our advantage.

There remained the principal business, the battle of the north—postponed owing to the necessity of waiting for the British army. On August 20th the concentration of our lines was finished and the Commander-in-Chief gave orders for our center and our left to take the offensive. Our center comprised two armies. Our left consisted of a third army, re-enforced to the extent of two army corps, a corps of cavalry, the reserve divisions, the British army, and the Belgian army, which had already been engaged for the previous three weeks at Liege, Namur, and Louvain.

The German plan on that date was as follows: From seven to eight army corps and four cavalry divisions were endeavoring to pass between Givet and Brussels, and even to prolong their movements more to the west. Our object was, therefore, in the first place, to hold and dispose of the enemy's center and afterward to throw ourselves with all available forces on the left flank of the German grouping of troops in the north.

On August 21st our offensive in the center began with ten army corps. On August 22nd it failed, and this reverse appeared serious.

The reasons for it are complex. There were in this affair individual and collective failures, imprudences committed under the fire of the enemy, divisions ill engaged, rash deployments, precipitate retreats, a premature waste of men and, finally, the inadequacy of certain of our troops and their leaders, both as regards the use of infantry and artillery.

In consequences of these lapses the enemy, turning to account the difficult terrain, was able to secure the maximum of profit from the advantages that the superiority of his subaltern complements gave him.

In spite of this defeat our maneuver had still a chance of success, if our left and the British army obtained a decisive result. This was unfortunately not the case. On August 22nd, at the cost of great losses, the enemy succeeded in crossing the Sambre and our left army fell back on the 24th upon Beaumont-Givet, being perturbed by the belief that the enemy was threatening its right.

On the same day (the 24th), the British army fell back after a German attack upon the Maubeuge-Valenciennes line. On the 25th and 26th its retreat became more hurried. After Landrecies and Le Cateau it fell back southward by forced marches. It could not from this time keep its hold until after crossing the Marne.

The rapid retreat of the English, coinciding with the defeat sustained in Belgian Luxemburg (at the Sambre), allowed the enemy to cross the Meuse and to accelerate, by fortifying it, the action of his right.

The situation at this moment may be thus summed up: Either our frontier had to be defended on the spot under conditions which the British retreat rendered extremely perilous, or we had to execute a strategic retirement which, while delivering up to the enemy a part of the national soil, would permit us, on the other hand, to resume the offensive at our own time with a favorable disposition of troops, still intact, which we had at our command. The Commander-in-Chief determined on the second alternative.

. . . . .

The counter-attacks, executed during the retreat, were brilliant and often fruitful. On August 26th we successfully attacked St. Quentin to disengage the British army. Two other corps and a reserve division engaged the Prussian Guard and the Tenth German Army Corps, which was debouching from Guise. By the end of the day, after various fluctuations the enemy was thrown back on the Oise and the British front was freed.

On August 27th we also succeeded in throwing back upon the Meuse the enemy, who was endeavoring to gain a foothold on the left bank. Our successes continued on the 28th in the woods of Marfee and of Jaulnay. Thanks to them we were able, in accordance with the orders of the Commander-in-Chief, to fall back on the Buzancy-LeChesne-Bouvellemont line.

Further to the right another army took part in the same movement and carried out successful attacks on August 25th on the Othian and in the region of Spincourt. On the 26th these different units recrossed the Meuse without being disturbed and were able to join in the action of our center. Our armies were, therefore, again intact and available for the offensive.

On August 26th a new army composed of two army corps, five reserve divisions, and a Moorish brigade was constituted. This army was to assemble in the region of Amiens between August 27th and September 1st and take the offensive against the German right, uniting its action with that of the British army, operating on the line of Ham-Bray-sur-Somme.

The hope of resuming the offensive was at this moment rendered vain by the rapidity of the march of the German right wing. This rapidity had two consequences, which we had to parry before thinking of advancing. On the one hand, our new army had not time to complete its detraining, and, on the other hand, the British army, forced back farther by the enemy, uncovered on August 31st our left flank. Our line, thus modified, contained waves which had to be redressed before we could pass to the offensive.

To understand this it is sufficient to consider the situation created by the quick advance of the enemy on the evening of September 2nd.

A corps of cavalry had crossed the Oise and advanced as far as Chateau-Thierry. The First German army (General von Kluck), comprising four active army corps and a reserve corps, had passed Compeigne.

The Second German army (General von Bulow), with three active army corps and two reserve corps, was reaching the Laon region.

The Third German army (General von Hausen), with two active army corps and a reserve corps, had crossed the Aisne between the Chateau Porcien and Attigny.

More to the east, the Fourth, Fifth, Sixth, and Seventh German armies, namely twelve army corps, four reserve corps, and numerous Ersatz formations, were in contact with our troops, the Fourth and Fifth Armies between Vouziers and Verdun and the others in the positions which have been indicated above, from Verdun to the Vosges.

It will, therefore, be seen that our left, if we accepted battle, might be in great peril through the British forces and the new French army, operating more to the westward, having given way.

A defeat in these conditions would have cut off our armies from Paris and from the British forces and at the same time from the new army that had been constituted to the left of the English. We should thus be running the risk of losing by a single stroke the advantage of the assistance that Russia later on was to furnish.

General Joffre chose resolutely for the solution that disposed of these risks, that is to say, for postponing the offensive and the continuance of the retreat. In this way he remained on the ground that he had chosen. He waited only until he could engage in better conditions.

In consequence, on September 1st, he fixed as an extreme limit for the movement of retreat, which was still going on, the line of Bray-sur-Seine, Nogent-sur-Seine, Arcis-sur-Aube, Vitry-le-François, and the region to the north of Bar-le-Duc. This line might be reached if the troops were compelled to go back so far. They would attack before reaching it, as soon as there was a possibility of bringing about an offensive disposition, permitting the cooperation of the whole of our forces.

On September 5th it appeared that this desired situation existed.

The first German army, carrying audacity to temerity, had continued its endeavor to envelop our left, had crossed the Grand Morin, and reached the region of Chaugry, to the south of Rebaix and of Eternay. It aimed then at cutting our armies off from Paris, in order to begin the investment of the capital.

The Second German army had its head on the line Champaubert, Etoges, Bergeres and Vertus.

The Third and Fourth German armies reached to Chalons-sur-Marne and Bussy-le-Repos. The Fifth German army was advancing on one side and the other from the Argonne as far as Triacourt-les-Islettes and Juivecourt. The Sixth and Seventh German armies were attacking more to the east.

But—and here is a capital difference between the situation of September 5th and that of September 2nd—the envelopment of our left was no longer possible.

In the first place, our left army had been able to occupy the line of Sezanne, Viller St. Georges and Courchamps. Furthermore, the British forces, gathered between the Seine and the Marne, flanked on their left by the newly created army, were closely connected with the rest of our forces.

This was precisely the disposition that the Commander-in-Chief had wished to see achieved. On the 4th he decided to take advantage of it, and ordered all the armies to hold themselves ready. He had taken from his right two new army corps, two divisions of infantry, and two divisions of cavalry, which were distributed between his left and his center.

On the evening of the 5th he addressed to all the commanders of armies a message ordering them to attack.

"The hour has come," he wrote, "to advance at all costs and to die where you stand rather than give way."

. . . .

The Beginnings of Trench Warfare

Although at the Marne the British and French successfully stopped the German onslaught through Belgium and northern France, their military operations could only be considered "barely" a success. The French offensive along the frontier, as called for under Plan XVII, had killed thousands of their soldiers, barely leaving enough reserves for Joffre to move north to stop the main German attack from fulfilling the Schleiffen Plan. The British Expeditionary Force (BEF) had barely arrived in time and barely found their footing to help Joffre and the French at the Marne. The Allies had barely saved the day.

After the Marne, the Germans fell back to a line along the Aisne River and began digging in. Both sides then began what has been called the "Race to the Sea." By the end of October 1914, both armies realized that a war of mobility would lead to more futile destruction, and "the whole battle line in Belgium and France had congealed."[23] In *Eye-Deep in Hell,* John Ellis writes that everyone was

> forced to dig deep holes in the ground and concentrate upon breaking up any attacks launched by their adversaries.
>
> The armies remained in these holes for the next four years, millions of men trapped in a desolate strip of territory, living and dying in a wilderness of trenches, dugouts, craters, shattered villages and forests of lifeless tree-stumps, a desert in the midst of civilization, that became more featureless with each passing day.[24]

Trench warfare had been around for centuries but nothing on the scale that would emerge during the next four years of fighting on the Western Front. Ellis writes that

> Few men went to the front utterly devoid of any patriotic feelings, a positive sense that what they [were] doing was for the good of their country and that that alone was a worthwhile thing....
>
> Love of country was bound up in a whole series of obligations that came together under the vague heading of honor and duty. Victorian and Edwardian education and propaganda, the whole ideology of the age, inculcated both officers and men with a sense of being duty-bound to come forward in the defense of their family, their country, even their country's allies. Many soldiers did not even bother to put their feelings into words; honor was not something that a gentleman talked about.[25]

The following excerpt is a report by an officer in the BEF. Notice the official military description of what he observes. He has no idea about the extent of the trench warfare to come.

FROM TRENCH WARFARE BEGINS ON THE AISNE, 18 SEPTEMBER 1914

World War I Document Archive,
http://www.lib.byu.edu/~rdh/wwi/1914/aisne.html

Col. Edward D. Swinton, DSO

September 14th, the Germans were making a determined resistance along the River Aisne. Opposition, which it was at first thought might possibly be of a rear-guard nature, not entailing material delay to our progress, developed and proved to be more serious than was anticipated.

The action, now being fought by the Germans along their line, may, it is true, have been undertaken in order to gain time for some strategic operation or move, and may not be their main stand. But, if this is so, the fighting is naturally on a scale which as to extent of ground covered and duration of resistance, makes it undistinguishable in its progress from what is known as a "pitched battle," though the enemy certainly showed signs of considerable disorganization during the earlier days of their retirement phase.

. . . . .

So far as we are concerned the action still being contested is the Battle of the Aisne. The foe we are fighting is just across the river along the whole of our front to the east and west. The struggle is not confined to the valley of that river, though it will probably bears its name.

The progress of our operations and the French armies nearest us for the 14th, 15th, 16th, and 17th will now be described:

On Monday, the 14th, those of our troops which had on the previous day crossed the Aisne, after driving in the German rear guards on that evening, found portions of the enemy's forces in prepared defensive positions on the right bank and could do little more than secure a footing north of the river. This, however, they maintained in spite of two counter-attacks delivered at dusk and 10 p. m., in which the fighting was severe.

During the 14th, strong re-enforcements of our troops were passed to the north bank, the troops crossing by ferry, by pontoon bridges, and by the remains of permanent bridges. Close cooperation with the French forces was maintained and the general progress made was good, although the opposition was vigorous and the state of the roads, after the heavy rains, made movements slow. One division alone failed to secure the ground it expected to.

The First Army Corps, after repulsing repeated attacks, captured 600 prisoners and twelve guns. The cavalry also took a number of prisoners. Many of the Germans taken belong to the reserve and *Landwehr* formations, which fact appears to indicate that the enemy is compelled to draw on other classes of soldiers to fill the gaps in his ranks.

There was a heavy rain throughout the night of September 14th-15th, and during the 15th. The situation of the British forces underwent no essential change. But it became more and more evident that the defensive preparations made by the enemy were more extensive than was at first apparent.

In order to counterbalance these, measures were taken by us to economize our troops and to secure protection from the hostile artillery fire, which was very fierce; and our men continued to improve their own entrenchments. The Germans bombarded our lines nearly all day, using heavy guns, brought, no doubt, from before Maubeuge, as well as those with the corps.

All their counter attacks, however, failed, although in some places they were repeated six times. One made on the Fourth Guard Brigade was repulsed with heavy slaughter.

An attempt to advance slightly, made by part of our line, was unsuccessful as regards gain of ground, but led to the withdrawal of part of the enemy's infantry and artillery.

Further counter-attacks made during the night were beaten off. Rain came on toward evening and continued intermittently until 9 a.m. on the 16th. Besides adding to the discomfort of the soldiers holding the line, the wet weather to some extent hampered the motor transport service, which was also hindered by broken bridges.

On Wednesday, the 16th, there was little change in the situation opposite the British. The efforts made by the enemy were less active than on the previous day, although their bombardment continued throughout the morning and evening. Our artillery fire drove the defenders of one of the salients of their position but they returned in the evening. Forty prisoners were taken by the Third Division.

On Thursday, the 17th, the situation still remained unchanged in its essential. The German heavy artillery fire was more active than on the previous day. The only infantry attacks made by the enemy were on the extreme right of our position, and, as had happened before, were repulsed with heavy loss, chiefly, on this occasion, by our field artillery.

In order to convey some idea of the nature of the fighting it may be said that along the greater part of our front the Germans have been driven back from the forward slopes on the north of the river. Their infantry are holding strong lines of trenches among and along the edge of the numerous woods that crown the slopes. These trenches are elaborately constructed and cleverly concealed. In many places there are wire entanglements and length of rabbit fencing.

Both woods and open are carefully aligned, so that they can be swept by rifle fire and machine guns, which are invisible from our side of the valley. The ground in front of the infantry trenches is also, as a rule, under crossfire from the field artillery placed on neighboring features and under high-angle fire from pieces placed well back behind the woods on top of the plateau.

A feature of this action, as of the previous fighting, is the use by the enemy of their numerous heavy howitzers, with which they are able to direct long-range fire all over the valley and right across it. Upon these they evidently place great reliance....

So far as the British are concerned, the greater part of this week has been passed in bombardment, in gaining ground by degrees, and in beating back severe counter-attacks with heavy slaughter. Our casualties have been severe, but it is probable that those of the enemy are heavier.

On our right and left the French have been fighting fiercely, and have also been gradually gaining ground. One village has already during this battle been captured and recaptured twice by each side, and at the time of writing remains in the hands of the Germans.

The fighting has been at close quarters and of the most desperate nature, and the streets of the village are filled with dead on both sides.

The Germans are a formidable enemy, well trained, long prepared, and brave. Their soldiers are carrying on the contest with skill and valor. Nevertheless they are fighting to win anyhow, regardless of all the rules of fair play, and there is evidence that they do not hesitate at anything in order to gain victory.

A large number of the tales of their misbehaviors are exaggeration and some of the stringent precautions they have taken to guard themselves against the inhabitants of the areas traversed are possibly justifiable measures of war. But, at the same time, it has been definitely established that they have committed atrocities on many occasions.

Among the minor happenings of interest is the following: During a counter-attack by the German Fifty-third Regiment on positions of the Northampton and Queen's Regiments on Thursday, the 17th, a force of some 400 of the enemy were allowed to approach right up to the trench occupied by a platoon of the former regiment owing to the fact that they had held up their hands and made gestures that were interpreted as signs that they wished to surrender. When they were actually on the parapet of the trench held by the Northamptons they opened fire on our men at point-blank range.

Unluckily for the enemy, however, flanking them and only some 400 yards away, there happened to be a machine gun manned by a detachment of the Queen's. This at once opened fire, cutting a lane through their mass, and they fell back to their own trench with great loss. Shortly afterward they were driven further back, with additional loss, by a battalion of Guards which came up in support.

Thomas Reginald Part and the Daily War Diary

Marshal Joffre and Col. Swinton (later Major General Swinton) were members of the social and political elite; their education and social status would have been quite different than that of the vast majority of soldiers who fought in the war. The following excerpts are from men whose words were written completely outside the aristocratic, political arena; they are primarily members of the middle class. There is a rough honesty to what these soldiers have to say about the war they variously fought in. Many of them could only jot down a few notes in the trenches before the next engagement. Anyone who was doing a lot of writing received the unfavorable attention of the officer corps. The thinking was that morale at home was just as important as it was at the front, and in military logic, the people back home don't need to know everything about the war. Mail was completely censored. Therefore, some writers probably turned to their diaries to express themselves about the conditions that they were in. As a consequence, there are quite a few unpublished diaries of the war, but some have been properly published since.

Most of the potential great memoirists, those educated at public schools, were killed off in the early phase of the war. As such, Samuel Hynes, in *Soldiers' Tale: Bearing Witness to Modern War,* underscores the point that most memoirs of the war came from

the middle class volunteers who became the war's junior officers. That's understandable. The middle class is the great self-recording class that keeps diaries and journals and considers that the preservation of one's daily life is an appropriate and interesting activity for an individual. In modern times it has also been the imagining class, out of which have come most of the novels and poems and plays that constitute Western literature. Until 1914 that recording and imagining class had not gone to war much—through the whole nineteenth century, for example, no major British writer had any direct experience of battle. But in 1914–18 that changed; middle-class men did go, and then wrote what they had seen. Their testimonies taken together are what we know about what the First World War was like. They are our collective memory.[26]

The following excerpt is from the diary of Thomas Reginald Part, a member of the Australian and New Zealand Army Corps (ANZAC), who saw extensive action in the failed Gallipoli Campaign before supplementing the British army on the continent. Part's diary is rough and unfinished, which underscores the tragic fact that he, like Paul Bäumer, did not live to return home. However, whereas Bäumer's narrative was actually written by a novelist, Reginald Part's was not. While Part's story remains frozen in its unfinished and unvarnished condition, that precisely is the basis of its authentic power. Hynes comments that personal narratives, such as Part's,

> work at a level below the big words and the brave sentiments, down on the surface of the earth where men fight. They don't glorify war, or aestheticize it, or make it literary or heroic; they speak in their own voices, in their own plain language. They are against war, not antiwar—that is they are not polemics against war; they simply tell us what it is like. They make war actual, without making it familiar. They bear witness.[27]

While Part's narrative witness is thus plainly written "at a level below the big words," it is also rich in the descriptive details of death and dying and other hardships of combat. He abbreviates military names and units (Bn. stands for battalion, for example) because they are so familiar to him that he does not feel the need to spell the words out. He also maddeningly capitalizes all the letters in proper names as if to emphasize their importance, their concreteness, and their precedent over abstract ideas. Part horribly misspells words—evidence of a soldier on the run and exhausted from duty. Ultimately, the exact understanding of these abbreviations and misspelled words, and reasons for other eccentricities, is futile because other issues are more pressing. His recollections represent a personal argot, seemingly written down to jog his memory for revision at a later date—an occasion regrettably he did not live to experience. What is important about this narrative is the matter-of-fact detailing of the loss of life and destruction that he bears witness to, the accumulation of the daily routine of a soldier at the front, and names of rivers and cities and units and men. The reader has to remember that we are uninvited guest into his world.

Part was a lance corporeal and signaler, assigned to the headquarters detachment of the 24th Battalion in the Imperial Australian Forces. As his diary demonstrates, Part and the ANZACs became a well-traveled and experienced group of soldiers. Part's diary actually begins when he leaves Australia and then describes his subsequent experiences at Gallipoli and in the Mediterranean and the trip into France. This excerpt starts seven days after the opening of the 1916 Battle of the Somme. Part was a member of the large group of reinforcements called up to replace those who had been wounded or killed in the 1 July 1916 assault. Part's unit was assigned to the Fricourt Salient of the Somme battlefield, a sector that was attempting to take a heavily fortified ridge that ran from Pozières to Thiepval in France. Part and the ANZACs, who were commanded by General Birdwood, would lose 23,000 casualties during these engagements. Part's unit remained with the British Fourth Army until after the last great massed assault on 15 September 1916. (There is no entry in Part's diary on that day, indicating he had been too busy fighting to write.) Part and his unit were subsequently moved to Belgium for only a few days in support of British forces that were concentrating in the Ypres Salient; he and his unit were then returned back to the Somme battlefield in time to participate in more fighting for the remainder of the war. The Australians fortified trenches in that sector of the battlefield after British offensive operations ceased on the Somme battlefield.

The best way to get oriented as to where Part was fighting and writing about on the Western Front on any given day is to refer to Arthur Banks's *A Military Atlas of the First World War*. Just as Frederic Henry suggested, the names of the nearby French villages or local rivers are a good indication of where Part was at any given time.

FROM THE DIARY OF THOMAS REGINALD PART, AN AUSTRALIAN SOLDIER WHO FOUGHT IN WORLD WAR I, 15 DECEMBER 1915

World War I Document Archive,
http://www.scotch.sa.edu.au/WarDiary/RegPart.html

. . . .

[1916]

La Creche—Amiens Trip

July 8 Left "LA CRECHE" at 1.30PM & arrived at "MERRIS" (a small village of "Pradelle") at 7PM.

9 Left "PRADELLE" at 11AM & arrived at "EBBLINGHEM" & put up at the Mayor's residence.

10 Left "EBBLINGHEM" at 10AM for "WARDRECQUES".

11 Left "WARDRECQUES" at 7.15AM with transports (in charge of panniers) & arrived at "ARQUES" at 9AM to entrain.

12 Left "ARQUES" at 11.30AM by train passed through ST. OMER thence through BOLOGNE, past ETAPLES (the Aust. training camp) thence through St. ELOI. The railway practically follows the RIVER SOMME all the way. We finally arrived at ARMIENS where we dis-entrained. The scenery of the country was unsurpassed & the trip one to be always remembered. It was like the MARSEILLE—PARIS—AIRE trip. We arrived at ARMIENS at 8PM & untrucked transports etc. From the railway siding the whole body marched through the main streets of ARMIENS. The French people especially the girls were hilarious with

Armiens—Toutencourt

12 joy, they threw kisses & pressed wine etc. upon us. "VOOLAY VOU MOMBRASSAY" was what most girls asked, hand shakes & souvenirs collectors in galore. This was the first occasion of Australian troops passing through their City. We marched past nearly 4 miles of buildings & splendid avenues. It was a never-to-be-forgotten sight & experience. We had a spell about 3 1/2 miles out & had tea & then proceeded on to "St. SAVAEUR"

13 We are now billeted at ST. SAVAEUR. This is a fair sized village & 3 of our Bns. are camped here.

16 Bn. moved this morning at 10.30AM for RAINNEVILLE 8 1/4 miles march, arrived at 2.40PM.

17 This morning lined up & inspected by a French woman who was trying to identify some suspected individual who stole 400 Francs from her shop. This village has rather a forlorn & dilapidated appearance.

18 Left RAINVILLE at 11AM & rested by roadside for lunch, some cows even close by & some of our chaps milked them. Gen. BIRDWOOD has just passed us.

19 Arrived at TOUTENCOURT at 4PM yesterday light showers falling

Pozieres

July 19 Sleeping in huts, no sleep last night on a/c of extreme cold so got up & promenaded for a spell.

21 Left TOUTENCOURT at 9AM & arrived at VARANNES at 1PM & then went for a walk to German prisoners camp.

27 Left VARANNES at 5AM & arrived at ALBERT at 8AM Our Bde. takes over firing line tonight; we in supports. We are busy cleaning rifles & having tin diamond discs put on our backs.

28 Arrived at destination last night 5 1/2 miles from "Albert" & have taken over trenches. Lost & wandering in No Mans land. Shrapnel & H.Es is simply hellish sigs acting as runners & guides. Sigs are in deep German dugout 20 ft. deep electric lights were used here, fittings still remain. In large hand painted letters over the mess room are the words "GOTT, STRAFF ANGLAIS".

29 6th & 7th Bdes charged & endeavoured to take 2 lines of trenches. There was a bollocks up, 7th Bde. failed to take their position & 23 Bn. had to fall back one trench on a/c of their Right flank not being covered.

Pozieres

July 29 Our Bn. casualties up to now today 168. Both yesterday & today it was a perfect "HELL". This evening while returning to "SAUSAGE VALLEY" (after having guided a party in) BILLY HILL was shot through the heart by machine gun bullet.

Bn. now camped in saps at SAUSAGE VALLEY near the "CRATER" on the Albert-Bapaume Rd.

30 Last night I had the first nights sleep for 4 nights. I slept only 10 yds from guns of battery which were going all night. We've had plenty to eat since being here. An aeroplane left FRANCE & flew to BERLIN & dropped "PAMPHLETS" thence on to RUSSIA & when over AUSTRIA had to descend on a/c of dirty sparkling plugs & he was captured. He did 850 miles in one lap. At POZIERES, one could take a 1000 acre patch & you wouldn't a piece of ground not turned up, on which you could place a threepenny piece, so heavy are the bombardments in this area. A chap feels like shaking hands with himself when he gets out. Today the weather is very hot. Our casualties in this area to date approx 250.

Pozieres

Aug. 3 The 1st & 2nd of month the enemy fire was normal. Last night we bombarded Fritz severely—The Anniversary of the French declaration of War on the "Huns". Tonight we hop the parapets. My "Kingdom" for a Blighty says many.

4 Left SAUSAGE VALLLEY at 6PM for trenches got mixed up with the 22nd Bn. & kept with MAJOR McKIE (since killed in charge this evening). We were blocked in sap by 7th Bde & others whilst in "DINKUM ALLEY". Fritz kept up a deadly barrage & gave us "HELL" one shell landing near top of sap buried 3 of us, got out alright. From "DINKUM ALLEY" hopped sap & did a dash along road for "KAY" got blocked there, so made back for CONCRETE HOUSE (on GIBRALTER) thence struck out along old sunken road for "CEMETARY" HQRS.

Machine gun bullets, 77s & HEs in abundance. Earth torn up everywhere, our chaps scattered about. We were walking over scores of our own dead & wounded in the semi-darkness.

Pozieres

Aug. This evening it was "HELL" with a vengeance we passed a 22nd Bn. C.S.M. who had gone mad. We 9 sigs who had started off together found ourselves scattered 3 of us were together at front line & were on our way back—while charge was on— looking for HQRS near the cemetery, when Vic Hughes got his Blighty, Alex Munro & Arthur Kay burn? also wounded—3 sigs at a time. 3 other sigs stopped in dugout near "GIBRALTER" and wouldn't venture out & come up. I found HQRS, the first sig to report & straight away I had to run out a line to Cement house (3/4 mile) got tear shelled while running out line, fixed everything up but the line had been chewed up while running it out. I was absolutely "buggered" having been buried 3 times & gassed within two hours, so I took a good pull at the "Demijohn" (Rum) & had an hours spell at Bde. before returning.

·····

Pozieres

Aug. 5 of us sigs acted as runners, 3 evacuated wounded, 1 shell shock, & 3 others who wouldn't venture out of their warren. Heavy fire was kept up all day, in the evening Fritz put up a heavy barrage & completely demolished "KAY SAP", & a pitiful sight it was, as I cut across it, from Cemetery H.Q to Bde. HQ with a message at 4.30AM—scores & scores of our men buried & 1/2 buried, about 50 were lying about severely wounded, nothing but shell holes & dead & wounded was left to mark what was once "KAY SAP". No stretcher-bearers were available to carry away the wounded for a while.

6 We moved out of trenches to "TARA" HILL. 4th Div. relieved us, & just as we were preparing to go to sleep Fritz lobbed shells around & one went into the deserted gun pit where COL. R. WATSON, Mjr. MANNING, CAPT. TATNALL, CAPT. PLANT & Lt. CARVISK? were asleep. Only COL. WATSON escaped with severe shell shock, the others were killed, 4 of our best officers gone in a second.

7 Moved out this morning & billeted at WARLOY-BAILLON

·····

Berteaucourt—Pozieres

Aug. 12 runs the Railway AMIENS-PARIS etc.(Marseilles &...) & also the SOMME river.

16 Here we have several hours a day drilling on the valley slopes. I visited several villages from here ST. GUEU etc.

17 This evening had night operations 3/4 mile from...

18 Moved off from BERTEAUCOURT at 8AM & arrived at LA VICOGNE.

19 Left LA VICOGNE at 9AM & arrived at TOUTENCOURT at 12 noon we slept in wooden huts this evening.

20 Left TOUTENCOURT at 10AM & arrived at HARPONVILLE near ALBERT.

21 Left HARPONVILLE at 11.30AM & arrived at ALBERT at 6PM.

22 We move off to SAUSAGE VALLEY this morning.

23 Arrived at trenches 21st 23rd & 24th Bns. in & 22nd Bn. in reserve doing fatigue work.

25 21st & 24th Bns. advanced this morning at 4AM taking two lines of trenches. The position is well maintained. MORAY FARM was their object but found too heavily garrisoned. Several of 21st Bn. captured owing to them going beyond their objective. We "sigs" carried bombs for this stunt up to F. line.

Pozieres—Gezaincourt

Aug. 27 Relieved from trenches by 15th Bn. 4th Div. at 2AM this morning & walked out independently to ALBERT. Slept in billet on a/c of rain.

28 Left ALBERT at 8AM & arrived at WARLOY at 12AM & slept in our old billets of our previous visit.

29 Left WARLOY for HERRISART at 8AM Our allotted billets at HERRISART are flooded out accomodation hard to find. Lieut? Les Nicholls & I induced a Frenchy to take us in for the night. Francs does wonders, the others had a sit-up sleep.

30 Moved off from HERRISART at 7AM & arrived at BONNEVILLE at 10.30PM. On our way through CONTAY we passed several Canadian units who are to relieve the Australians.

Sep. 1 Still at BONNEVILLE, not a bad place but estaminets are scarce. Yes Lt. Gen. BIRDWOOD presented ribbons for valour shown at POZIERES.

3 Left BONNEVILLE at 8AM & arrived at GEZAINCOURT this afternoon at 4PM.

4 Rained heavily this morning.

Doullens—Ouderdom

France—Belgium

Sep. 5 The anniversary of our Bde. landing at ANZAC. This afternoon we leave at 5.10PM to entrain at 7.30PM at DOULLENS & proceed to destination unknown. Moved off at 8PM in dirty horse boxes & after a long journey, raining all the

6 time we disentrained at PROVEN (BELGIUM) at 3AM Left the station at 3.30AM & marched to "WINNIPEG" CAMP ("DICKIEBUSCH"—"OUDERDOM"). This camp was taken over from the Canadians. The weather during the trip was rather chilly, but I slept nearly all the way from Doullens to Proven. The roads on the way from the stn to camp was in a rotten condition.

7 Ran out wires to Bde.

8 Cricket match H.QRS versus A. Coy. we won but...by an innings.

9 Went to Gas school for two days instruction & I in turn instruct H.QRS on new bore respirator etc. Gas school was held at BUSEBOOM.

11 Sports of all kinds on today, Bn. sports 500 Francs in prize money, weather perfect. Went to Scottish woods to see Bob McKing who is in the 44th Bn.?

Ouderdom—Ypres

Sep. 27 Mjr. NICHOLAS left on leave to England & Lt. COL. FITZGERALD has taken over the command of battalion.

Oct. 2 At Bde. for 3 days telephone school.

5 Finished school & visited POPERINGHE & had a fling about the town.

7 Concert & movies in hall.

14 Left OUDERDOM at 6.30PM & marched to railway station & entrained for YPRES. On alighting, a moonlight night, we marched through that once beautiful

city, now absolutely in ruins, every building practically razed to the ground. We arrived in supports at 11PM H.Q. supports only 3/4 miles from the City.

16 Visited different sections around firing line.

17 Now sitting at FULLERPHONE devilish cold draught here.

20 Left YPRES supports at 1AM relieved by the 23rd London Bn. marched to Stn. & entrained to BELGIUM-FRANCE border & then landing in France we proceeded by foot to STEENEVOORDE arriving at our billets at 4.30AM night cold & icy.

21 Cold & shivery last night but slept warm as Les Readman & I bunked together.

Oct. 22 Left STEENEVOORDE at 10AM & marched 12 miles to NOORD-PEENE arriving here at 5.30PM We are billeted at a beautiful Chateau, formally the property of a French general, who presented this beautiful place to the French Govt. A splendid—well laid out—garden & moat surrounds the Chateau. We HQs slept on the 2nd floor of this mansion.

22 Left NOORDPEENE at 9.30 AM, a grand day for a march, we passed through deep valleys, the scenery was great, we enjoyed the march, in spite of our heavy packs.

24 After a journey of 8 miles we arrived at BAYENGHEM (near ST. OMER) at 2.55PM After a rest we continued our journey at 11.30 .m. along the road to

26 ST. OMER & arrived there at 2AM We got into horse-boxes ("filthy" isn't the word) & after a journey of approx 140 miles we landed at LONGPRE—20 miles either side to ABBOTSFORD & ARMIENS. Thence a march of 6 1/2 miles to BRU-CAPMS, where we are now billeted.

27 This morning at 10AM we were picked up 4 miles from billets

Armiens—Crest Trench

Oct. 27 on the ARMIENS-ALBERT road by motor omnibuses. The 6th & 7th Bde. all in motor transport 600 motors in all followed each other in one long line through ARMIENS thence on to BUIRE a place of slush & mud & very poor billeting accomodation. Our Bde. is all quartered here. The 1st Div. has relieved the 5th Div.

28 Raining all day

31 Still raining

Nov. 2 Left Buire for MONTAUBAN by train, thence a march through 6" to 1 ft. of slush up to DELVILLE WOOD, where we bivouacked for the night on wet ground.

3 Everyone wet through. This morning we got sand bags & tarpaulins to make a hut, had barely finished when the rain came down in torrents.

4 Left this morning for CREST TRENCH. Crest Trench—shallow sap water 1 ft. deep no dugouts no covering & raining all the time.

Crest Trench—Delville Wood

Nov. 4 Pulled out of CT this evening to carry ration up the line to & Bde. my first time in gum boots. Fell into shell hole (4 to 5 ft. of water inside of it) & got a good ducking. Oh! what a beautiful night, dark, raining, shell holes everywhere slippery (This night has caused the re-writing of the old diary). After tramping about all night, or rather slipping about, since it was all I could do to walk, without using the rifle as a crutch.

5 Got back to C.T. at 2.30AM all clothes wet & doing a shiver. Got permission at Noon to go back to camp to dry clothes. "B" Coy had to do 2 trips to the trenches.

6 The 7th Bde. had a charge (25th & 27th Bns.) at 6AM. It was fascinating to watch the bombardment from Crest Trench. Returned to "Delville Wood". &th Bde. men suffering badly from trench feet & rheumatism.

8 Doing buzzer practice in canvas hut, when shells burst all around our hut, killed 1 O/R, wounded 2 O/R. It got too hot for us, so we went over to Division to get out of

Flers—Fricourt

Nov. 8 range & while there, watched two "TANKS" crawling along over 2 ft. of slush & negotiating shell holes with ease.

9 Urgently ordered up to "TURK" LANE & stayed in sap all night & did a freeze.

11 C & D Coys in trenches did a stunt, 1 O/R killed they took 2 trenches & straightened up our line.

12 Came out of trenches last night.

14 Off to trenches again at FLERS, we pozied on the TERRACE, ground frozen, shelling fairly quiet, except on the ridge & around disabled 'TANK".

15 The thaw set in, result ground in a horribly boggy condition, we are acting as runners & guides as well as manning the phones.

21 Relieved by Nth. LANES—1st Div. "A devil of a night."

22 Left the QUARRY by train & arrived at "DERNANCOURT".

24 Marched back to FRICOURT, "SYDNEY" CAMP ground like elsewhere, very boggy, but huts "Tres Bon." Companies on road repairing.

29 3 of us at "Adelaide" camp with C 7 D Coys.

. . . .

Dec. 10 Battalion moved to POMMIERS REDOUBT camp, we are billeted in huts.

12 Heavy fall of snow this morning.

13 Leave to AMIENS, two days TRES BON.

23 Left "POMMIERS" & whole Bn. moved to "ADELAIDE" CAMP.

24 Saw Lt. Gen. BIRDWOOD strolling around

25 Spent Christmas Day in peace at "Adelaide" camp.

1917

Jan. 1 "New Years Eve". Every one jovial & very merry.

3 Left "ADELAIDE" CAMP for NEEDLE TRENCH. We put in 2 days there & 3 days in the firing line. THISTLE TRENCH.

8 Back to "NEEDLE" TRENCH & at 12PM two companies & HQs moved back to ADELAIDE CAMP & two companies stopped at C & D camps.

15 Left ADELAIDE camp to entrain at the "QUARRY" MONTAUBAN thence per trucks to BUIRE & a march from there to RIBEMONT.

16 Now billeted in various broken down houses, raining heavily.

Ribemont

Jan. 17 Snowing very heavily.

. . . .

21 Weather very cold, all water frozen. billets very draughty, 10 below zero.

24 Gen' parade on field of snow & Bde. inspected by GEN. SMYTHE.

25 Bn. practicing new French manouvres.

29 We leave at 10AM & march to BECOURT (8 miles).

Feb. 1 Left BECOURT for "SCOTS" REDOUT. T.L. READMAN retns. from leave.

4 We leave here tomorrow evening for the trenches.

5 In the trenches—I'm neutral.

9 Bn. retd. from supports, now camped at GORDON camp.

14 Moved from GORDON camp to C. CAMP FRICOURT.

17 Bn. moved into the line this evening

18 Arrived at trenches H.Q 2000 yds behind firing line (something unusual). Took over phones at 10PM.

19 Col. & Adj. lose their heads on a/c of Phones. . . . (buzzer unit) & a 100 & 1 different things going wrong we've never had such a crook time before.

The Evacuation—Warlencourt

Feb. 20 Have finished reading "Daddy long legs" (by Jean Webster) which I read at odd moments. It is a real human book & I enjoyed reading it. This last 2 evenings have been to rations dump, pitch dark, plenty of slips in the mud & slush & plenty of swearing by some, our dug out is 150 yds from H.Q & situated in a sunken road with steep sides & a chap visiting his dugout always takes a header in the dark.

23 Came out of trenches last night & had a 7 mile march back in the dark & got back after several sprawls in the slush.

24 10PM All "standing to" word just come through that Germans are evacuating opposite our positions. 1/2 fighting strength ordered up to supports.

25 "Stand down" at 1AM At 2PM we left for firing line 26th Avenue. Germans have gone back 20 miles in places. Now in dug out of 22nd Bn. uncertain as to where we take over.

"The Advance"—Warlencourt

Feb. 25 Orders to take over from 22nd Bn. Major JAMES asked for 2 HQ sigs to go up top with him so Charlie Mitchell & I toddle up. We ran out line following up infrantry Bn. makes a new line, we have communication 1/2 hour after taking over new possy. We establish HQ at WARLENCOURT in Pigeon house.

27 Relieved at 12 Midnight by 27 & 28 Bns. & we return to camp at PRICOURT "C".

Mch. 2 We leave for the line again this evening.

3 Last night we took over from 26th Bn. at the Right of the BUTTE DE WARLENCOURT, conditions fairly quiet.

6 We were relieved last night by the 23rd Bn. & we returned to SUSSEX CAMP (RESERVES).

7 Came up to LE SARS, now in trenches, dug-outs very cold.

8 Heavy snow this morning.

10 Moved up to supports (21st in line).

12 This evening Fritz is moving back. Bn. moved up with 21st Bn. towards LOUPART Wood & GREVILLERS (village).

13 We relieve 21st Bn. & continue the advance through GREVILLERS.

Grevillers—"The Advance"

Mch. 13 Asked to take charge in keeping up

14 communications with front line & Bn. Could

15 not get wire from Bde. so had to roll up old 'Fritz' wire & join up with what we had. It was rather hellish up there, the worst I've experienced more so than Pozieres, it was absolutely marvelous the way I escaped being killed for 2–1/2 hrs in the thickest bombardment & being sniped at as well. Communication well kept up by the section during our stunts. Section heartily congratulated by our Colonel (Smile, Boys, Smile!).

16 Back to Reserves at Seven Elms.

17 Retd. to camp at BAZENTIN to straighten up.

18 A Bonzer day, like Ausy weather we expect to move up tomorrow to BAPAUME which was taken on the 16th.

19 Moving this afternoon to "BECOURT" Camp.

20 At BECOURT Camp have taken over Bde sig offices until 6th Bde arrive.

22 Left "BECOURT" this morning, now at "LE SARS" companies doing salvage work principally from EUCOURT LE ABBS. Bn. has salvaged over L.8,000 worth of munitions etc.

Mametz—Noreuil

Mch. 28 Back to "MAMETZ" Bde camp. Out for a rest at last, begining with jerks & drill.

30 Moved from MAMETZ this morning to BECOURT camp.

Apr. 1 Took charge of Bde signal office at Transport lines "La BOISELLE."

4 Very heavy snow fall also heavy rains.

5 Took a trip on motor lorry from LA BOISELLE to BAPAUME, a very interesting journey.

6 Raining like—all day. Good Friday.

13 Finish of telephone. Bde. transports & all move up to VAULX, we camp in open. Visit of Jack's.

14 We moved up to NOREUIL, we all dig in, ground sloppy. Along this gully are several gun batteries & many units of troops, shelling here fairly light.

15 This morning between 5 & 6AM Fritz drove our boys back from near BULLECOURT—QUEANT line to just outside NOREUIL. Our 18 p'drs firing point blank on the advancing Fritzs. By 7AM we had them back to their original line &

ourselves—our own. Over 2000 Fritzs were mown down & 300 odd captured. Les & I doss in make-shift shanty.

Noreuil—Bougnatre

Apr. 16 We take up supports tonight & our front line charge forward then we move up to their possies. Fritz shelled valley this morning very consistently, causing over 60 casualties in our unit.

17 The great stunt postponed. This gully getting well tickled up NO BON! What?

18 We are relieved by 27th Bn. 7th Bde taking over 5th & 6th Bdes line, while we have 4 days (approx.) out thence in again for the big forward stunt.

19 Arrived at BOUGNATRE last night.

21 Drill & stunt manouvres all day.

"Probably leave to England tomorrow.

22 Recd. leave pass. ("At Last") Tres Bon! Eh?

23 Spent last night in Albert (sitting around a fire)

24 Arrived "BOULOGNE" at 1AM this morning.

In billets—"Good-O". Glorious weather. Left Boulogne at 1.30PM & arrived at FOLKSETON at 2.45PM & thence on to VICTORIA STN. LONDON arriving there at about 5PM At "PEEL HOUSE"

25 ANZAC DAY.

[Reginald Part was killed on 25 April, 1918 and is buried, along with five other Australians, in Lavieville, on the road to Albert, France.]

A German Deserter's Narrative

Despite their superhuman reputation, which was born out of a Prussian mythology of military superiority, German soldiers proved to be just as human as the soldiers on the other side of the line. In fact, as the war continued, their suffering was probably more intense than their British or French counterparts, and their dissatisfaction with the war was probably as contentious (although there were never any large-scale mutinies, such as occurred in the French army). Before the war, Germany was deeply divided over various social perspectives. There were as many Germans who considered themselves Socialists (and therefore antimilitary) at the time as there were those who were comfortable with Prussian imperialism. The German soldier who wrote the following narrative was a Socialist before the war, and his commitment to the fighting was ambivalent at best. This narrative is vastly different than Part's in that it is written far from the war's front and is based on his memory of what had happened; it is not a daily war diary. Therefore, it lacks the immediacy of Part's writing, while at the same time it lacks the idiosyncrasies of the war diary. For one thing, his spelling is regular. Both narratives, however, are informative of how the war was fought on the Western Front. As the translator's note indicates, the narrative was originally written and published in the *Volkszeitung,* a New

York periodical that represented the émigré German Socialists living in New York at the time. According to the translator, this soldier was a reluctant fighter but one whose "word can be relied upon."

FROM THE GERMAN DESERTER'S WAR EXPERIENCE [ANONYMOUS], TRANSLATED BY J. KOETTGEN, 1917

(New York: B. W. Huebsch, 1917), World War I Document Archive, http://www.lib.byu.edu/~rdh/wwi/memoir/Deserter/GermanTC.htm

Translator's Preface

The following narrative first appeared in German in the columns of the New York *Volkszeitung,* the principal organ of the German-speaking Socialists in the United States. Its author, who escaped from Germany and military service after 11 months of fighting in France, is an intelligent young miner. He does not wish to have his name made public, fearing that those who will be offended by his frankness might vent their wrath on his relatives. Since his arrival in this country his friends and acquaintances have come to know him as an upright and truthful man whose word can be relied upon.

The vivid description of the life of a common German soldier in the present war aroused great interest when the story presented in these pages to the English speaking reader was published in serial form. For here was an historian of the war who had been through the horrors of the carnage as one of the "Huns," one of the "Boches"; a soldier who had not abdicated his reason; a warrior against his will, who nevertheless had to conform to the etiquette of war; a hater of militarism for whom there was no romance in war, but only butchery and brutality, grime and vermin, inhuman toil and degradation. Moreover, he was found to be no mean observer of men and things. His technical training at a school of mining enabled him to obtain a much clearer understanding of the war of position than the average soldier possesses.

Most soldiers who have been in the war and have written down their experiences have done so in the customary way, never questioning for a moment the moral justification of war. Not so our author. He could not persuade his conscience to make a distinction between private and public morality, and the angle from which he views the events he describes is therefore entirely different from that of other actual observers of and participators in war. His story also contains the first German description of the retreat of the Teutonic armies after the battle of the Marne. The chief value of this soldier's narrative lies, however, in his destructive, annihilating criticism of the romance and fabled virtues of war. If some of the incidents related in this book appear to be treated too curtly it is solely due to this author's limited literary powers. If, for instance, he does not dwell upon his inner experiences during his terrible voyage to America in the coal bunker of a Dutch ship, it is because he is not a literary artist, but a simple workman.

The translator hopes that he has succeeded in reproducing faithfully the substance and the spirit of the story, and that this little book will contribute in combating one of the forces that make for war—popular ignorance of war's realities. Let each individual fully grasp and understand the misery, degradation, and destruction that await him in war, and the barbarous ordeal by carnage will quickly become the most unpopular institution on earth.

J. Koettgen

German Deserter's War Experience

VII

In Pursuit

AFTER a short rest we were commanded to search the burning houses for wounded men. We did not find many of them, for most of the severely wounded soldiers who had not been able to seek safety unaided had been miserably burnt to death, and one could only judge by the buttons and weapons of the poor wretches for what "fatherland" they had suffered their terrible death by fire. With many it was even impossible to find out the nationality they belonged to; a little heap of ashes, a ruined house were all that was left of whole families, whole streets of families.

It was only the wine cellars, which were mostly of strong construction that had generally withstood the flames. The piping hot wine in bottles and barrels, proved a welcome refreshment for the soldiers who were wet to their skins and stiff with cold. Even at the risk of their lives (for many of the cellars threatened to collapse) the soldiers would fetch out the wine and drink it greedily, however hot the wine might be.

And strangely enough, former scenes were repeated. After the hot wine had taken effect, after again feeling refreshed and physically well, that same brutality which had become our second nature in war showed itself again in the most shameful manner. Most of us behaved as if we had not taken part in the unheard-of events of the last hours, as if we did not see the horrible reminders of the awful slaughter, as if we had entirely forgotten the danger of extinction, which we had so narrowly escaped. No effort was made to do honor to the dead though every one had been taught that duty by his mother from the earliest infancy; there was nothing left of that natural shyness which the average man feels in the presence of death. The pen refuses even to attempt a reproduction of the expressions used by officers and soldiers or a description of their actions, when they set about to establish the nationality or sex of the dead. Circumstances were stronger than we men, and I convinced myself again that it was only natural that all feelings of humanity should disappear after the daily routine of murdering and that only the instinct of self-preservation should survive in all its strength. The longer the war lasted the more murderous and bestial the men became.

Meanwhile the fight between our troops that had crossed the river and the French on the other side of the Meuse had reached its greatest fury. Our troops had suffered great losses; now our turn came. While we were crossing, the German artillery pounded the enemy's position with unheard-of violence. Scarcely had we landed and taken our places when our section proceeded to the assault. The artillery became silent, and running forward we tried to storm the slope leading to the enemy positions. We got as

near as 200 yards when the French machine-guns came into action; we were driven
back with considerable losses. Ten minutes later we attempted again to storm the positions, but had only to go back again exactly as before. Again we took up positions
in our trenches, but all desire for fighting had left us; every one stared stupidly in front
of him. Of course we were not allowed to lose courage, though the victims of our useless assaults were covering the field, and our dead mates were constantly before our
eyes.

The artillery opened fire again; reinforcements arrived. Half an hour later we
stormed for the third time over the bodies of our dead comrades. That time we went
forward in rushes, and when we halted before the enemy's trench for the last time,
some twenty yards away from it, our opponent withdrew his whole first line. The rid-
dle of that sudden retreat we were able to solve some time later. It turned out that the
main portions of the French army had retreated long ago; we had merely been engaged in rear-guard actions, which, however, had proved very costly to us.

During the next hour the enemy evacuated all the heights of the Meuse. When we
reached the ridge of those heights we were able to witness a horrifying sight with our
naked eyes. The roads, which the retreating enemy was using, could be easily surveyed.
In close marching formation the French were drawing off. The heaviest of our artillery
(21cm.) was pounding the retreating columns, and shell after shell fell among the
French infantry and other troops. Hundreds of French soldiers were literally torn to
pieces. One could see bodies and limbs being tossed in the air and being caught in the
trees bordering the roads.

We sappers were ordered to rally and we were soon going after the fleeing enemy.
It was our task to make again passable for our troops the roads which had been
pounded and dug up by the shells; that was all the more difficult in the mid-day sun,
as we had first to remove the dead and wounded. Two men would take a dead soldier
by his head and feet and fling him in a ditch. Human corpses were here treated and
used exactly as a board in bridge building. Severed arms and legs were flung through
the air into the ditch in the same manner. How often since have I not thought of these
and similar incidents, asking myself whether I thought those things improper or im-
moral at the time? Again and again I had to return a negative answer, and I am therefore fully convinced of how little the soldiers can be held responsible for the brutalities
which all of them commit, to whatever nation they belong. They are no longer civilized human beings, they are simply bloodthirsty brutes, for otherwise they would be
bad, very bad soldiers.

. . . . .

The dead horses and shattered batteries had also to be removed. We were not strong
enough to get the bodies of the horses out of the way so we procured some horse roam-
ing about without a master, and fastened it to a dead one to whose leg we had attached
a noose, and thus we cleared the carcass out of the road. The portions of human bodies hanging in the trees we left, however, undisturbed. For who was there to care about
such "trifles"?

We searched the bottles and knapsacks of the dead for eatable and drinkable things, and enjoyed the things found with the heartiest appetite imaginable. Hunger and thirst are pitiless customers that cannot be turned away by fits of sentimentality.

Proceeding on our march we found the line of retreat of the enemy thickly strewn with discarded rifles, knapsacks, and other accouterments. French soldiers that had died of sunstroke were covering the roads in masses. Others had crawled into the fields to the left and right, where they were expecting help or death. But we could not assist them for we judged ourselves happy if we could keep our worn-out bodies from collapsing altogether. But even if we had wanted to help them we should not have been allowed to do so, for the order was "Forward!"

At that time I began to notice in many soldiers what I had never observed before—they felt envious. Many of my mates envied the dead soldiers and wished to be in their place in order to be at least through with all their misery. Yet all of us were afraid of dying—afraid of dying, be it noted, not of death. All of us often longed for death, but we were horrified at the slow dying lasting hours, which is the rule on the battle-field, that process which makes the wounded, abandoned soldier die piecemeal. I have witnessed the death of hundreds of young men in their prime, but I know of none among them who died willingly. A young sapper of the name of Kellner, whose home was at Cologne, had his whole abdomen ripped open by a shell splinter so that his entrails were hanging to the ground. Maddened by pain he begged me to assure him that he would not have to die. Of course, I assured him that his wounds were by no means severe and that the doctor would be there immediately to help him. Though I was a layman who had never had the slightest acquaintance with the treatment of patients I was perfectly aware that the poor fellow could only live through a few hours of pain. But my words comforted him. He died ten minutes later.

We had to march on and on. The captain told us we had been ordered to press the fleeing enemy as hard as possible. He was answered by a disapproving murmur from the whole section. For long days and nights we had been on our legs, had murdered like savages, had had neither opportunity nor possibility to eat or rest, and now they asked us worn-out men to conduct an obstinate pursuit. The captain knew very well what we were feeling, and tried to pacify us with kind words.

The cavalry divisions had not been able to cross the Meuse for want of apparatus and bridges. For the present the pursuit had to be carried out by infantry and comparatively small bodies of artillery. Thus we had to press on in any case, at least until the cavalry and machine-gun sections had crossed the bridges that had remained intact farther down stream near Sédan. Round Sommepy the French rear-guard faced us again. When four batteries of our artillery went into action at that place our company and two companies of infantry with machine guns were told off to cover the artillery.

The artillery officers thought that the covering troops were insufficient, because aeroplanes had established the presence of large masses of hostile cavalry, an attack from whom was feared. But reinforcements could not be had, as there was a lack of troops for the moment. So we had to take up positions as well as we could. We dug shallow trenches to the left and right of the battery in a nursery of fir trees, which were about a yard high. The machine-guns were built in and got ready, and ammunition was made ready for use in large quantities. We had not yet finished our preparations when the shells of our artillery began to whizz above our heads and pound the ranks of our opponent. The fir nursery concealed us from the enemy, but a little wood, some 500 yards in front of us, effectively shut out our view.

We were now instructed in what we were to do in case of an attack by cavalry. An old white-haired major of the infantry had taken command. We sappers were distributed among the infantry, but those brave "gentlemen," our officers, had suddenly disappeared. Probably the defense of the fatherland is in their opinion only the duty of the common soldier. As those "gentlemen" are only there to command and as we had been placed under the orders of infantry officers for that undertaking, they had become superfluous and had taken French leave.

Our instructions were to keep quiet in case of an attack by cavalry, to take aim, and not allow ourselves to be seen. We were not to fire until a machine-gun, commanded by the major in person, went into action, and then we were to fire as rapidly as the rifle could be worked; we were not to forget to aim quietly, but quickly.

Our batteries fired with great violence, their aiming being regulated by a biplane, soaring high up in the air, by means of signals, which were given by rockets whose signification experts, only could understand.

One quarter of an hour followed the other, and we were almost convinced that we should be lucky enough that time to be spared going into action. Suddenly things became lively. One man nudged the other, and all eyes were turned to the edge of the little wood some five hundred yards in front of us. A vast mass of horsemen emerged from both sides of the little wood and, uniting in front of it, rushed towards us. That immense lump of living beings approached our line in a mad gallop. Glancing back involuntarily I observed that our artillery had completely ceased firing and that its crews were getting their carbines ready to defend their guns.

But quicker than I can relate it misfortune came thundering up. Without being quite aware of what I was doing I felt all over my body to find some place struck by a horse's hoof. The cavalry came nearer and nearer in their wild career. Already one could see the hoofs of the horses, which scarcely touched the ground and seemed to fly over the few hundred yards of ground. We recognized the riders in their solid uniforms; we even thought we could notice the excited faces of the horsemen who were expecting a sudden hail of bullets to mow them down. Meanwhile they had approached to a distance of some 350 yards. The snorting of the horses was every moment becoming more distinct. No machine-gun firing was yet to be heard. Three hundred yards—250. My neighbor poked me in the ribs rather indelicately, saying, "Has the old mass murderer (I did not doubt for a moment that he meant the major) gone mad! It's all up with us, to be sure!" I paid no attention to his talk. Every nerve in my body was hammering away; convulsively I clung to my rifle, and awaited the calamity. Two hundred yards! Nothing as yet. Was the old chap blind or—? One hundred and eighty yards! I felt a cold sweat running down my back and trembled as if my last hour had struck. One hundred and fifty! My neighbor pressed close to me. The situation became unbearable. One hundred and thirty—an infernal noise had started. Rrrrrrrr—An overwhelming hail of bullets met the attacking party and scarcely a bullet missed the lump of humanity and beasts.

The first ranks were struck down. Men and beasts formed a wall on which rolled the waves of succeeding horses, only to be smashed by that terrible hail of bullets. "Continue firing!" rang out the command, which was not needed. "More lively!" The murderous work was carried out more rapidly and with more crushing effect. Hundreds of volleys were sent straight into the heap of living beings struggling against death. Hundreds were laid low every second. Scarcely a hundred yards in front of us lay more than six hundred men and horses, on top of each other, beside each other, apart, in every imaginable position. What five minutes ago had been a picture of strength, proud horsemen, joyful youth, was now a bloody, shapeless, miserable lump of bleeding flesh.

And what about ourselves? We laughed about our heroic deed and cracked jokes. When danger was over we lost that anxious feeling which had taken possession of us. Was it fear? It is, of course, supposed that a German soldier knows no fear—at the most he fears God, but nothing else in the world—and yet it was fear, low vulgar fear that we feel just as much as the French, the English, or the Turks, and he who dares to contradict this and talk of bravery and the fearless courage of the warrior, has either never been in war, or is a vulgar liar and hypocrite.

Why were we joyful and why did we crack jokes? Because it was the others and not ourselves who had to lose their lives that time. Because it was a life and death struggle. It was either they or we. We had a right to be glad and chase all sentimentality to the devil. Were we not soldiers, mass murderers, barbarians?

. . . . .

X

Sacking Suippes

THE inhabitants of the place who had not fled were all quartered in a large wooden shed. Their dwelling places had almost all been destroyed, so that they had no other choice but live in the shed that was offered them. Only one little, old woman sat, bitterly crying, on the ruins of her destroyed home, and nobody could induce her to leave that place.

In the wooden shed one could see women and men, youths, children and old people, all in a great jumble. Many had been wounded by bits of shell or bullets; others had been burned by the fire. Everywhere one could observe the same terrible misery— sick mothers with half-starved babies for whom there was no milk on hand and who had to perish there; old people who were dying from the excitement and terrors of the last few days; men and women in the prime of their life who were slowly succumbing to their wounds because there was nobody present to care for them.

A soldier of the *landwehr*, an infantryman, was standing close to me and looked horror-struck at some young mothers who were trying to satisfy the hunger of their babes. "I, too," he said reflectively, "have a good wife and two dear children at home. I can therefore feel how terrible it must be for the fathers of these poor families to know their dear ones are in the grip of a hostile army. The French soldiers think us to be still worse barbarians than we really are, and spread that impression through their letters among those left at home. I can imagine the fear in which they are of us everywhere. During the Boxer rebellion I was in China as a soldier, but the slaughter in Asia was child's play in comparison to the barbarism of civilized European nations that I have had occasion to witness in this war in friend and foe." After a short while he continued: "I belong to the second muster of the *landwehr*, and thought that at my age of 37 it would take a long time before my turn came. But we old ones were no better off than you of the active army divisions—sometimes even worse. Just like you we were sent into action right from the beginning, and the heavy equipment, the long marches in the scorching sun meant much hardship to our worn-out proletarian bodies so that many amongst us thought they would not be able to live through it all.

"How often have I not wished that at least one of my children were a boy? But today I am glad and happy that they are girls; for, if they were boys, they would have to shed their blood one day or spill that of others, only because our rulers demand it." We now became well acquainted with each other. Conversing with him I got to know that dissatisfaction was still more general in his company than in mine and that it was only the ruthless infliction of punishment, the iron discipline, that kept the men of the *landwehr*, who had to think of wife and children, from committing acts of insubordination. Just as we were treated they treated those older men for the slightest breach of discipline; they were tied with ropes to trees and telegraph poles.

"Dear Fatherland, may peace be thine;
Fast stands and firm the
Watch on the Rhine."

A company of the Hessian *landwehr*, all of them old soldiers, were marching past with sore feet and drooping heads. They had probably marched for a long while. Officers were attempting to liven them up. They were to sing a song, but the Hessians, fond of singing and good-natured as they certainly are known to be, were by no means in a mood to sing. "I tell you to sing, you swine!" the officer cried, and the pitifully helpless-looking "swine" endeavored to obey the command. Here and there a thin voice from the ranks of the overtired men could be heard to sing, "Deutschland, Deutschland über alles, über alles in der Welt." With sore feet and broken energy, full of disgust with their "glorious" trade of warriors, they sang that symphony of super-germanism that sounded then like blasphemy, nay, like a travesty "Deutschland, Deutschland über alles, über alles in der Welt."

Some of my mates who had watched the procession like myself came up to me saying, " Come, let's go to the bivouac. Let's sleep, forget, and think no more."

We were hungry and, going "home," we caught some chicken, "candidates for the cooking pot," as we used to call them. They were eaten half cooked. Then we lay down in the open and slept till four o'clock in the morning when we had to be ready to march off. Our goal for that day was Suippes. Before starting on the march an army order was read out to us. "Soldiers," it said, "His Majesty, the Emperor, our Supreme War Lord, thanks the soldiers of the Fourth Army, and expresses to all his imperial thankfulness and appreciation. You have protected our dear Germany from the invasion of hostile hordes. We shall not rest until the last opponent lies beaten on the ground, and before the leaves fall from the trees we shall be at home again as victors. The enemy is in full retreat, and the Almighty will continue to bless our arms."

Having duly acknowledged receipt of the message by giving those three cheers for the "Supreme War Lord" which had become almost a matter of daily routine, we started on our march and had now plenty of time and opportunity to talk over the imperial "thankfulness." We were not quite clear as to the "fatherland" we had to "defend" here in France. One of the soldiers thought the chief thing was that God had blessed our arms, whereupon another one, who had been president of a freethinking religious community in his native city for many a long year, replied that a religious man who babbled such stuff was committing blasphemy if he had ever taken religion seriously.

All over the fields and in the ditches lay the dead bodies of soldiers whose often sickening wounds were terrible to behold. Thousands of big flies, of which that part of the country harbors great swarms, were covering the human corpses, which had partly begun to decompose and were spreading a stench that took away one's breath. In between these corpses, in the burning sun, the poor, helpless refugees were camping, because they were not allowed to use the road as long as the troops were occupying it. But when were the roads not occupied by troops!

Once, when resting, we chanced to observe a fight between three French and four German aeroplanes. We heard above us the well-known hum of a motor and saw three French and two German machines approach one another. All of them were at a great altitude when all at once we heard the firing of machine-guns high up in the air. The two Germans were screwing themselves higher up, unceasingly peppered by their opponents, and were trying to get above the Frenchmen. But the French, too, rose in great spirals in order to frustrate the intentions of the Germans. Suddenly one of the German flying-men threw a bomb and set alight a French machine which at the same time was enveloped in flames and, toppling over, fell headlong to the ground a few seconds after. Burning rags came slowly fluttering to the ground after it. Unexpectedly two more strong German machines appeared on the scene, and then the Frenchmen took to flight immediately, but not before they had succeeded in disabling a German Rumpler-Taube by machine-gun fire to such an extent that the damaged aeroplane had to land in a steep glide. The other undamaged machines disappeared on the horizon.

That terrible and beautiful spectacle had taken a few minutes. It was a small, unimportant episode, which had orphaned a few children, widowed a woman—somewhere in France.

In the evening we reached the little town of Suippes after a long march. The captain said to us, "Here in Suippes there are swarms of franctireurs. We shall therefore not take quarters but camp in the open. Anybody going to the place has to take his rifle and ammunition with him." After recuperating a little we went to the place in order to find something to eat. Fifteen dead civilians were lying in the middle of the road. They were inhabitants of the place. Why they had been shot we could not learn. A shrugging of the shoulders was the only answer one could get from anybody. The place itself, the houses, showed no external damage.

I have never in war witnessed a greater general pillaging than here in Suippes. It was plain that we had to live and had to have food. The inhabitants and storekeepers having fled, it was often impossible to pay for the things one needed. Men simply went into some store, put on socks and underwear, and left their old things; they then went to some other store, took the food they fancied, and hid themselves to a wine-cellar to provide themselves to their hearts' content. The men of the ammunition trains who had their quarters in the town, as also the men of the transport and ambulance corps and troopers went by the hundred to search the homes and took whatsoever pleased them most. The finest and largest stores—Suippes supplied a large tract of country and had comparatively extensive stores of all descriptions—were empty shells in a few hours. Whilst men were looking for one thing others were ruined and broken. The drivers of the munitions and transport trains dragged away whole sacks full of the finest silk, ladies' garments, linen, boots, and shoved them in their shot-case. Children's shoes, ladies' shoes, everything was taken along, even if it had to be thrown away again soon after. Later on, when the field-post was running regularly, many things acquired in that manner were sent home. But all parcels did not reach their destination on account of the unreliable service of the field-post, and the maximum weight that could be sent proved another obstacle. Thus a pair of boots had to be divided and each sent in a separate parcel if they were to be dispatched by field-post. One of our sappers had for weeks carried about with him a pair of handsome boots for his fiancée and then had them sent to her in two parcels. However, the field-post did not guarantee delivery; and thus the war bride got the left boot, and not the right one.

An important chocolate factory was completely sacked, chocolates and candy lay about in heaps trodden under foot. Private dwellings that had been left by their inhabitants were broken into, the wine-cellars were cleared of their contents, and the windows were smashed—a speciality of the cavalry.

As we had to spend the night in the open we tried to procure some blankets, and entered a grocer's store in the market-place. The store had been already partly demolished. The living-rooms above it had remained, however, untouched, and all the rooms had been left unlocked. It could be seen that a woman had had charge of that house; everything was arranged in such a neat and comfortable way that one was immediately seized by the desire to become also possessed of such a lovely little nest. But all was surpassed by a room of medium size where a young lady had apparently lived. Only with great reluctance we entered that sanctum. To our surprise we found hanging on the wall facing the door a caustic drawing on wood bearing the legend in German: "Ehret die Frauen, sie flechten und weben himmlische Rosen ins irdische Leben." (Honor the women, they work and they weave heavenly roses in life's short reprieve.) The occupant was evidently a young bride, for the various pieces of the trousseau, trimmed with dainty blue ribbons, could be seen in the wardrobes in a painfully spick and span condition. All the wardrobes were unlocked. We did not touch a thing. We were again reminded of the cruelty of war. Millions it turned into beggars in one night; the fondest hopes and desires were destroyed. When, the next morning, we entered the house again, driven by a presentiment of misfortune, we found everything completely destroyed. Real barbarians had been raging here, who had lost that thin varnish with which civilization covers the brute in man. The whole trousseau of the young bride had been dragged from the shelves and was still partly covering the floor. Portraits, photographs, looking-glasses, all lay broken on the floor. Three of us had entered the room, and all three of us clenched our fists in helpless rage.

Having received the command to remain in Suippes till further orders we could observe the return of many refugees the next day. They came back in crowds from the direction of Châlons-sur-Marne, and found a wretched, dreary waste in the place of their peaceful homes. The owner of a dry-goods store was just returning as we stood before his house. He collapsed before the door of his house, for nothing remained of his business. We went up to the man. He was a Hebrew and spoke German. After having somewhat recovered his self-possession he told us that his business had contained goods to the value of more than 8000 francs, and said: "If the soldiers had only taken what they needed I should have been content, for I expected nothing less; but I should have never believed of the Germans that they would destroy all of my possessions." In his living-rooms there was not even a cup to be found. The man had a wife and five children, but did not know where they were at that time. And his fate was shared by uncounted others, here and elsewhere.

I should tell an untruth if I were to pretend that his misery touched me very deeply. It is true that the best among us—and those were almost always the men who had been active in the labor movement at home, who hated war and the warrior's trade from the depth of their soul—were shaken out of their lethargy and indifference by some especially harrowing incident, but the mass was no longer touched even by great tragedies.

When a man is accustomed to step over corpses with a cold smile on his lips, when he has to face death every minute day and night he gradually loses that finer feeling for human things and humanity. Thus it must not surprise one that soldiers could laugh and joke in the midst of awful devastation, that they brought wine to a concert room in which there was a piano and an electric organ, and had a joyful time with music and wine. They drank till they were unconscious; they drank with sergeants and corporals, pledging "brotherhood"; and they rolled arm in arm through the streets with their new "comrades."

The officers would see nothing of this, for they did not behave much better themselves, even if they knew how to arrange things in such a manner that their "honor" did not entirely go to the devil. The "gentleman" of an officer sends his orderly out to buy him twenty bottles of wine, but as he does not give his servant any money wherewith to "buy," the orderly obeys the command the best he can. He knows that at any rate he must not come back without the wine. In that manner the officers provide themselves with all possible comforts without losing their "honor." We had five officers in our company who for themselves alone needed a wagon with four horses for transporting their baggage. As for ourselves, the soldiers, our knapsack was still too large for the objects we needed for our daily life.

· · · · ·

XII

At the Marne—In the Maw of Death

WE got in the neighborhood of the line of defense, and were received by a rolling fire
from the machineguns. We went up to the improvised trenches that were to protect
us, at the double-quick. It was raining hard. The fields around were covered with dead
and wounded men who impeded the work of the defenders. Many of the wounded
contracted tetanus in consequence of contact with the clayey soil, for most of them
had not been bandaged. They all begged for water and bread, but we had none ourselves. In fact, they implored us to give them a bit of bread. They had been in that hell
for two days without having eaten a mouthful.

We had scarcely been shown our places when the French began to attack in mass formation. The occupants of those trenches, who had already beaten back several of those
attacks, spurred us on to shoot and then began to fire themselves into the on-rushing
crowd as if demented. Amidst the shouting and the noise one could hear the cries of the
officers of the infantry: "Fire! Fire! More lively!" We fired until the barrels of our rifles became quite hot. The enemy turned to flee. The heap of victims lying between us and our
opponents had again been augmented by hundreds. The attack had been beaten back.

It was dark, and it rained and rained. From all directions one heard in the darkness
the wounded calling, crying, and moaning. The wounded we had with us were likewise moaning and crying. All wanted to have their wounds dressed, but we had no
more bandages. We tore off pieces of our dirty shirts and placed the rags on those sickening wounds. Men were dying one after the other. There were no doctors, no bandages; we had nothing whatever. You had to help the wounded and keep the French
off at the same time. It was an unbearable, impossible state of things. It rained harder
and harder. We were wet to our skins. We fired blindly into the darkness. The rolling
fire of rifles increased, then died away, then increased again. We sappers were placed
among the infantry. My neighbor gave me a dig in the ribs.

"I say," he called out.

"What do you want? " I asked.

"Who are you?"

"A sapper."

"Come here," he hissed. "It gives you an uncanny feeling to be alone in this hell of
a night. Why are you here too?—They'll soon come again, those over there; then
there'll be fine fun again. Do you hear the others cry?"

He laughed. Suddenly he began again: "I always shoot at those until they leave off
crying that's great fun."

Again he laughed, that time more shrilly than before.

I knew what was the matter. He had become insane. A man passed with ammunition. I begged him to go at once and fetch the section leader. The leader, a lieutenant
of the infantry, came up. I went to meet him and told him that my neighbor was continually firing at the wounded, was talking nonsense, and was probably insane. The
lieutenant placed himself between us. "Can you see anything?" he asked the other

man. "What? See? No; but I hear them moaning and crying, and as soon as I hit one—well, he is quiet, he goes to sleep—" The lieutenant nodded at me. He took the gun away from the man. But the latter snatched it quickly away again and jumped out of the trench. From there he fired into the crowd of wounded men until, a few seconds after, he dropped down riddled by several bullets.

The drama had only a few spectators. It was scarcely over when it was forgotten again. That was no place to become sentimental. We continued shooting without any aim. The crying of the wounded became louder and louder. Why was that so? Those wounded men, lying between the two fighting lines, were exposed to the aimless fire of both sides. Nobody could help them, for it would have been madness to venture between the lines. Louder and more imploring became the voices that were calling out, "Stretcherbearer! Help! Help! Water!" For an answer they got at most a curse or a malediction.

Our trench was filled with water for about a foot water and mud. The dead and wounded lay in that mire where they had dropped. We had to make room. So we threw the dead out of the trench. At one o'clock in the night people came with stretchers and took away part of the wounded. But there was no help at all for the poor fellows between the lines.

To fill the cup of misery we received orders, in the course of the night, to attack the enemy's lines at 4:15 o'clock in the morning. At the time fixed, in a pouring rain, we got ready for storming. Received by a terrible fire from the machine-guns we had to turn back half-way. Again we had sacrificed uselessly a great number of men. Scarcely had we arranged ourselves again in our trench when the French began a new attack. They got as far as three yards from our trenches when their attack broke down under our fire. They, too, had to go back with enormous losses. Three times more the French attacked within two hours, each time suffering great losses and achieving not the slightest success.

We did not know what to do. If help did not arrive soon it would be impossible for us to maintain our position. We were tormented by hunger and thirst, were wet to the skin, and tired enough to drop down. At ten o'clock the French attacked a fourth time. They came up in immense masses. Our leaders recognized at last the danger in which we were and withdrew us. We retreated in waves abandoning the wounded and our material. By exerting our whole strength we succeeded in saving the machine-guns and ammunition. We went back a thousand yards and established ourselves again in old trenches. The officers called to us that we should have to stay there whatever happened; reinforcements would soon come up. The machine-guns were in their emplacements in a jiffy. Our opponents, who were following us, were immediately treated to a hail of bullets. Their advance stopped at once. Encouraged by that success we continued firing more wildly than ever so that the French were obliged to seek cover. The reinforcements we had been promised did not arrive. Some 800 yards behind us were six German batteries which, however, maintained but a feeble fire.

An officer of the artillery appeared in our midst and asked the commander of our section whether it would not be wise to withdraw the batteries. He said he had been informed by telephone that the whole German line was wavering. Before the commander had time to answer another attack in mass formation took place, the enemy being five or seven times as numerous as we were. As if by command, we quitted our position without having been told to do so, completely demoralized; we retired in full flight, leaving the six batteries (36 guns) to the enemy. Our opponent had ceased his curtain of fire fearing to endanger his own advancing troops. The Germans used that moment to bring into battle reinforcements composed of a medley of all arms. Portions of scattered infantry, dismounted cavalry, sappers without a lord and master, all had been drummed together to fill the ranks. Apparently there were no longer any proper complete reserve formations on that day of battle.

Again we got the order, "Turn! Attention!"

The unequal fight started again. We observed how the enemy made preparations to carry off the captured guns. We saw him advance to the assault. He received us with the bayonet. We fought like wild animals. For minutes there was bayonet fighting of a ferocity that defies description. We stabbed and hit like madmen—through the chest, the abdomen, no matter where. There was no semblance of regular bayonet fighting; that, by the way, can only be practised in the barracks yard. The butt-ends of our rifles swished through the air. Every skull that came in our way was smashed-in. We had lost helmets and knapsacks. In spite of his great numerical superiority the enemy could not make headway against our little barrier of raving humanity. We forgot all around us and fought bloodthirstily without any calculation. A portion of our fellows had broken through the ranks of the enemy, and fought for the possession of the guns.

Our opponent recognized the danger that was threatening him and retired, seeking with all his might to retain the captured guns. We did not allow ourselves to be shaken off, and bayoneted the retiring foes, one after the other. But the whole mass of the enemy gathered again round the guns. Every gun was surrounded by corpses, every minute registered numerous victims. The artillery who took part in the fight attempted to remove the breech-blocks of the guns. To my right, around the third gun, three Germans were still struggling with four Frenchmen; all the others were lying on the ground dead or wounded. Near that one gun were about seventy dead or wounded men. A sapper could be seen before the mouth of the gun. With astonishing coolness he was stuffing into the mouth of that gun one hand grenade after another. He then lit the fuse and ran away. Friends and enemies were torn into a thousand shreds by the terrible explosion that followed. The gun was entirely demolished. Seventy or eighty men had slaughtered each other for nothing—absolutely nothing.

After a struggle lasting nearly one hour all the guns were again in our possession. Who can imagine the enormous loss of human lives with which those lost guns had been recaptured! The dead and wounded, infantry, cavalry, sappers and artillery, together with the Frenchmen, hundreds and hundreds of them, were covering the narrow space, that comparatively small spot which had been the scene of the tragedy.

We were again reinforced, that time by four regular companies of infantry, which had been taken from another section of the battle-field. Though one takes part in everything, one's view as an individual is very limited, and one has no means of informing oneself about the situation in general. Here, too, we found ourselves in a similar situation. But those reinforcements composed of all arms, and the later arrivals, who had been taken from a section just as severely threatened as our own, gave us the presentiment that we could only resist further attacks if fresh troops arrived soon. If only we could get something to quiet the pangs of hunger and that atrocious thirst!

The horses of the guns now arrived at a mad gallop to take away the guns. At the same moment the enemy's artillery opened a murderous fire, with all sizes of guns, on that column of more than thirty teams that were racing along. Confusion arose. The six horses of the various teams reared and fled in all directions, drawing the overturned limbers behind them with wheels uppermost. Some of the maddest animals ran straight into the hottest fire to be torn to pieces together with their drivers. Then our opponent directed his fire on the battery positions which were also our positions. We had no other choice—we had either to advance or retire. Retire? No! The order was different. We were to recapture our lost first positions, now occupied by the French, who were now probably getting ready for another attack. Had we not received fresh food for cannon so that the mad dance could begin again? We advanced across a field covered with thousands upon thousands of torn and bleeding human bodies.

No shot was fired. Only the enemy's artillery was still bombarding the battery positions. We were still receiving no fire from the artillery; neither did the enemy's infantry fire upon us. That looked suspicious; we knew what was coming. We advanced farther and farther without being molested. Suddenly we found ourselves attacked by an army of machine-guns. An indescribable hail of bullets was poured into us. We threw ourselves to the ground and sought cover as well as we could. "Jump forward! March, march!" Again we ran to meet our fate. We had lost already more than a third of our men. We halted again, exhausted. Scarcely had we had time to take up a position when we were attacked both in front and the flank. We had no longer strength enough to withstand successfully a simultaneous frontal and flank attack. Besides, we were being almost crushed by superior numbers. Our left wing had been completely cut off, and we observed our people on that wing raising their hands to indicate that they considered themselves prisoners of war. However, the French gave no quarter—exactly as we had acted on a former occasion. Not a man of our left wing was spared; every one was cut down.

We in the center could give them no help. We were getting less from minute to minute. "Revenge for Sommepy!" I heard it ringing in my ears. The right wing turned, drew us along, and a wild stampede began. Our direct retreat being cut off, we ran backwards across the open field, every one for himself, with beating hearts that seemed ready to burst, all the time under the enemy's fire.

After a long run we reached a small village to the northeast of Vitry-le-François. There we arrived without rifles, helmets or knapsacks; one after the other. But only a small portion could save themselves. The French took plenty of booty. All the guns we fought for were lost, besides several others. Of the hundreds of soldiers there remained scarcely one hundred. All the others were dead, wounded or missing. Who knew?

Was that the terrible German war machine? Were those the cowardly, degenerated Frenchmen whom we had driven before us for days? No; it was war, terrible, horrid war, in which fortune is fickle. To-day it smiles upon you; to-morrow the other fellow's turn comes.

We sought to form up again in companies. There were just twelve men left of our company. Little by little more came up from all directions until at last we counted twenty. Then every one began to ask questions eagerly; every one wanted to know about his friend, mate, or acquaintance. Nobody could give an answer, for every one of us had been thinking merely of himself and of nobody else. Driven by hunger we roamed about the place. But our first action was drinking water, and that in such quantities as if we wanted to drink enough for a lifetime. We found nothing to eat. Only here and there in a garden we discovered a few turnips which we swallowed with a ravenous appetite without washing or even cleaning them superficially.

But where was our company? Nobody knew. We were the company, the twenty of us. And the officers? "Somewhere," a soldier observed, "somewhere in a bomb-proof shelter." What were we to do? We did not know. Soon after a sergeant-major of the field gendarmes came up sitting proudly on his steed. Those "defenders of the Fatherland" have to see to it that too many "shirkers" do not "loiter behind the front." "You are sappers, aren't you?" he roared out. "What are you doing here? 30th. Regiment?" He put a great many questions, which we answered, as well as we were able to. "Where are the others?" "Over there," said a young Berliner, and pointed to the battle-field, "dead or prisoners; maybe some have saved themselves and are elsewhere!" "It doesn't matter," roared out our fierce sergeant-major for whom the conversation began to become unpleasant. "Wait till I come back." "Where are the officers?" Again nobody could answer him. "What are their names? I daresay I shall find them. Maybe they are at Vitry?" We gave him their names—Captain Menke, First Lieutenant Maier, Lieutenants of the Reserves Spahn, Neesen and Heimbach. He gave us a certificate with which to prove the purpose of our "loitering" to other overseers and disappeared. "Let's hope the horse stumbles and the fellow breaks his neck." That was our pious wish which one of our chaps sent after him.

We went into one of the houses that had been pillaged like all the rest, lay down on mattresses that were lying about the rooms and slept—slept like door-mice.

Henry Sheehan and the Battle of Verdun

No single battle of World War I exemplifies the futility and utter waste of humanity than does the one fought at Verdun, France. The historical significance of Verdun dates back to the Romans, who gave the city its original name "Virodunium."[28] Situated on the western frontier of France, the ring of fortresses that surround the city was the essential defense against invading armies from the west. Without the defenses of Verdun, Paris—the soul of France—was completely vulnerable. Verdun, therefore, was a sacred place in the hearts and mind of the French people. The French would defend Verdun at any costs. And the Germans knew it, which is exactly why they chose that particular spot on the map to attack.

Operation Judgment, the name the Germans gave their offensive, began on 21 February 1916 with a bombardment that rained 80,000 shells in one day on the French army at Verdun. German general Erich von Falkenhayn's plan for the offensive was to bleed the French army white, which underscored the brutal nature of combat during this war. Nowhere in the history of warfare had the objective of one army against another been primarily to kill soldiers, and by the end of fighting in that sector, Verdun indeed proved to be a meat grinder of historic proportions. According to Alistair Horne, in *The Price of Glory: Verdun 1916,*

> Estimates on the total casualties inflicted at Verdun vary widely; the accounting in human lives was never meticulous in that war. France's Official War History (published in 1936) sets her losses at Verdun during the ten months of 1916 at 277,231, of which 162,308 were killed or missing, though calculations based on Churchill's "The World Crisis" (1929) would put them as high as 469,600. The most reliable assessment of German losses for the same period comes to roughly 337,000 (Churchill: just under 373,000), and contemporary German lists admitted to over 700,000. Nor is that all, for although strictly speaking the "Battle of Verdun" was limited to the fighting of 1916, in fact a heavy toll of lives had been enacted there long before Falkenhayn's offensive, and bitter fighting continued on its blood-sodden ground through 1917. One recent French estimate that is probably not excessive places the total French and German losses on the Verdun battlefield at 420,000 dead, and 800,000 gassed or wounded; nearly a million and a quarter in all. Supporting this figure is the fact that after the war some 150,000 unidentified and unburied corpses—or fragments of corpses—alone were collected from the battlefield and interred in the huge, forbidding Ossuaire. Still to this day remains are being discovered.[29]

In *Back to the Front: An Accidental Historian Walks the Trenches of World War I,* Stephen O'Shea describes his impressions of this battlefield seventy years after the war:

> Fort Douaumont is in the heart of the battlefields of the right bank. It is the Western Front's ring of desolation.... The forests surrounding it give way to great clearings of tortured ground and landscapes of mass graveyards. It is the Frenchman's postcard image of *la guerre de quatorze.*
>   I stand atop the fort on a morning so gray that no distinction can be made between ground and sky. Even the earth and heavens have deserted the prominence of Douaumont today, preferring to leave the place in some intermediate limbo. Nearby is a neatly kept graveyard with 15,000 headstones stretching off beyond the mist. Beside that, a lighthouse sticks up into the grayness, its top lopped off by low-hanging clouds. At the base of the beacon is an ossuary containing the remains of 150,000 soldiers whose blasted skeletons were found scattered around the vicinity after the war. You can walk around inside the base,

peering through windows at the heaps of bones piled high. Femurs go with femurs, tibias with tibias, skulls, and so on. Off in the woods, wild boars dig up
unrecovered skeletal parts and make a meal.[30]

Such are the horrors of the Verdun battlefield even today. The following excerpt is from an American volunteer ambulance driver in Section II of the
French army, which became officially operational (but with a French officer
commanding) in October 1915. This chapter from Sheehan's book is about
his experiences during the opening days of the Battle of Verdun.

American volunteers for ambulance driving during the war were largely Ivy
Leaguers (one notable exception of course was Ernest Hemingway); Sheehan
was a Harvard man and this well-written narrative belies his education.

FROM *A VOLUNTEER POILU,* HENRY SHEEHAN, 1916

(Boston, 1916), World War I Document Archive,
http://www.lib.byu.edu/~rdh/wwi/memoir/Sheahan/Sheahan1.htm

Chapter X

The Great Days of Verdun

I

THE Verdun I saw in April, 1913, was an out-of-the-way provincial city of little importance outside of its situation as the nucleus of a great fortress. There were two
cities—an old one, *la ville des évêques,* on a kind of acropolis rising from the left bank
of the Meuse, and a newer one built on the meadows of the river. Round the acropolis Vauban had built a citadel whose steep, green-black walls struck root in the mean
streets and narrow lanes on the slopes. Sunless by-ways, ill-paved and sour with the
odor of surface drainage, led to it. Always picturesque, the old town now and then
took on a real beauty. There were fine, shield-bearing doorways of the Renaissance to
be seen, Gothic windows in greasy walls, and here and there at a street corner a hud-
dle of half-timbered houses in a high contrast of invading sunlight and retreating shade.
From the cathedral parapet, there was a view of the distant forts, and a horizontal
sweep of the unharvested, buff-brown moorlands.

"Un peu morte," say the French who knew Verdun before the war. The new town
was without distinction. It was out of date. It had none of the glories that the province
copies from Paris, no boulevards, no *grandes aertères.* Such life as there was, was military. Rue Mazel was bright with the gold braid and scarlet of the *fournisseurs militaires,*
and in the late afternoon chic young officers enlivened the provincial dinginess with
a brave show of handsome uniforms. All day long squads of soldiers went flick! flack!
up and down the street and bugle-calls sounded piercingly from the citadel. The soldiery submerged the civil population.

With no industries of any importance, and becoming less and less of an economic center as the depopulation of the Woevre continued, Verdun lived for its garrison. A fortress since Roman days, the city could not escape its historic destiny. Remembering the citadel, the buttressed cathedral, the soldiery, and the military tradition, the visitor felt himself to be in a soldier's country strong with the memory of many wars.

II

The next day, at noon, we were ordered to go to M———, and at 12.15 we were in convoy formation in the road by the barracks wall. The great *route nationale* from Bar-le-Duc to Verdun runs through a rolling, buff-brown moorland, poor in villages and arid and desolate in aspect. Now it sinks through moorland valleys, now it cuts bowl-shaped depressions in which the spring rains have bred green quagmires, and now, rising, leaps the crest of a hill commanding a landscape of ocean-like immensity.

Gray segments of the road disappear ahead behind fuzzy monticules; a cloud of wood-smoke hangs low over some invisible village in a fold of the moor, and patches of woodland lie like mantles on the barren slopes. Great swathes of barbed wire, a quarter of a mile in width, advancing and retreating, rising and falling with the geographical nature of the defensive position, disappear on both sides to the horizon. And so thick is this wire spread, that after a certain distance the eye fails to distinguish the individual threads and sees only rows of stout black posts filled with a steely, purple mist.

We went though several villages, being greeted in every one with the inevitable error, *Anglais!* We dodged interminable motor-convoys carrying troops, the *poilus* sitting unconcernedly along the benches at the side, their rifles tight between their knees. At midnight we arrived at B———, four miles and a half west of Verdun. The night was clear and bitter cold; the ice-blue winter stars were westering. Refugees tramped past in the darkness. By the sputtering light of a match, I saw a woman go by with a cat in a canary cage; the animal moved uneasily, its eyes shone with fear. A middle-aged soldier went by accompanying an old woman and a young girl. Many pushed baby carriages ahead of them full of knick-knacks and packages.

The crossroad where the ambulances turned off was a maze of beams of light from the autos. There was shouting of orders that nobody could carry out. Wounded, able to walk, passed through the beams of the lamps, the red of their bloodstains, detached against the white of the bandages, presenting the sharpest of contrasts in the silvery glare. At the station, men who had died in the ambulances were dumped hurriedly in a plot of grass by the side of the roadway and covered with a blanket. Never was there seen such a bedlam! But on the main road the great convoys moved smoothly on as if held together by an invisible chain. A smouldering in the sky told of fires in Verdun.

From a high hill between B——— and Verdun I got my first good look at the bombardment. From the edge of earth and sky, far across the moorlands, ray after ray of violet-white fire made a swift stab at the stars. Mingled with the rays, now seen here, now there, the reddish-violet semicircle of the great mortars flared for the briefest instant above the horizon. From the direction of this inferno came a loud roaring, a rumbling and roaring, increasing in volume—the sound of a great river tossing huge rocks through subterranean abysses. Every little while a great shell, falling in the city, would blow a great hole of white in the night, and so thundering was the crash of arrival that we almost expected to see the city sink into the earth.

Terrible in the desolation of the night, on fire, haunted by specters of wounded men who crept along the narrow lanes by the city walls, Verdun was once more undergoing the destinies of war. The shells were falling along rue Mazel and on the citadel. A group of old houses by the Meuse had burnt to rafters of flickering flame, and as I passed them, one collapsed into the flooded river in a cloud of hissing steam.

In order to escape shells, the wounded were taking the obscure by-ways of the town. Our wounded had started to walk to the ambulance station with the others, but, being weak and exhausted, had collapsed on the way. They were waiting for us at a little house just beyond the walls. Said one to the other, "As-tu-vu Maurice?" and the other answered without any emotion, "Il est mort."

The 24th was the most dreadful day. The wind and snow swept the heights of the desolate moor, seriously interfering with the running of the automobiles. Here and there, on a slope, a lorry was stuck in the slush, though the soldier passengers were out of it and doing their best to push it along. The cannonade was still so intense that, in intervals between the heavier snow-flurries, I could see the stabs of fire in the brownish sky. Wrapped in sheepskins and muffled to the ears in knitted scarves that might have come from New England, the territorials who had charge of the road were filling the ruts with crushed rock. Exhaustion had begun to tell on the horses; many lay dead and snowy in the frozen fields. A detachment of khaki-clad, red-fezzed colonial troops passed by, bent to the storm. The news was of the most depressing sort. The wounded could give you only the story of their part of the line, and you heard over and over again, "*Nous avons reculés.*" A detachment of cavalry was at hand; their casques and dark-blue mantles gave them a crusading air. And through the increasing cold and darkness of late afternoon, troops, cannons, horsemen, and motor-trucks vanished toward the edge of the moor where flashed with increasing brilliance the rays of the artillery.

I saw some German prisoners for the first time at T——, below Verdun. They had been marched down from the firing-line. Young men in the twenties for the most part, they seemed even more war-worn than the French. The hideous, helot-like uniform of the German private hung loosely on their shoulders, and the color of their skin was unhealthy and greenish. They were far from appearing starved; I noticed two or three who looked particularly sound and hearty. Nevertheless, they were by no means as sound-looking as the ruddier French.

The *poilus* crowded round to see them, staring into their faces without the least malevolence. At last—at last—*voilà enfin des Boches!* A little to the side stood a strange pair, two big men wearing an odd kind of grayish protector and apron over their bodies. Against a near-by wall stood a kind of flattish tank to which a long metallic hose was attached. The French soldiers eyed them with contempt and disgust. I caught the words, "Flame-throwers!"

· · · · ·

III

A few miles below Verdun, on a narrow strip of meadowland between the river and the northern bluffs, stood an eighteenth-century château and the half-dozen houses of its dependents. The hurrying river had flooded the low fields and then retreated, turning the meadows and pasturages to bright green, puddly marshes, malodorous with swampy exhalations. Beyond the swirls and currents of the river and its vanishing islands of pale-green pebbles, rose the brown, deserted hills of the Hauts de Meuse. The top of one height had been pinched into the rectangle of a fortress; little forests ran along the sky-line of the heights, and a narrow road, slanting across a spur of the valley, climbed and disappeared.

The château itself was a huge, three-story box of gray-white stone with a slate roof, a little turret *en poivrière* at each corner, and a graceless classic doorway in the principal façade. A wide double gate, with a coronet in a tarnished gold medallion set in the iron arch-piece, gave entrance to this place through a kind of courtyard formed by the rear of the château and the walls of two low wings devoted to the stables and the servants' quarters. Within, a high clump of dark-green myrtle, ringed with muddy, rutscarred turf, marked the theoretical limits of a driveway. Along the right-hand wall stood the rifles of the wounded, and in a corner, a great snarled pile of bayonets, belts, cartridge-boxes, gas-mask satchels, greasy tin boxes of anti-lice ointment, and dented helmets. A bright winter sunlight fell on walls dank from the river mists, and heightened the austerity of the landscape. Beyond a bend in the river lay the smoke of the battle of Douaumont; shells broke, pin-points of light, in the upper fringes of the haze.

The château had been a hospital since the beginning of the war. A heavy smell of ether and iodoform lay about it, mixed with the smell of the war. This effluvia of an army, mixed with the sharper reek of anesthetics, was the atmosphere of the hospital. The great rush of wounded had begun. Every few minutes the ambulances slopped down a miry byway, and turned in the gates; tired, putty-faced hospital attendants took out the stretchers and the nouveaux clients; mussy bundles of blue rags and bloody blankets turned into human beings; an overworked, nervous *médecin* chef shouted contradictory orders at the *brancardiers,* and passed into real crises of hysterical rage.

"Avancez!" he would scream at the bewildered chauffeurs of the ambulances; and an instant later, "Reculez! Reculez!"

The wounded in the stretchers, strewn along the edges of the driveway, raised patient, tired eyes at his snarling.

Another doctor, a little bearded man wearing a white apron and the red velvet képi of an army physician, questioned each batch of new arrivals. Deep lines of fatigue had traced themselves under his kindly eyes; his thin face had a dreadful color. Some of the wounded had turned their eyes from the sun; others, too weak to move, lay stonily blinking. Almost expressionless, silent, they resigned themselves to the attendants as if these men were the deaf ministers of some inexorable power.

The surgeon went from stretcher to stretcher looking at the diagnosis cards attached at the *poste de secours,* stopping occasionally to ask the fatal question, "As-tu craché du sang? " (Have you spit blood?) A thin oldish man with a face full of hollows like that of an old horse, answered "Oui," faintly. Close by, an artilleryman, whose cannon had burst, looked with calm brown eyes out of a crooked and bluish face. Another, with a soldier's tunic thrown capewise over his naked torso, trembled in his thin blanket, and from the edges of a cotton and lint-pad dressing hastily stuffed upon a shoulder wound, an occasional drop of blood slid down his lean chest.

A little to one side, the cooks of the hospital, in their greasy aprons, watched the performance with a certain calm interest. In a few minutes the wounded were sorted and sent to the various wards. I was ordered to take three men who had been successfully operated on to the barracks for convalescents several miles away.

A highway and an unused railroad, both under heavy fire from German guns on the Hauts de Meuse, passed behind the château and along the foot of the bluffs. There were a hundred shell holes in the marshes between the road and the river, black-lipped craters in the sedgy green; there were ugly punches in the brown earth of the bluffs, and deep scoops in the surface of the road. The telephone wires, cut by shell fragments, fell in stiff, draping lines to the ground. Every once in a while a shell would fall into the river, causing a silvery gray geyser to hang for an instant above the green eddies of the Meuse. A certain village along this highway was the focal point of the firing. Many of the houses had been blown to pieces, and fragments of red tile, bits of shiny glass, and lumps of masonry were strewn all over the deserted street.

As I hurried along, two shells came over, one sliding into the river with a Hip! and the other landing in a house about two hundred yards away. A vast cloud of grayish-black smoke befogged the cottage, and a section of splintered timber came buzzing through the air and fell into a puddle. From the house next to the one struck, a black cat came slinking, paused for an indecisive second in the middle of the street, and ran back again. Through the canvas partition of the ambulance, I heard the voices of my convalescents. "No more marmites!" I cried to them as I swung down a road out of shell reach. I little knew what was waiting for us beyond the next village.

A regiment of Zouaves going up to the line was resting at the crossroad, and the regimental wagons, drawn up in waiting line, blocked the narrow road completely. At the angle between the two highways, under the four trees planted by pious custom of the Meuse, stood a cross of thick planks. From each arm of the cross, on winesoaked straps, dangled, like a bunch of grapes, a cluster of dark-blue canteens; rifles were stacked round its base, and under the trees stood half a dozen clipped-headed, bull-necked Zouaves. A rather rough-looking adjutant, with a bullet head disfigured by a frightful scar at the corner of his mouth, rode up and down the line to see if all was well. Little groups were handing round a half loaf of army bread, and washing it down with gulps of wine.

"Hello, sport!" they cried at me; and the favorite "All right," and "Tommy!"

The air was heavy with the musty smell of street mud that never dries during winter time, mixed with the odor of the tired horses, who stood, scarcely moving, backed away from their harnesses against the mire-gripped wagons. Suddenly the order to go on again was given; the carters snapped their whips, the horses pulled, the noisy, lumbering, creaky line moved on, and the men fell in behind, in any order.

I started my car again and looked for an opening through the *mêlée*.

Beyond the cross, the road narrowed and flanked one of the southeastern forts of the city. A meadow, which sloped gently upward from the road to the abrupt hillside of the fortress, had been used as a place of encampment and had been trodden into a surface of thick cheesy mire. Here and there were the ashes of fires. There were hundreds of such places round the moorland villages between Verdun and Bar-le-Duc. The fort looked squarely down on Verdun, and over its grassy height came the drumming of the battle, and the frequent crash of big shells falling into the city.

In a corner lay the anatomical relics of some horses killed by an air-bomb the day before. And even as I noted them, I heard the muffled Pom! Pom! Pom! of anti-aircraft guns. My back was to the river and I could not see what was going on.

"What is it?" I said to a Zouave who was plodding along beside the ambulance.

"Des Boches—crossing the river."

The regiment plodded on as before. Now and then a soldier would stop and look up at the aeroplanes.

"He's coming!" I heard a voice exclaim.

Suddenly, the adjutant whom I had seen before came galloping down the line, shouting, "Arrêtez! Arrêtez! Pas de mouvement!"

A current of tension ran down the troop with as much reality as a current of water runs down hill. I wondered whether the Boche had seen us.

"Is he approaching?" I asked.

"Yes."

Ahead of me was a one-horse wagon, and ahead of that a wagon with two horses carrying the medical supplies. The driver of the latter, an oldish, thick-set, wine-faced fellow, got down an instant from his wagon, looked at the Boche, and resumed his seat. A few seconds later, there sounded the terrifying scream of an air-bomb, a roar, and I found myself in a bitter swirl of smoke. The shell had fallen right between the horses of the two-horse wagon, blowing the animals to pieces, splintering the wagon, and killing the driver. Something sailed swiftly over my head, and landed just behind the ambulance. It was a chunk of the skull of one of the horses. The horse attached to the wagon ahead of me went into a frenzy of fear and backed his wagon into my ambulance, smashing the right lamp. In the twinkling of an eye, the soldiers dispersed. Some ran into the fields. Others crouched in the wayside ditch. A cart upset. Another bomb dropped screaming in a field and burst; a cloud of smoke rolled away down the meadow.

When the excitement had subsided, it was found that a soldier had been wounded. The bodies of the horses were rolled over into the ditch, the wreck of the wagon was dragged to the miry field, and the regiment went on. In a very short time I got to the hospital and delivered my convalescents.

My way home ran through the town of S——, an ugly, overgrown village of the Verdunois, given up to the activities of the staff directing the battle. The headquarters building was the *hôtel de ville,* a large eighteenth-century edifice, in an acre of trampled mud a little distance from the street. Before the building flowed the great highway from Bar-le-Duc to Verdun; relays of motor lorries went by, and gendarmes, organized into a kind of traffic squad, stood every hundred feet or so. The atmosphere of S—— at the height of the battle was one of calm organization; it would not have been hard to believe that the motor-lorries and unemotional men were at the service of some great master-work of engineering. There was something of the holiday in the attitude of the inhabitants of the place; they watched the motor show exactly as they might have watched a circus parade.

"Les voilà," said somebody.

A little bemedaled group appeared on the steps of the *hôtel de ville*. Dominating it was Joffre. Above middle height, silver-haired, elderly, he has a certain paternal look which his eye belies; Joffre's eye is the hard eye of a commander-in-chief, the military eye, the eye of an Old Testament father if you will. De Castelnau was speaking, making no gestures—an old man with an ashen skin, deep-set eye and great hooked nose, a long cape concealed the thick, age-settled body. Poincaré stood listening, with a look at once worried and brave, the ghost of a sad smile lingering on a sensitive mouth. Last of all came Pétain, the protégé of De Castelnau, who commanded at Verdun—a tall, square-built man, not un-English in his appearance, with grizzled hair and the sober face of a thinker. But his mouth and jaw are those of a man of action, and the look in his gray eyes is always changing. Now it is speculative and analytic, now steely and cold.

In the shelter of a doorway stood a group of territorials, getting their first real news of the battle from a Paris newspaper. I heard "Nous avons reculé—huit kilometers— le général Pétain." A motor-lorry drowned out the rest.

That night we were given orders to be ready to evacuate the château in case the Boches advanced. The drivers slept in the ambulances, rising at intervals through the night to warm their engines. The buzz of the motors sounded through the tall pines of the château park, drowning out the rumbling of the bombardment and the monotonous roaring of the flood. Now and then a trench light, rising like a spectral star over the lines on the Hauts de Meuse, would shine reflected in the river. At intervals attendants carried down the swampy paths to the chapel the bodies of soldiers who had died during the night. The cannon flashing was terrific. Just before dawn, half a dozen batteries of "seventy-fives" came in a swift trot down the shelled road; the men leaned over on their steaming horses, the harnesses rattled and jingled, and the cavalcade swept on, outlined a splendid instant against the mortar flashes and the streaks of day.

On my morning trip a soldier with bandaged arm was put beside me on the front seat. He was about forty years old; a wiry black beard gave a certain fullness to his thin face, and his hands were pudgy and short of finger. When he removed his helmet, I saw that he was bald. A bad cold caused him to speak in a curious whispering tone, giving to everything he said the character of a grotesque confidence.

"What do you do *en civil?*" he asked.

I told him.

"I am a pastry cook," he went on; "my specialty is Saint-Denis apple tarts."

A marmite intended for the road landed in the river as he spoke.

"Have you ever had one? They are very good when made with fresh cream." He sighed.

"How did you get wounded?" said I.

"Éclat d'obus," he replied, as if that were the whole story. After a pause he added, "Douaumont—yesterday."

I thought of the shells I had seen bursting over the fort.

"Do you put salt in chocolate?" he asked professionally.

"Not as a rule," I replied.

"It improves it," he pursued, as if he were revealing a confidential dogma. "The Boche bread is bad, very bad, much worse than a year ago. Full of crumbles and lumps. *Dégoutant!*"

The ambulance rolled up to the evacuation station, and my pastry cook alighted.

"When the war is over, come to my shop," he whispered benevolently," and you shall have some *tartes aux pommes à la mode de Saint-Denis* with my wife and me."

"With fresh cream?" I asked.

"Of course," he replied seriously.

I accepted gratefully, and the good old soul gave me his address.

In the afternoon a sergeant rode with me. He was somewhere between twenty-eight and thirty, thick-set of body, with black hair and the tanned and ruddy complexion of outdoor folk. The high collar of a dark-blue sweater rose over his great coat and circled a muscular throat; his gray socks were pulled country-wise outside of the legs of his blue trousers. He had an honest, pleasant face; there was a certain simple, wholesome quality about the man. In the piping times of peace, he was a *cultivateur* in the Valois, working his own little farm; he was married and had two little boys. At Douaumont, a fragment of a shell had torn open his left hand.

"The Boches are not going to get through up there?"

"Not now. As long as we hold the heights, Verdun is safe." His simple French, innocent of argot, had a good country twang. "But oh, the people killed! Comme il y a des gens tués! He pronounced the final s of the word *gens* in the manner of the Valois.

"Ça s'accroche aux arbres," he continued.

The vagueness of the *ça* had a dreadful quality in it that made you see trees and mangled bodies. "We had to hold the crest of Douaumont under a terrible fire, and clear the craters on the slope when the Germans tried to fortify them. Our 'seventy-fives' dropped shells into the big craters as I would drop stones into a pond. *Pauvres gens!*"

The phrase had an earth-wide sympathy in it, a feeling that the translation "poor folks" does not render. He had taken part in a strange incident. There had been a terrible corps-à-corps in one of the craters that had culminated in a victory for the French; but the lieutenant of his company had left a kinsman behind with the dead and wounded. Two nights later, the officer and the sergeant crawled down the dreadful slope to the crater where the combat had taken place, in the hope of finding the wounded man. They could hear faint cries and moans from the crater before they got to it. The light of a pocket flash-lamp showed them a mass of dead and wounded on the floor of the crater—"un tas de mourants et de cadavres," as he expressed it.

After a short search they found the man for whom they were looking; he was still alive but unconscious. They were dragging him out when a German, hideously wounded, begged them to kill him.

"Moi, je n'ai plus jambes," he repeated in French; "pitié, tuez-moi."

He managed to make the lieutenant see that if he went away and left them, they would all die in the agonies of thirst and open wounds. A little flickering life still lin-

The rubble and ruins of what was once a village along the Western Front. In the modern age, what sometimes took centuries to build, now—with high explosive artillery shells—only took minutes to destroy. Photo by the author.

gered in a few; there were vague *râles* in the darkness. A *rafale* of shells fell on the slope; the violet glares outlined the mouth of the crater.

"Ferme tes yeux:" (shut your eyes), said the lieutenant to the German. The Frenchmen scrambled over the edge of the crater with their unconscious burden, and then, from a little distance, threw hand-grenades into the pit till all the moaning died away.

Two weeks later, when the back of the attack had been broken and the organization of the defense had developed into a trusted routine, I went again to Verdun. The snow was falling heavily, covering the piles of *débris* and sifting into the black skeletons of the burned houses. Untrodden in the narrow streets lay the white snow. Above the Meuse, above the ugly burned areas in the old town on the slope, rose the shell-spattered walls of the citadel and the cathedral towers of the still, tragic town. The drumming of the bombardment had died away. The river was again in flood. In a deserted wine-shop on a side street well protected from shells by a wall of sandbags was a post of territorials.

To the tragedy of Verdun, these men were the chorus; there was something Sophoclean in this group of older men alone in the silence and ruin of the beleaguered city. A stove filled with wood from the wrecked houses gave out a comfortable heat, and in an alley-way, under cover, stood a two-wheeled hose cart, and an old-fashioned see-

saw fire pump. There were old clerks and bookkeepers among the soldier firemen—
retired gendarmes who had volunteered, a country schoolmaster, and a shrewd peasant from the Lyonnais. Watch was kept from the heights of the citadel, and the
outbreak of fire in any part of the city was telephoned to the shop. On that day only
a few explosive shells had fallen.

"Do you want to see something odd, *mon vieux?*" said one of the *pompiers* to me;
and he led me through a labyrinth of cellars to a cold, deserted house. The snow had
blown through the shell-splintered window-panes. In the dining-room stood a table,
the cloth was laid and the silver spread; but a green feathery fungus had grown in a
dish of food and broken straws of dust floated on the wine in the glasses. The territorial took my arm, his eyes showing the pleasure of my responding curiosity, and
whispered,

"There were officers quartered here who were called very suddenly. I saw the servant of one of them yesterday; they have all been killed."

Outside there was not a flash from the batteries on the moor. The snow continued
to fall, and darkness, coming on the swift wings of the storm, fell like a mantle over
the desolation of the city.

·····

Aviation

The airplane made its combat debut during World War I, and aviation
quickly developed as an important force in modern warfare. In *Technology and
War: From 2000 B.C. to the Present,* Martin Van Creveld describes the airplane's
rise to prominence:

> When war broke out in 1914, aerial operations were initially conducted on a
> very modest scale—all belligerents put together only had around 500 aircraft
> among them. This situation, however, soon changed. With the exception of the
> signal services, there was no arm in World War I which expanded as fast as the
> various air corps.... A technical arm *per excellence,* the air corps of all the bel-
> ligerents were mostly staffed by well-schooled young men of bourgeois ori-
> gins.... [T]he prevailing values were solidly technological and middle class. The
> combination of these values with the spirit of adventure, freedom, and indi-
> vidual heroism offered by aviation proved too strong for the heads of many.[31]

Alone up in the air, the World War I pilots' experiences were totally different
from their earth-bound comrades, the soldiers who were dug into the ground
and crowded into trenches. The increasing lethality of the airplane's mission,
including being the eyes of the artillery, added to the destruction and suffering

of the infantry, which initiated a rivalry between these two disparate arms of military service. Despite the airplane being a modern technology, the military tradition that pilots primarily pursued was old-fashioned chivalry. At the same time, however, all forms of chivalry were being eradicated on the ground.

Flyers and soldiers just did not get along; even those serving under the same flag quarreled. Byron Farwell states in *Over There: The United States in The Great War, 1917–1918* that "much of the friction between flyers and ground forces was caused by mutual ignorance. The infantry had no understanding of the capabilities and restraints of the Air Service nor did the pilots and observers understand the needs of the infantry."[32] Basically, the infantry wanted close air support either to destroy the enemy in front or to help keep the enemy's head down until they did it themselves; the flyers chafed at such work. Their thinking was that it was hard to distinguish friend from foe in the tangled mess below, and such missions lacked the glamour of air-to-air combat. Besides, one does not become an ace by shooting at the ground. In *The First World War,* John Keegan observes that while the airplane served primarily as "at the level of artillery observation, 'balloon busting' and dogfighting to gain or retain air superiority," the war in the air in 1918 "would take a dramatic leap forward into the fields of ground attack and long-range strategic bombing."[33]

Captain Alfred A. Cunningham was the first American military aviator to witness the war firsthand. He would eventually command the 1st Marine Aviation Force as a lieutenant colonel, which was comprised of 149 officers and 842 enlisted men. This unit launched its first mission in October 1918 and by the "end of the war had flown in fourteen raids and dropped 27,000 pounds of bombs. Between four and twelve enemy planes were destroyed by these Marines; four Marine flyers died in air actions."[34]

In his 1917 diary, Cunningham lacks the philosophical insight to know what the new machines of war would do to increase the suffering of mankind. This was decades before Tokyo fire bombings, Dresden, and Hiroshima. He is, however, only a soldier and not a poet or philosopher. Yet his observations are important to note because they underscore how essential this new technology would be to the war effort. What makes Cunningham's observations essential reading is that they are a detailed inventory of the modern machines of war. Also, Cunningham's pragmatic observations are an interesting glimpse of life crossing the U-boat-infested Atlantic and behind the lines in war-torn France. In his diary, he writes, "I have received the best impression of the business side of the war here." War business is exactly what Captain Cunningham is all about.

FROM DIARY, MARINE FLYER IN FRANCE CAPTAIN ALFRED A. CUNNINGHAM, NOVEMBER 1917 TO JANUARY 1918

World War I Document Archive,
http://www.lib.byu.edu/~rdh/wwi/memoir/marines/cunning/flyer.html

Saturday, November 3, 1917
New York and S.S. "St. Paul"

Got up 6:30 a.m. after only 2:45 sleep. Went to paymasters for mileage checks. Saw Mrs. Whiting and received box from her to take to Ken Whiting in Paris. Got money changed and went on Board the St. Paul at 11:30 a.m. We sailed at 12:30 with only 47 first class passengers and apparently not many 2nd class. I have seen three women and a small boy. Had my last glimpse of Long Island about 3 p.m. Suppose there are a great many experiences in store for me before I see it again. I have stateroom 29 all to myself and think I am lucky to be on the Promenade Deck. Weather bad and ship cold and uncomfortable.

. . . . .

Saturday, November 10, 1917
S.S. "St. Paul," In War Zone

Our first day in the submarine danger zone is over safely, but it was one of the most strenuous days I have passed. I went on watch at 6 a.m. Twilight is the most dangerous time of the day and everyone is extremely alert then. I stayed on watch until 10 a.m., went back on at 2 p.m. and stayed until after evening twilight. This looking for submarines is the most nerve straining duty I ever did. You must see them first, and, as their periscope is very small, the Odds are against you. You feel that the slightest negligence on your part might lose the ship and all on board. I freely strained my eyesight while on watch today. I am confident that I saw the periscope of a submarine today, but, as it did not reappear I might have been mistaken. The ten minutes after I saw it were anxious ones. We met our convoy of two U.S. destroyers (Conyngham and Jacob Jones) at 4 p.m. and were much relieved to see them. They were mottled all over with the most crazy colors and designs but they looked good to us, even if they were camouflaged to the limit. We were glad to see them, not so much for the slight additional protection they give as to the fact that if we are sunk, they will pick us up from the lifeboats. No merchant vessel is allowed to stop to pick up survivors of a torpedo ship. Without the destroyers we would have to drift around in lifeboats until some passing destroyer found us. I personally have no desire to drift around the North Atlantic in an open boat for several days this time of the year. On the last trip this ship passed twelve lifeboats full of people from a torpedo ship and could not stop to pick them up. They were found two days later by a destroyer. We passed some wreckage this afternoon but could not make out just what it was. I have had a most strenuous day and am all worn out.

. . . . .

Thursday, November 22, 1917

Grand Hotel, Paris, France

Got up at 9 o'clock and went to the bank and drew out 500 fcs. Went over to the Invalides and saw all kinds of captured German guns and howitzers. Also the 4 nacelles of the Zeppelin L-49 captured recently and saw sections of the aluminum framework. They had on view one Fokker monoplane, an L.V.G. biplane and a Rumpler 2 seater which were captured in excellent condition. They were all interesting, especially the motors, one of which had 5 valves to each cylinder, 3 intake and 2 exhaust. The most interesting thing I saw was Capt. Guynemer's little Spad, the "Veaux Charles," which means Charles, old fellow. He downed 19 boches with this machine. The French have it decorated profusely with the tri-color and flowers all over it. I spent all afternoon looking for something to carry back to my little sweetheart. I remember she wanted an ivory toilet set and decided she would have it if it could be found. It looked hopeless until I asked Milling if he knew of a lady who would help me. He got the Comptesse to go with me and we finally found a shop that agreed to make one to order for me within three weeks. I hope I get it before I go back and I hope my little wife likes it. I thought I would have my photo taken to send her but found that it would take 3 weeks to get the proofs and *6 months* after that to get the photos! At night I went over to the Latin quartier with a crowd to a studio and we went to the Theatre Femina. To bed at 11:30.

· · · · ·

Friday, November 23, 1917

Hotel de l'Univers Tours, France

Got up at 9. Tried to buy films for kodak. Could only find one store in Paris that had them and they would only sell 3 rolls. Left Gare de Orsay on 2:35 p.m. train for Tours. We passed through a very pretty country. There did not seem to be many men in the small towns. All the farming and plowing along the way seemed to be done by young boys. I saw very few women at work in the fields. I was surprised at the number of airplanes I saw flying. They were flying all around us all the way down and appeared to all be slow pushers. Probably Caudron training machines. I arrived in Tours at 6:20 p.m. and went to the Hotel l'Universe. There are a number of U.S. Army officers here who say they are guarding the Line of Communications. They have more than a regiment here at Tours out for the life of me I can't see why they are loafing around here or what there is here to guard. I should think they would have them up near the front getting ready to fight. Maj. Dunsworth came in the Hotel after supper and is going to send an auto in for me in the morning. The aviation camp, which has been taken over by the U.S. Army is about 4 miles out of town. Tours is where that pretty blue and gold china is made. The factories are closed now, however.

· · · · ·

Saturday, November 24, 1917

Army Ecole de Aviation, Tours, France

Got up at 7 a.m. and Maj. Dunsworth had his Hudson at Hotel for me at 8. Rode out to the Ecole de Aviation, which is 2 1/2 miles from town. The weather was misty with a strong wind. Dunsworth met me and Lt. Knight showed me around the place. It is quite a big place with 10 very large wooden hangars and several Bessioneau canvas hangars. No flying on account of the wind. They have about 65 Caudron training planes and 2 Nieuport of chasse model but old. This place can be made into an excellent school but is in bad shape now. Saw my first German prisoners at work on the grounds. They appear satisfied with their lot and are good workers. There was one officer (not working) who strutted around as if he owned the place. I was surprised to see how loosely they were guarded. At 3 p.m. the wind let up and about 20 machines flew until dark. The Caudrons fly better than they look. There was some looping. Saw the twin motored Caudrons and large Breguet used for the defense of Paris. They use Anzani and LeRhone motors in training machines. Seems to be very, especially the LeRhone. Am afraid Dunsworth is not much of a C.O. Most of the men who handle the machines are Algerians. There are a great many women working in the shops. Rode back to the Hotel with Dunsworth and had dinner with him. Wrote to my little sweetheart. Tours must be pretty in summer but is cold and foggy now. Is on the bank of the Loire. Has a very fine Cathedral. Wish the weather would improve.

. . . . .

Monday, November 26, 1917
Ecole de Aviation Francaise, Avord, France
Got up at daylight and walked 1 1/2 miles to station almost frozen. The sun was shining today the first time since I can remember but it has been very cold. Arrived in Avord at 9:30 a.m. and found that the aviation school was 2 miles from the station and no way to ride. I started out on foot in mud 2 inches deep and my feet were wet and freezing when I arrived. Was introduced to the Commandant, Col. Fabre, and the Chief of Flying, Capt. Levy. Both were extremely nice. The Colonel cannot speak English so I cannot know him well. Capt. Levy was manager of a South American railroad and speaks English very well. He is the real head of the school and has a very fine organization. This school is larger than all the other schools in France combined. They have 800 airplanes in commission and have 11 flying fields besides the big one at the main station. There are 3000 mechanics here. They have every kind of machine here made in France. This afternoon I made 10 flights to the different schools with Capt. Levy. He has the reputation of being very reckless and he lives up to it. I was asked to mess with the Commandant and the 3 senior officers, which the other officers seemed to think is a special honor. I have a room in the officers' quarters which is a wooden shack and cold as a stable. I will certainly be glad to get back to Paris and be warm again. My bed consists of a cot with one blanket and a sheet. I am going to sleep in my underclothes and put my overcoat over me and expect to freeze anyway. I have received the best impression of the business side of the war here. Everyone here is in dead earnest and you can realize the grimness of it when you realize that an average of one man a day is killed flying here. This afternoon we flew low over the wreck of a machine in which a pilot was killed yesterday. They keep the deaths as quiet as possible and I do not know if anyone was killed today or not. I talked to several pilots who have flown over the lines and Lieut. Privat, who has 4 boches to his credit is going to show me his log tomorrow and tell me some of his experiences. I wish I could

stay here longer as it is a most interesting place. The pilots from all the primary schools in France come here to prepare for the finishing schools at Pau, Cazaux and LeCrotoy. There is an American ex-ambulance driver here named de Roode, who is a lieut. in the French Army now. He is detailed as my guide around the place. I am afraid he is somewhat of a jack-leg, but he has been very nice and accommodating to me. I spent a few hours tonight in the officers' club, or Circle Officers, where all the officers gather and have tea or coffee and play cards when off duty. There are 4 Russians and 2 Cossack officers here training. They do not seem to be very popular with the French.

. . . . .

Sunday, December 2, 1917
Hotel de France, Pau, France
Got up late as today is a repose day at the Ecole and there will be no flying: Walked around with Rolph and met Capt. Levy from Avord. At 1:15 went out to the Ecole and found everything locked up except the hangars. Saw some captured German machines and all the wrecks which have happened in the last few days. Saw the machine in which young Fowler was killed day before yesterday. It was certainly a wreck and had blood all over the cockpit. I saw pieces of Fowler's flesh still hanging to the windshield. They kill here more than 1 pilot every day, which, when one thinks of it, is an enormous percentage. There must be some fault with their training methods. The Ecole is much smaller than at Avord and they use only the Nieuport machine. There is the main field and four small fields nearby. It is 10 miles from Pau on a dinky train road. We came back to the hotel and had dinner and afterwards Bradley, an American in the French Flying Corps played the piano and another man sang. In our little party was the Duchess (who is 18) and Countess Bourg. I am certainly getting chummy with the aristocracy. I must get up very early in the morning so had best get to bed. I wish I could see my sweet little wife tonight or at least know what she was doing and thinking about. It is only 7 o'clock at home now.

. . . . .

Saturday, December 15, 1917
Paris and Villacoublay, France
Got up at 8 a.m. and went to Maj. Wills' office to see about expense account. From there I went to Aviation Headquarters to see if my orders to the front had come. They had not, so I went out to see the Spad Factory. It was extremely interesting. The workmanship is wonderful. It hardly seems to be possible to build a machine lighter than they have and it is strongly built too. The way they mounted the 1 1/2" cannon in the motor and the automatic loader were interesting. Their 300 h.p. experimental machine flew the wings off of it and buried the pilot 9 ft. After lunch I drove out to Villacoublay, the largest aviation station in France. It was well worth the trip. It is where all the new types of machines are tried out. I never saw so many different types before. From the big Voisin triplane that looks like a battleship down to the little 150 m.p.h. Morane parasol. The Morane and Nieuport Monosoupape are so fast that you

wonder how a man can live in them. I came back at dark. My orders have not come yet, which means I will have to stay here another day. At the hotel tonight I met Maj.——— about half full with a disgustingly painted up little French street walker he calls Lulu. It makes me sick the way some of these married officers in France have already contracted diseases. I was tired after dinner and came up to my room and have been writing up my notes. My rheumatism is uncomfortable tonight. I feel like a new man since I heard from my precious little wife yesterday. I bet I have read her letter fifty times and expect to read it some more. I am afraid these lazy Army officers are going to mess up my plans by delaying my orders to the front. They never seem to do anything on time or well.

. . . . .

Monday, December 17, 1917
Front of 4th French Army
Got up frozen stiff and left after breakfast in a staff car for the 13th Groupe of combat machines. They are just behind the line of balloons with hangars around the edge of a wood. The Groupe is composed of the 65th, 85th, 15th and 124th Escadrilles. The 124th is the LaFayette Escadrille at LaCheppe. The others are at La Noblette. Saw quite a lot of the LaFayette pilots. The pilots live in huts of rough boards and the wind whistles through with little obstruction. Can't describe anything as my hands are numb with cold. There is a line of old trenches on side of field which soldiers off duty use in practice drills. These poor soldiers are really pitiful and are thoroughly sick of the war. Just in front of us are the line of sausage balloons. They look queer hanging up there. It cleared up in the afternoon and I saw very interesting sights of antiaircraft shells bursting around our machines. Two or 3 boches came out and I saw our pilots go for them. It was certainly pretty but the boches all got away. It is so cold I can hardly write. At dark 2 of our pilots had not returned and we were uneasy about them. At 8 p.m. we called up the advanced artillery and they said the last they saw of them they were in German territory fighting 3 boches. We were worried until I came in on foot at 9 p.m. and said they had gotten lost and landed several miles away and walked to camp. At night I noticed the artillery more. It sounded like a pitched battle to me but it is just the ordinary thing. Too cold to write more.

. . . . .

Tuesday, December 18, 1917
Same Locality
Got up frozen stiff. The weather fairly clear. Persuaded a French pilot of a biplane fighting Spad to take me over the lines. We went up like an elevator and talk about speed! We were over the lines in no time and I was all eyes. The archies bursting near us worried me some and made it hard to look all the time for boches. I saw something to one side that looked like a fountain of red ink. Found it was the machine gun tracer bullets from the ground. After a few minutes we sighted a boche 2 seater just below

us. We made for him. It was the finest excitement I ever had. I got my machine gun ready. Before we got to him he dived and headed for home. On 1 of our rolls I let loose a couple of strings of 6 at him but it was too far for good shooting. After following him a ways over the lines we turned to look for another. None were out so we came home. Finest trip I ever had. If the boche had not turned quite so soon, I think I might have got him. Watched pilots doing stunts in afternoon. At about 8 p.m. we were huddled around a small fire in the hut when we heard 3 boche machines fly over very low. Two of them did not locate our place and went on. We went outside and saw the other 1 flying around trying to locate the hangars so we made for the machine gun pit. He finally flew down the line and let go a couple of bombs, as he came over we opened on him but the gun jammed and no one could fix it in the dark. He made 3 trips and let go 2 bombs each trip. Then he left us. We found he had dropped them all in the woods and no machines were hurt. We went back and tried to sleep but every time a big gun would go off I thought it was another raid. I am writing this Wednesday night with my hands blue from cold. There is certainly no lack of excitement around here.

· · · · ·

Wednesday, December 19, 1917
French front near Suippes
Walked 6 miles before daylight and went in the trenches. They are filthy and horrible. Don't see how the men stand it. The stink of dead Huns in front is awful even in this cold weather. Soon after daylight I followed a party cleaning out an old communicating trench with hand grenades. I went until I saw 4 boches killed by grenades and 2 bayoneted and 1 poilu shot through the head. It was sickening but I suppose I would get used to it. Everyone does. Late in afternoon the boches began shelling the trench and we retired to dugouts. I stood in the observation post a few minutes to see the show but only until a shell landed near and the shock nearly knocked me over. I hunted the dugout also. One observer was wounded. After dark we started for the rear and I was relieved to get some pure air. After walking miles in the cold I am writing this. The shells bursting at night are very pretty. It has been a rather exciting day.

· · · · ·

Friday, December 28, 1917
Dunkirk and British Front
Still about half sick and rheumatism giving me fits. From our station went over to French and British seaplane stations. Then went out to R.N.A.S. bombing station near front. Bitter cold. The Handley Pages look like battleships, Quite a little artillery actions today. Drove back through Dunkirk. Is a sad deserted looking place. There is scarcely a whole pane of glass in the city and it is hard to find a building which has not been scarred or damaged by bombs. On a recent raid 1 bomb killed 50 people. I doubt if we have a raid tonight. Too many clouds. Walked home alone tonight. Weird

feeling walking through city without a single light or sign of life in it. Rheumatism hurting me so am going to bed now.

. . . . .

[Captain Cunningham's last entry in his diary is dated 12 January, 1918. He is at sea on the way home from his introductory trip to the Western Front.]

TOPICS FOR WRITTEN AND ORAL DISCUSSION

1. View one of the documentaries that are now available on video (the PBS series on the Great War is one suggestion), taking notes on what you see and hear. Using your notes, write a war diary of your own. Then, revise that diary into a memoir of your experience learning about World War I. Compare your memoir with an actual one from the war. Describe some similarities and differences.

2. Procure a modern road map of Western Europe and trace a line where the primary line of trenches flowed from the North Sea to Switzerland during the war. Make a list of some of the major cities along this line and look them up on the Internet. Describe what you see and compare and contrast these pictures with those you may find in histories of the war.

3. Research and debate the question as to who started the Great War. Was it Wilhelm II or the ambitions of Great Britain? How far back can one trace the origins of the war?

4. Is Frederic Henry a coward for deserting the Italian army? Why does he shoot the enlisted man in his ambulance unit? Is Henry a moral person or is he an opportunist? Which character do you favor in the novel, Catherine Barkley or Frederic Henry? Why exactly does Catherine adore Henry so much?

5. On 11 September 2001, terrorists flew planes into the World Trade Center in New York City and destroyed that building complex. Research the news coverage of that event and the U.S.'s response. Pay careful attention to the words that were being used and debate whether the world was being manipulated into war or not. Research the words of the terrorists as well.

6. Define the meaning of *irony*. It has become an overused word that has lost its meaning in the modern context. Come up with one strict definition and find as many instances of it as you can in *A Farewell to Arms, All Quiet on the Western Front,* and *Good-bye to All That.* Now compare and contrast the instances of your definition of irony in the documents and narratives found elsewhere in chapter 1.

7. Although it could be a gruesome exercise, go through each of the memoirs that have been excerpted in this chapter and count the number of the dead that are mentioned in them. Also, when you're reading the books of literature discussed in this chapter, take a count of the dead in them as well. You will be surprised how many you come up with. However, you may also be surprised to discover how many people die each day in the very city you live in. Take a similar survey of those who are killed in your hometown by reading the newspaper. It could be argued that World War I and the great number of ordinary citizens who were trained to kill started the explosion of homicides in the last century, which is also carrying over to this one. Write an essay for or against this argument.

NOTES

1. Ernest Hemingway, *A Farewell to Arms* (New York: Scribners Paperback Fiction Edition, 1995 [1929]), 184–85. All subsequent citations are from this text and page numbers are indicated parenthetically.

2. Kirk Curnutt, *Ernest Hemingway and the Expatriate Modernist Movement* (Detroit, Mich.: Gale, 2000).

3. Henry S. Villard and James Nagel, *Hemingway in Love and War: The Lost Diary of Agnes von Kurowsky* (Boston: Northeastern University Press, 1989), 197–269.

4. *Merriam-Webster's Encyclopedia of Literature* (Springfield, Mo.: Merriam-Webster, 1995), 938.

5. Erich Maria Remarque, *All Quiet on the Western Front* (New York: Ballantine, 1929), 140. All subsequent citations are from this text and page numbers are indicated parenthetically.

6. Patrick J. Quinn, *The Great War and the Missing Muse* (London: Susquehanna University Press, 1994), 10.

7. Quinn, *Missing Muse,* 25.

8. Paul Fussell, *The Great War and Modern Memory* (London: Oxford, 1975), 203–4.

9. Robert Graves, *Good-bye to All That* (New York: Anchor, 1957 [1929]), 83–84. All subsequent citations are from this text and page numbers are indicated parenthetically.

10. Martin Gilbert, *The First World War: A Complete History* (New York: Henry Holt, 1994), 16–17.

11. Ibid., 23.

12. See also *Collected Documents Relating to the Outbreak of the European War* (London: Her Majesty's Stationery Office, 1915), 392.

13. Ibid., 28.

14. John Keegan, *The First World War* (New York: Alfred Knopf, 1999), 28.

15. Barbara W. Tuchman, *The Guns of August* (New York: Ballantine, 1962), 124.

16. John Keegan, *An Illustrated History of the First World War* (New York: Alfred Knopf, 2001), 71.

17. Woodrow Wilson, Message to Congress, 63rd Cong., 2d sess., 1914. S. Doc. 566, 3–4.

18. Keegan, *The First World War,* 135.

19. Gilbert, *First World War,* 541.

20. Tuchman, *Guns,* 439–40.

21. Keegan, *The First World War,* 112.

22. Hew Strachan, *The First World War: To Arms* (London: Oxford, 2001), 261.

23. John Ellis, *Eye-Deep in Hell: Trench Warfare in World War I* (Baltimore, Md.: Johns Hopkins University Press, 1976), 4.

24. Ellis, *Hell,* 4–5.

25. Ellis, *Hell,* 162.

26. Samuel Hynes, *Soldiers' Tale: Bearing Witness to Modern War* (New York: Allen Lane, 1997), 32.

27. Hynes, *Soldiers' Tale,* 30.

28. Alistair Horne, *The Price of Glory: Verdum 1916* (London: Penguin, 1993), 46.

29. Horne, *Glory,* 327–28.

30. Stephen O'Shea, *Back to the Front: An Accidental Historian Walks the Trenches of World War I* (New York: Avon Books, 1996), 163–64.

31. Martin Van Creveld, *Technology and War: From 2000 B.C. to the Present* (New York: Free Press, 1991), 188–189.

32. Byron Farwell, *Over There: The United States in The Great War, 1917–1918* (New York: Norton, 1999), 202.

33. Keegan, *The First World War,* 359.

34. Farwell, *Over There: The United States in The Great War, 1917–1918,* 202.

SUGGESTIONS FOR FURTHER READING

Aldington, Richard. *Death of a Hero.* London: Four Square Books, 1958 (1929).

Anthony, Patricia. *Flanders.* New York: Berkley, 1998.

Banks, Arthur, *A Military Atlas of the First World War.* London: Leo Cooper, 1998.

Barbusse, Henri. *Under Fire: The Story of a Squad.* London: Arden, 1986.

Blunden, Edmund. *Undertones of War.* London: Oxford University Press, 1956 (1928).

Clark, Alan. *The Donkeys.* London: Pimlico, 1961.

cummings, e. e. *The Enormous Room.* New York: Liveright, 1978 (1922).

Curnutt, Kirk. *Ernest Hemingway and the Expatriate Modernist Movement.* Detroit, Mich.: Gale, 2000.

Dos Passos, John. *Three Soldiers.* Boston: Houghton Mifflin, 1921.

Eksteins, Modris. *Rites of Spring: The Great War and the Birth of Modern Age.* Boston: Marnier, 1989.

Ellis, John. *Eye-Deep in Hell: Trench Warfare in World War I.* Baltimore, Md.: Johns Hopkins University Press, 1976.

Farwell, Byron. *Over There: The United States in the Great War, 1917–1918.* New York: W. W. Norton, 1999.

Faulkner, William. *A Fable.* New York: Vintage, 1978 (1950).

Fussell, Paul. *The Great War and Modern Memory.* London: Oxford University Press, 1975.

Gilbert, Martin. *The First World War: A Complete History.* New York: Henry Holt, 1994.

Hannah, John. *The Great War Reader.* College Station: Texas A&M University Press, 2000.

Hart, B. H. Liddell, Captain. *The Real War: 1914–1918.* Boston: Back Bay, 1930.

Hemingway, Ernest. *In Our Time.* New York: Scribners, 1923.

———. *The Sun Also Rises.* New York: Scribners, 1925.

Holmes, Richard. *The Western Front: Ordinary Soldiers and the Defining Battles of World War I.* London: TV Books, 1999.

Horne, Alistair. *The Price of Glory: Verdun 1916.* London: Penguin, 1993 (1962).

Keegan, John. *The First World War.* New York: Knopf, 1999.

Prior, Robin, and Trevor Wilson. *Passchendaele: The Untold Story.* New Haven, Conn.: Yale University Press, 1996.

Reynolds, Michael. *Literary Masters: Ernest Hemingway.* Detroit, Mich.: Gale, 2000.

Sassoon, Siegfried. *The Complete Memoirs of George Sherston.* London: Faber and Faber, 1972 (1937).

Tuchman, Barbara W. *The Guns of August.* New York: Ballantine, 1962.

Villard, Henry, and James Nagel. *Hemingway in Love and War: The Lost Diary of Agnes von Kurowsky.* Boston: Northeastern University Press, 1989.

Ziegler, Robert H. *America's Great War: World War I and the American Experience.* Oxford: Rowman and Littlefield, 2000.

2

Women and the Home Front:

An Analysis of Edith Wharton's *A Son at the Front* (1922)

During World War I, noncombatants on the home front also suffered their share of hardships, especially in those areas of France and Belgium where the Western Front stretched from the English Channel to the Swiss border. Homes and towns were destroyed, families were displaced, and livelihoods were lost. All along the Western Front, people were in peril of starving to death. The war spread depression and despair like a medieval plague. What is often overlooked is that World War I was fought on two fronts—on the battlefield and at home. Both fronts involved a life-or-death struggle for survival. While men primarily fought the war on the battlefield, women significantly took up the struggle at home.

The analysis in this chapter examines how American writer Edith Wharton represents this suffering in two important areas: (1) in fiction, by presenting the sorrows of mothers and fathers who have lost their sons in the war; (2) in reality, by helping to provide relief for those who were directly impacted by the war. Edith Wharton's *A Son at the Front* portrays the suffering of two parents as they see their son off to war, only to see him return back to them wounded and dead. The ultimate tragedy of this scenario is that it was repeated all over the world during the years 1914–1918, a condition that brought with it universal depression as millions of family members grieved over the loss of their loved ones. Moreover, Wharton organized several relief agencies in France to help refugees find work and adequate food, shelter, and health care.

In a similar vein, the suffering of noncombatants in the Belgian war zone is poignantly conveyed in the excerpt from Charlotte Kellogg's *The Women of*

Belgium: Turning Tragedy to Triumph. When Kellogg wrote her narrative, she and others around her were afraid that "the story of Belgium will never be told." However, as we now know, her fears were unfounded because the story of how the Belgian people survived is here for everyone to read and heed. Despite their different subject matter, there is a great unity in Wharton's *A Son at the Front* and Kellogg's *The Women of Belgium* in that both are about people desperately trying to save their children.

LITERARY ANALYSIS

A Son at the Front (1922)

During war, any war, there are few words that evoke as much trepidation from people as having to say they have a son at the front. The title of Wharton's novel, thus, comes from a universal fear of having a son, a loved one, in the war. Wharton writes:

> A son at the front—
>
> The words followed [John] Campton down the stairs. What did it mean, and what must it feel like, for parents in this safe denationalized modern world to be suddenly saying to each other with white lips: A son in the war?[1]

White lips denote the parents' abject fear of losing their son at the front. Since this fear concerns an issue so close, so vital, to the heart of all people, Wharton's *A Son at the Front* should be easily recognizable, then, as an antiwar novel. By making the experience of war personal rather than political, Wharton attempts to demonstrate that the loss of one human life can still be a tragedy in a century where the death of millions has merely become a statistic.

The novel opens on 30 July 1914 in Paris. John Campton, an American painter of portraits, is standing in his Montmartre studio, waiting for his only child, George, to arrive back from the United States. He is focused on his son's return, seemingly unaware of the political turmoil that is brewing in Europe after the assassination of Archduke Ferdinand in the summer of 1914. It is appropriate that he is a portrait painter because Wharton's narrative perspective in this novel is that of portraiture, as she paints the very personal tragedy of the loss of a son and its impact on his family—the father, John Campton; the mother, Julia Brant; and the stepfather, Mr. Anderson Brant, a prominent banker. Interestingly, their son had already escaped death once, having previously contracted tuberculosis. He had been cured, and his parents hoped that having had the disease would preclude him from military service in the French army. They were wrong because the son had other ideas when it seemed that war was about to break out. Although he was only half French, he still had been required to register for mobilization; yet he had done so willingly. George, like a lot of young men in that generation, wanted to experience the romance of war. He wanted to be a man.

Why were so many young men eager to go to war in 1914?

Without having to probe too deeply into human psychology, anxieties about masculine identity seem easily identifiable in this particular question. Leo Braudy writes, in *From Chivalry to Terrorism: War and the Changing Nature of Masculinity,* that

> Men at war are on the front line of a more exacting and more one-sided defi-
> nition of what it means to be a man than ever faces men at peace. By its em-
> phasis on the physical prowess of men enhanced by their machines, by its
> distillation of national identity into the abrupt contrast between winning and
> losing, war enforces an extreme version of male behavior as the ideal model for
> all such behavior. Just as epic formulas focus on the hero with his undying fame,
> war focuses attention on certain ways of being a man and ignores or arouses sus-
> picions about others. Wartime masculinity is a top-down and bottom-up effort
> to emphasize a code of masculine behavior more single-minded and more tra-
> ditional than the wide array of circumstances and personal nature that influ-
> ences the behavior of men in nonwar situations.[2]

Campton's son was thus typical among the World War I generation in his desire to get to the front and to test himself in combat. That being said, what
was historically unique to this particular war was the confluence of forces that
not only magnified those masculine anxieties but also conspired against the
millions of young men and put them on the battlefield in such large numbers.
As will be further discussed in chapter 4, propaganda and mass-media technology led to the slaughter of a whole generation of young men, setting them
up to be killed with great efficiency on the battlefields of 1914. In France's
particular case, while the level of technology allowed the government to mobilize great numbers of its male citizens for war, it did not develop ways to
protect those men, either with advanced weapons or tactics, on the battlefield—
resulting in great initial slaughter. However, as the grim reality of the war
emerged, the motivations for going to war grew more complicated and quite
possibly more heroic. Wharton captures the personal impact of this historical
situation in an instance of introspection by George's father:

> In the careless pre-war world, as George himself had once said, it had seemed
> unbelievable that people should ever again go off and die in a ditch to oblige any-
> body. Even now, the automatic obedience of the millions of the untaught and
> the unthinking, though it had its deep pathetic significance, did not move Camp-
> ton like the clear-eyed sacrifice of the few who knew why they were dying. (99)

While Campton's son is in a unique situation, since his citizenship was half American and half French, he is also very typical in his desire to get to the front, not only to test himself in combat but to fight for a cause he believed in, which was the freedom of France. George demonstrates great resolve in defying his parents' desire to keep him safe. His stepfather had used his considerable influence and arranged a safer rear headquarter assignment for George, but as the family soon discovers, their son had made arrangements of his own for the front line, keeping his combat duties a secret from his family until he is severely wounded. Subsequently, George is wounded twice and his second wound turns out to be fatal. His death is excruciatingly prolonged and the death watch painful to witness.

After much rumination, Campton finally answers why his son wanted to be at the front so badly when he probably did not have to go:

> "But George, in the beginning, was—frankly indifferent to the war, wasn't he?"
> "Yes; intellectually he was. But he told me that when he saw the first men on their way back from the front—with the first mud on them—he knew he belonged where they'd come from. I tried hard to persuade him when he was here that his real job was on a military mission to America—and it was. Think what he might have done out there! But it was no use. His orderly's visit did the trick. It's the thought of their men that pulls them all back. Look at Louis Dastrey—they couldn't keep him American. That's something in all their eyes; I don't know what. *Dulce et decorum,* perhaps." (206)

As we'll see in chapter 3, the British poet Wilfred Owen in his poem "Dulce et Decorum Est, Pro Patria Mori," will turn that phrase on its head by asserting that this modern war has changed the meaning of these ancient, heroic words. In the modern context, it is neither fitting nor sweet to die in a ditch for one's country. But that did not stop George from needing to get mud on his uniform, or to die in a ditch with so many of his young comrades—even though he supposedly knew better.

In the prewar days, honor would have easily been definable, but World War I had totally devalued honor's meaning in a modern context. While having a son fighting at the front should have been a matter of honor, it had lost its meaning in a war that was being fought seemingly without meaning, and no amount of government propaganda would make a family feel better about their situation. In fact, they might even feel worse knowing that their government was trying to manipulate their feelings about the war through propaganda, which would then only intensify their cynicism.

While George's death inspires another American, Boylston, to commit to the war effort and join the American army, it does little to alleviate his father's pain. Campton can find no solace in the martyrdom of his son. Boylston states:

"My dear sir, haven't you guessed? It's George's wonderful example...his inspiration...I've been converted! We men of culture can't stand by while the ignorant and illiterate are left to die for us. We must leave that attitude to the Barbarian. Our duty is to set an example. I'm off to-night for America—for Plattsburg [the US army officer training base]."

Boylston burst into the studio the next day. "What did I tell you, sir" George's influence—it wakes up everybody.... (208)

Although he does not agree, Campton can at least understand why young men like George and Boylston had to get involved:

Yes, they were all being swept into it together—swept into the yawning whirlpool. Campton felt that as clearly as all these young men; he felt the triviality, the utter unimportance, of all their personal and private concerns, compared with this great headlong outpouring of life on the altar of conviction. And he understood why for youths like George and Boyslon, nothing, however close and personal to them, would matter till the job was over. (209)

Understanding, however, doesn't necessarily mean the acceptance of his loss. In the end, all that he and the other grieving family members can think to do is to build a monument to George, which is a similar response to the loss that whole nations would later undergo in trying to mollify the collective guilt over losing so many young men during the war.

The novel ends, therefore, almost as it began: Campton is in his studio waiting for his son to appear. George, of course, is gone. Campton will have to memorialize him. Wharton writes, "He pulled out all the sketches of his son from the old portfolio, spread them before him on the table, and began" (223). He began making a monument to his beloved dead son. In summary, this novel portrays one universal aspect of the suffering that occurred on the home front—the loss of a son at the front. For practically every young man or women who died or was severely wounded on the battlefield there was a mother and a father who were suffering too.

While the mobilization of the son—and exploring his complex motivations for going to war—is the primary focus of the novel, the petty intrigues of the various groups that were organized to provide relief for the refugees and those suffering from the calamity of this first global war play an interesting, if minor, role in the story's overall plot. For the purposes of this study, however, this analysis has primarily focused on the personal issue of a family facing the initial trauma of having a son at the front and the even more traumatic experience in facing his eventual death. Yet it is also essential to examine Wharton's role in organizing her own relief group to combat the enormous human suffering that the war caused throughout French and European society.

Despite her association with American and European aristocracy, Edith Wharton exhausted herself helping the common people of Belgium and France during the war. Alan Price notes, in *The End of the Age of Innocence: Edith Wharton and the First World War,* that Wharton's relief work began inauspiciously enough in the summer of 1914:

> With the mobilization, hundreds of shops, cafes, and small business in Paris closed, leaving previously employed women without a means of support. In her workroom, Wharton offered employment to many as ninety French women at a time. They received a nutritious lunch and a modest daily stipend.... With a few weeks, Wharton's sewing room had established a reputation for producing lingerie as well as bandages for the hospitals and knitted socks and gloves for the men in the trenches.[3]

In his biography of Wharton, R.W.B. Lewis describes what moved this woman of privilege to work so strenuously at helping the helpless. In trying to find an occupation to provide assistance beyond her sewing room, Lewis comments that Wharton

> Found one immediately in what developed into an enormous effort to provide succor for the civilian refugees who straggled into the city, driven from their homes during the [1st] Battle of the Marne, and even more in the savage fighting in October [1914] around Ypres—the town in Flanders.... They began to arrive in great waves, utterly destitute, deafened by the bombardments and dazed with the horrors they had seen and undergone. They slept on benches in the street and on straw in the railroad stations; by day they wandered helplessly about—some of them, the Flemish, unable to speak French—looking with little success for food and shelter. They brought with them stories that froze the blood and wrenched the heart, stories they mumbled out between appeals for help while their children stared ahead with vacant eyes.[4]

After the war began, Wharton quickly organized what became known as the American Hostels for Refugees, which complemented other organizations such as the Foyer Franco-Belge. Although she had no experience as an administrator of large-scale organizations, Wharton did have considerable energy and drive, and she also had a host of affluent friends who provided her with the resources to do the job. Lewis states that for the year 1915, Wharton had received $100,000 in contributions, which helped 9,330 refugees, serving 235,000 meals and handing out 48,000 garments. Her organization also helped 7,700 individuals with medical care and assisted 3,300 in finding jobs.[5]

Edith Wharton was born Edith Newbold Jones on 24 January 1862, in New York City, and according to Lewis, war was a central experience in her life. Lewis observes that she was born in the middle of the Civil War, America's bloodiest conflict, was emotionally affected when several of her friends, including Theodore Roosevelt, marched off to war during the Spanish-American conflict, and was living in war-torn France during most of World War I. After that war, Wharton continued her distinguished writing career, publishing her most famous novel, *An Age of Innocence,* in 1920. Wharton lived the rest of her life primarily as an expatriate in St.-Brice-sous-Forêt, France, where she died on 11 August 1937. She is buried in Cimetière des Gonards, Versailles. Charles Scribner's Sons of New York, Wharton's primary publisher throughout her career, first published *A Son at the Front* in 1923.

HISTORICAL CONTEXT AND DOCUMENTS

Charlotte Kellogg's *The Women of Belgium*

Herbert Hoover, the 31st president of the United States, was a great American if only for the tremendous work he performed in organizing the Belgium relief effort during and after World War I. During the initial 1914 invasion by Germany, and later as a prolonged battlefield during the war, Belgium experienced horrendous deprivations. Charlotte Kellogg's *The Women of Belgium: From Tragedy to Triumph* is a narrative based on her experiences as the only female member of the U.S. Commission for the Relief of Belgium, which was chaired by Hoover. She and the Commission visited Belgium in 1915. Her husband, Dr. Vernon Kellogg, was another U.S. representative. In his introduction to Kellogg's book, Hoover writes that "Every street corner and every crossroad is marked by a bayonet, and every night resounds with the march of armed men, the mark of national subjection. Belgium is a little country and the sound of the guns along a hundred miles of front strikes the senses hourly, and the hopes of the people rise and fall with the rise and fall in tones which follow the atmospheric changes and the daily rise and fall of battle."[6]

The commission was organized in September 1914 and by December 1914 began delivering $5 million worth of food and other assistance per month on 35 ships. At its peak of relief assistance, the commission was providing 80,000 tons of food and other necessities per month, which was still not enough, however, to avoid mass starvation in Belgium during the winter of 1916–17.[7] After the United States declared war on Germany in 1917, the commission had to be reconstituted into the Comité Hispano-Néderlandais (Spain and the Netherlands remained neutral throughout the war) in order to continue its nonalliance support.

With extraordinary humanity, Kellogg's narrative tells the story of a nation's struggle to exist both as a government and as a people. Reading her story one realizes just how much ordinary people had to suffer. Funk and Wagnalls of New York and London first published *The Women of Belgium: Turning Tragedy to Triumph* in 1917.

FROM *THE WOMEN OF BELGIUM: TURNING TRAGEDY TO TRIUMPH*, CHARLOTTE KELLOGG

http://www.lib.byu.edu/~rdh/wwi/memoir/CKellogg/WBelg1.htm

Introduction

By Herbert Hoover

BELGIUM, after centuries of intermittent misery and recuperation as the cockpit of Europe, had with a hundred years of the peaceful fruition of the intelligence, courage, thrift, and industry of its people, emerged as the beehive of the Continent. Its population of 8,000,000 upon an area of little less than Maryland was supported by the importation of raw materials, and by their manufacture and their exchange over-seas for two-thirds of the vital necessities of its daily life.

When in the summer of 1914 the people were again drawn into the European maelstrom, 600,000 of them became fugitives abroad, and the remainder were reduced to the state of a city which, captured by a hostile army, is in turn besieged from without. Thus, its boundaries were a wall of bayonets and a blockading fleet.

Under modern economic conditions, no importing nation carries more than a few weeks' reserve stock of food, depending as it does upon the daily arrivals of commerce; and the cessation of this inflow, together with the destruction and requisition of their meager stocks, threatened the Belgians with an even greater catastrophe—the loss of their very life.

With the stoppage of the industrial clock, their workpeople were idle, and destitution marched day and night into their slender savings, until today three and a half million people must be helped in charity. The Belgians are a self-reliant people who had sought no favors of the world, and their first instinct and continuing endeavor has been to help themselves. Not only were all those who had resources insistent that they should either pay now or in the future for their food, but far beyond this, they have insisted upon caring for their own destitute to the fullest extent of those remaining resources—the charity of the poor toward the poor. They have themselves set up no cry for benevolence, but the American Relief Commission has insisted upon pleading to the world to help in a burden so far beyond their ability.

This Commission was created in order that by agreement with the belligerents on both sides, a door might be opened in the wall of steel, through which those who had resources could re-create the flow of supplies to themselves; that through the same channel, the world might come to the rescue of the destitute, and beyond this that it could guarantee the guardianship of these supplies to the sole use of the people.

Furthermore, due to the initial moral, social, and economic disorganization of the country and the necessary restriction on movement and assembly, it was impossible for the Belgian people to project within themselves, without an assisting hand, the organization for the distribution of food supplies and the care of the impoverished. Therefore the Relief Organization has grown to a great economic engine that with its collateral agencies monopolizes the import food supply of a whole people, controlling directly and indirectly the largest part of the native products so as to eliminate all waste and to secure justice in distribution; and, above all, it is charged with the care of the destitute.

To visualize truly the mental and moral currents in the Belgian people during these two and a half years one must have lived with them and felt their misery. Overriding all physical suffering and all trial is the great cloud of mental depression, of repression and reserve in every act and word, a terror that is so real that it was little wonder to us when in the course of an investigation in one of the large cities we found the nursing period of mothers has been diminished by one-fourth. Every street corner and every crossroad is marked by a bayonet, and every night resounds with the march of armed men, the mark of national subjection. Belgium is a little country and the sound of the guns along a hundred miles of front strikes the senses hourly, and the hopes of the people rise and fall with the rise and fall in tones which follow the atmospheric changes and the daily rise and fall of battle. Not only do hope of deliverance and anxiety for one's loved ones fighting on the front vibrate with every change in volume of sound, but with every rumor which shivers through the population. At first the morale of a whole people was crushed: one saw it in every face, deadened and drawn by the whole gamut of emotions that had exhausted their souls, but slowly, and largely by the growth of the Relief Organization and the demand that it has made upon their exertion and their devotion, this morale has recovered to a fine flowering of national spirit and stoical resolution. The Relief Commission stands as an encouragement and protection to the endeavors of the Belgian people themselves and a shield to their despair. By degrees an army of 55,000 volunteer workers on Relief had grown up among the Belgian and French people, of a perfection and a patriotism without parallel in the existence of any country.

To find the finance of a nation's relief requiring eighteen million dollars monthly from economic cycles of exchange, from subsidies of different governments, from the world's public charity; to purchase 300,000,000 pounds of concentrated foodstuffs per month of a character appropriate to individual and class; to secure and operate a fleet of seventy cargo ships, to arrange their regular passages through blockades and war zones; to manage the reshipment by canal and rail and distribution to 140 terminals throughout Belgium and Northern France; to control the milling of wheat and the making of bread; to distribute with rigid efficiency and justice not only bread but milk, soup, potatoes, fats, rice, beans, corn, soap and other commodities; to create the machinery of public feeding in canteens and soup kitchens; to supply great clothing establishments; to give the necessary assurances that the occupying army receives no benefit from the food supply; to maintain checks and balances assuring efficiency and integrity—all these things are a man's job. To this service the men of Belgium and Northern France have given the most steadfast courage and high intelligence.

Beyond all this, however, is the equally great and equally important problem—the discrimination of the destitute from those who can pay, the determination of their individual needs—a service efficient, just and tender in its care of the helpless. To create a network of hundreds of canteens for expectant mothers, growing babies, for orphans and debilitated children; to provide the machinery for supplemental meals for the adolescent in the schools; to organize workrooms and to provide stations for the distribution of clothing to the poor; to see that all these reliefs cover the field, so that none fall by the wayside; to investigate and counsel each and every case that no waste or failure result; to search out and provide appropriate assistance to those who would rather die than confess poverty; to direct these stations, not from committee meetings after afternoon tea, but by actual executive labor from early morning till late at night—to go far beyond mere direction by giving themselves to the actual manual labor of serving the lowly and helpless; to do it with cheerfulness, sympathy and tenderness, not to hundreds but literally to millions, this is woman's work.

This service has been given, not by tens, but by thousands, and it is a service that in turn has summoned a devotion, kindliness and tenderness in the Belgian and French women that has welded all classes with a spiritual bond unknown in any people before. It has implanted in the national heart and the national character a quality which is in some measure a compensation for the calamities through which these people are passing. The soul of Belgium received a grievous wound, but the women of Belgium are staunching the flow—sustaining and leading this stricken nation to greater strength and greater life.

We of the Relief have been proud of the privilege to place the tools in the hands of these women, and have watched their skilful use and their improvement in method with hourly admiration. We have believed it to be so great an inspiration that we have daily wished it could be pictured by a sympathizing hand, and we confess to insisting that Mrs. Kellogg should spend some months with her husband during his administration of our Brussels office. She has done more than record in simple terms passing impressions of the varied facts of the great work of these women, for she spent months in loving sympathy with them. We offer her little book as our, and Mrs. Kellogg's, tribute in admiration of them and the inspiration which they have contributed to this whole organization.

This devotion and this service have now gone on for nearly 900 long days. Under unceasing difficulties the tools have been kept in the hands of these women, and they have accomplished their task. All of this time there have stood behind them our warehouses with from thirty to sixty days' supplies in advance, and tragedy has thus been that distance remote. Our share and the share of these women has therefore been a task of prevention, not a task of remedy. Our task and theirs has been to maintain the laughter of the children, not to dry their tears. The pathos of the long lines of expectant, chattering mites, each with a ticket of authority pinned to its chest or held in a grimy fist, never depresses the mind of childhood. Nor does fear ever enter their little heads lest the slender chain of finance, ships and direction which supports these warehouses should fail, for has the canteen ever failed in all these two and a half years? That the day shall not come when some Belgian woman amid her tears must stand before its gate to repeat: "Mes petites, il n'y en a plus," is simply a problem of labor and money. In this, America has a duty, and the women of America a privilege.

Herbert Hoover

I

The Leaders

THE story of Belgium will never be told. That is the word that passes oftenest between us. No one will ever by word of mouth or in writing give it to others in its entirety, or even tell what he himself has seen and felt. The longer he stays the more he realizes the futility of any such attempt, the more he becomes dumb. It requires a brush and color beyond our grasp; it must be the picture of the soul of a nation in travail, of the lifting of the strong to save the weak. We may, however, choose certain angles of vision from which we see, thrown into high relief, special aspects of an inexpressible experience.

One of these particular developments is the unswerving devotion of the women of Belgium to all those hurt or broken by the tragedy within and without her gates. How fortunate are these women, born to royal leadership, to have found in their Queen the leader typifying the highest ideal of their service, and the actual comrade in sorrow, working shoulder to shoulder with them in the hospitals and kitchens. The battle-lines may separate her wounded and suffering from theirs, but they know always that she is there, doing as they are doing, and more than they are doing.

Never were sovereigns more loved, more adored than Albert and Elizabeth. All through these two years people have been borne up by the vision of the day of their return. "But how shall we be able to stand it?" they say. "We shall go mad with joy! We shall not be able to speak for weeping and shouting! We shall march from the four corners of the country on foot in a mighty pilgrimage to Brussels, the King shall know what we think of him as man and leader!"

When they speak of the Queen all words are inadequate; they place her first as woman, as mother, as tender nurse. They are proud, and with reason, of her intelligence and sound judgment. Under her father, a distinguished oculist, she received a most rigorous education; she is equipped in brain as well as in heart for her incalculable responsibilities. I was told the other day that she dislikes exceedingly having her photograph as "nurse" circulate, feeling that people may think she wishes to be known for her good works. But whether she wishes it or not, she is known and will be known throughout history for her good works—for her clear, clean vision of right, her swift courage, and her utter devotion to each and all of her people. Albert and Elizabeth, A and E, these letters are written on the heart of Belgium.

If in the United States we have been too far away to realize in detail what the work of the Queen has been, we have had on our own shores the unforgettable example of her dear friend, Marie de Page, to prove to us the heroism of the women of Belgium.

Before she came, we knew of her. After the first two months of the war she had left her mother and father and youngest boy in Brussels—realizing that she was cutting herself off from all news of them—to follow her husband, who had himself followed his King to Le Havre. She worked her way across the frontier to Flushing, and finally to La Panne. The whole career of Doctor de Page had been founded on her devoted cooperation, and one has imagined the joy of that reunion in the great base hospital at La Panne, where he was in charge. Her eldest son was already in the trenches, the second, seventeen years old, was waiting his turn.

She worked as a nurse at her husband's side, day and night, until she could no longer bear to see the increasing needs of the wounded without being able to relieve them, and she determined to seek aid in America. This journey, even in peace time, is a much more formidable undertaking for a European than for an American woman, but Marie de Page started alone, encouraged always by her good friend, the Queen. And how swiftly, how enduringly, she won our hearts, as from New York to San Francisco she told so simply and poignantly her country's story!

She was a Belgian woman; so, even in her great trouble, she could not neglect her personal appearance, and after the fatiguing journey across the Continent, she looked fresh and charming as we met her in San Francisco. The first day at luncheon we were plying her with questions, until finally she laughed and said, "If you don't mind, I had better spread the map on the table—then you will see more quickly all the answers!" We moved our plates while she took the precious plan from her bag, and smoothed it across her end of the table. Then with her pencil she marked off with a heavy line the little part that is still free Belgium: she drew a star in front of La Panne Hospital and we were orientated! From point to point her pencil traveled as we put our eager questions. We marveled at the directness with which she brought her country and her people before us. We knew that her own son was in the trenches, but she made it impossible for us to think of herself.

Then, though there was much more to be done in America, she left. She must return to La Panne; her husband needed her. She had just received word that her seventeen-year-old son was to join his brother in the trenches; she hurried to New York. She did not wish to book on a non-neutral line, but further word showed her that her only chance to see her boy lay in taking the fastest possible ship. Fortunately the biggest, safest one was just about to leave, so she carried on board the money and supplies she was taking back to her people.

We settled down to doing what we could to carry forward her work. Then, on May 7, 1915, flashed the incredible, the terrible news—the greatest passenger liner afloat had been torpedoed! The *Lusitania*, had sunk in twenty-two minutes, 1,198 lives had been lost. We went about dazed. One by one the recovered bodies were identified, and among them was that of Marie de Page. We have found some little consolation in endowing beds in her memory in the hospital for which she gave her life. She is buried in the sand dunes not far from it; whenever Doctor de Page looks from his window, he looks on her grave. As the only American woman member of the Commission for Relief, I was permitted to enter Belgium in July 1916.

I already knew that this country held 3,000,000 destitute; that over one and one-quarter million depended for existence entirely on the daily "soups"; that between the soup-lines and the rich (who in every country, in every catastrophe, can most easily save themselves) there were those who, after having all their lives earned a comfortable living, now found their sources of income vanished, and literally faced starvation. For this large body, drawn from the industrial, commercial and professional classes, from the nobility itself, the suffering was most acute, most difficult to discover and relieve.

I knew that at the beginning of the war the great organizing genius of Herbert Hoover had seized the apparently unsolvable problem of the Relief of Belgium, and with an incredible swiftness had forced the cooperation of the world in the saving of this people who had not counted the cost of defending their honor. That because of this, every day in the month, ships, desperately difficult to secure, were pushing across the oceans with their cargoes of wheat and rice and bacon, to be rushed from Rotterdam through the canals to the C. R. B. warehouses throughout Belgium. It meant the finding of millions of money—$250,000,000 to date—begging of individuals, praying to governments, the pressing of the entire world to service.

I realized, too, that the Belgian men, under the active leadership of Messieurs Solvay, Francqui, de Wouters and Janssen, with a joint administration of Americans and Belgians, were organized into the Comité National, whose activities covered every square foot of the country, determining the exact situation, the exact need of each section, and who were responsible for the meeting of the situation locally and as a whole.

But I knew from the lips of the Chairman of the C. R. B. himself that despite all the work of the splendid men of these organizations, the martyrdom of Belgium was being prevented by its women. I was to learn in what glorious manner, in what hitherto undreamed of degree, this was true—that the women of Belgium, true to the womanhood and motherhood of all ages, were binding the wounds and healing the soul of their country!

II

The "Soupes"

I SHALL never think of Belgium without seeing endless processions of silent men and black-shawled women, pitchers in hand, waiting, waiting for the day's pint of soup. One and one-quarter million make a long procession. If you have imagined it in the sunshine, think of it in the rain!

. . . . .

The destitute must have a "supplement" to their daily ration of carbohydrates and fat which will give them protein—says the C. R. B., and thus we gave "Soupes";—but these dry statements of engineers now become dieticians convey to no one the human story of these dumb, waiting lines.

We can have little conception of what it means for just one city, the Agglomeration of Brussels, for instance, to keep 200,000 out of its 1,000,000 people on the "Soupes," not for a month or two, but for over two years! Nor does this include the soup made by the "Little Bees," an organization which cares especially for children, for the thousands in their canteens; or the soup served to the 8,500 children in sixty communal schools of central Brussels at four o'clock each afternoon, which is prepared in a special kitchen. These quantities are all over and above the regular soup served to 200,000—and do not think of soup as an American knows it, think more of a kind of stew; for it is thick, and, in the words of the C. R. B, "full of calories."

To make it for central Brussels the slaughter-house has been converted into a mighty kitchen, in charge of a famous pre-war maître d'hôtel. Ninety-five cooks and assistants from the best restaurants of the capital have been transferred from the making of pâtés and soufflés to the daily preparation of 25,000 quarts of soup! And they use the ingenuity born of long experience, to secure an appetizing variety while strictly following the orders of directing physicians. They had been doing this over 700 days when I visited the kitchen, but there was still a fresh eagerness to produce something savory and different. And one must remember that the changes can come only from shifting the emphasis from our dried American peas to beans, from carrots to cabbages, from macaroni to rice. The quantity of meat remains about the same, 1,200 pounds a day, which, though the committee kills its own cattle, costs almost fifty cents a pound. There must be, too, 10,000 pounds of potatoes. The great fear has been that this quantity might be cut, and unfortunately, in November 1916, that fear was realized to the extent of a 2,000 pound drop—and then remedied by the C R. B. with more beans, more rice, more peas!

Personal inspection of this marvelous kitchen is the only thing that could give an idea of its extraordinary cleanliness. The building offers great space, plenty of air and light and unlimited supply of water. The potato rooms, where each potato is put through two peeling processes, are in one quarter. Near them are the green vegetable rooms with their stone troughs, where everything is washed four or five times. The problem of purchasing the vegetables is so great that a special committee has been formed at Malines to buy for Brussels on the spot. One of the saving things for Belgium has been that she produces quantities of these delicious greens. In the smaller towns a committeeman usually goes each morning to market the day's supply. For instance, the lawyer who occupies himself with the vegetables for the Charleroi soup, makes his own selection at four o'clock each morning, and is extravagantly proud of the quality of his carrots and lettuces! The most important section, naturally, is that which cares for the meat and unsmoked bacon or "lard" the C. R. B. brings in. The more fat in the soup, the happier the recipient! With the little meat that can still be had in the butcher shop, selling at over one dollar a pound, one can imagine what it means to find a few pieces in the pint of soup! Then there is the great kitchen proper, with the one hundred and forty gas-heated caldrons, and the dozens of cooks hurrying from one to another. There seem to be running rivers of water everywhere, a perpetual washing of food and receptacles and premises.

The first shift of cooks arrives at two-thirty in the morning to start the gas under the one hundred and forty great kettles, for an early truck-load of cans must be off at 8 o'clock. That shift leaves at noon; the second works from 8 till 5, on an average wage of four francs a day and soupe! There are ten of the large trucks and 500 of the fifty-quart cans in constant use. As soon as the 8 o'clock lot come back, they are quickly cleaned, refilled, and hurried off on their second journey. Mostly they are hurried off through rain, for there are many more rainy than sunny days in Belgium.

One passes a long line of patient, wet, miserable-looking men and women with their empty pitchers, then meets with a thrill the red truck bringing the steaming cans. The bakers have probably already delivered the 25,000 loaves of bread, for a half loaf goes with each pint of soup. By following one of these steaming trucks I discovered "Soupe 18," with its line of silent hundreds stretching along the wet street.

· · · · ·

At the left, near the entrance, I was shown the office with all the records, and with the shelves of precious pots of jam and tiny packages of coffee and rice which are given out two or three times a month—in an attempt to make a little break in the monotony of the continual soup. No one can picture the heartbreaking eagerness in the faces of these thousands as they line up for this special distribution—these meager spoonfuls of jam, or handfuls of chopped meat.

We reviewed the army of cans stationed toward the rear, and the great bread-racks of either side. The committee of women arrived; we tasted the soup and found it good. I was asked to sit at the table with two men directors, where I might watch them stamp and approve the ration-cards as the hungry passed in. One may hate war, but never as it should be hated until he has visited the communal soupes and the homes represented by the lines. The work must be so carefully systematized that there is only time for a word or two as they pass the table. But that word is enough to reveal the tragedy!

There are sometimes the undeserving, but it is not often that any of the thousands who file by are not in pitiful straits. That morning the saddest were the very old—for them the men had always a kindly "How is it, mother? How goes it, father?"

The "Merci, Monsieur, merci beaucoup," of one sweet-faced old woman was so evidently the expression of genuine feeling that I asked about her. She had three sons, who had supported her well—all three were in the trenches. Another still older, said, "Thank you very much," in familiar English. She, too, had been caught in the net, and there was no work. A little Spanish woman had lost her husband soon after the war began, and the director who investigated the case was convinced that he had died of hunger. An old French soldier on a crutch, but not too feeble to bow low as he said "Merci," was an unforgettable figure.

Some of the very old and very weak are given supplementary tickets which entitle them to small portions of white bread, more adapted to their needs than the stern war bread of the C. R. B.; and every two days mothers are allowed additional bread for their children. One curly-haired little girl was following her mother and grandmother, and slipped out of the line to offer a tiny hand. Then came a tall, distinguished-looking man, about whom the directors knew little except that he was absolutely without funds. They put kindly questions to the poor hunchback, who had just returned to the line from the hospital, and congratulated the pretty girl of fifteen, who had won all the term's prizes in the communal school. There were those who had never succeeded; then there were those who two years before had been comfortable-railway employees, artists, men and women, young and old, in endless procession, a large proportion in carpet slippers, or other substitutes for leather shoes. Many were weak and ill-looking; all wore the stamp of war. Every day they must come for the pint of soup and the bread that meant life. 200,000 in Brussels alone; in Belgium one and a half million! These are the lowest in the scale of misery—those who it must have a supplement of protein, for meat never passes their lips but in soup. The questions were always swift, admitting no delay in the reply, and knowing the hearts of the questioners, I wondered a little at this. Till in a flash I saw: if the directors wished to know more they would go to the homes represented—but the line must not be held back! Every ten-minute halt means that those outside in the rain must stand ten minutes longer. On this particular day the committee put through a line representing 2,500 pints of soup and portions of bread in fifty minutes, an almost incredible efficiency, especially when you remember that every card is examined and stamped as well as every pitiful pitcher and string bag filled.

That day a woman who had not before served on the soupes offered her services to the seasoned workers. They were grateful, but smilingly advised her to go home, fill her bath tub with water, and ladle it out—to repeat this the following day and the following, until finally she might return, ready to endure the work, and above all, not to retard the "Line" five unnecessary minutes! Two and a half years have not dulled the tenderness of these women toward the wretched ones they serve.

At Home

Belgium is small. Until now I had been able to go and return in the same day. But on this particular evening I found myself too far south to get back. I was in a thickly forested, sparsely settled district, but I knew that farther on there was a great chateau belonging to the family of A., with numerous spare rooms.

. . . . .

After what seemed an endless time I saw the servant coming back through the great hall, followed by three women, who, I felt instinctively, had not come in welcome. But there was no turning about possible now—some one was already speaking to me. Her very first words showed she could not in the least have understood. And I swiftly realized this was not surprising since I had been there so short a time, and there had not before been a woman delegate. I explained that my sole excuse for sending in my stranger's card at that time of night was my membership in the C. R. B—and I uncovered my pin.

It was as if I had revealed a magic symbol—the door swung wide! They took my hands and drew me inside, overwhelming me with apologies, with entreaties to stop with them, to stay for a week, or longer. They would send for my husband—as Director he must be sorely in need of a few days' rest—we should both rest. Their district in the forest had many relief centers, they would see that I got to them all. A room was all ready for me on the floor above—if I did not like it I should have another. I must have some hot "tilleul" at once!

In the drawing-room I was presented to the other thirteen or fourteen members of the family, and in pages I could not recount their beautiful efforts, individually and together, to make me forget I had had to wait for one moment on their threshold.

Still later, two American men arrived.

They were known, and expected at any hour of the day or night their duties might bring them that way. One of them was ill, and not his own mother and sister could have been more solicitous in their care of him than were these kind women.

Do Americans wonder that it hurts us, when we return, to have people praise us for what we have given Belgium? In our hearts we are remembering what Belgium has given us.

III

The Cradles on the Meuse

Dinant made me think of Pompeii. It had been one of the pleasure spots of Belgium; gay, smiling, it stretched along the tranquil Meuse, at the base of granite bluffs and beech-covered hill-slopes. There were factories, it is true, at either end of the town; but they had not marred it. Every year thousands of visitors, chiefly English and Germans, had stopped there to forget life's grimness. Dinant could make one forget: she was joyous, lovable, laughing. Before the tragedy of her ruins, one felt exactly as if a happy child had been crushed or mutilated.

I came to Dinant in September 1916, by the way of one of the two cemeteries where her 600, shot in August 1914, are buried. This burial-ground is on a sunny hill-slope overlooking rolling wheat fields, and the martyred lie in long rows at the upper corner. A few have been interred in their family plots, but mostly they are gathered in this separate place.

Up and down I followed the narrow paths; the crowded plain white crosses with their laconic inscriptions spoke as no historian ever will. "Father, Husband, and Son"; "Brother and Nephew"; "Husband and Sons, one seventeen, and another nineteen"; "Brother and Father"; "Husband and Brother"; "Brother, Sons and Father"; "Father and Son"—the dirge of the desolation of wives and sisters and mothers! War that had left them the flame-scarred skeletons of their homes, had left them the corpses of their loved ones as well!

Dinant was not entirely destroyed, but a great part of it was. A few days after the burning, people began to crawl back. They came from hiding-places in the hills, from nearby villages, from up and down the river, to take up life where they had left it. Human beings are most extraordinarily adaptable: people were asked where they were living; no one could answer exactly, but all knew that they were living somewhere, somehow—in the sheltered corner of a ruined room, perhaps in a cave, or beside a chimney! The relief committee hurried in food and clothing, hastily constructed a few temporary cottages; a few persons began to rebuild their original homes, and life went on.

I was walking through a particularly devastated section, nothing but skeleton façades and ragged walls in sight, when suddenly from the midst of the devastation I heard the merry laughter of children. I pushed ahead to look around the other side of a wall, and there was a most incredible picture. In front of a low temporary building tucked in among the ruins, was a series of railed-in pens for children to play in. And there they were romping, riotously—fifty-two golden-haired, lovely babies, all under four! Along the front of the enclosure was a series of tall poles carrying gaily painted cocks and cats and lions. That is the Belgian touch; no relief center is too discouraging to be at once transformed into something cheering, even beautiful. The babies had on bright pink-and-white checked aprons. I let myself in, and they dashed for me, pulling my coat, hiding in the folds of my skirt, deciding at once that I was a good horse.

Then happened a horrible thing. One of the tiniest, with blue eyes and golden curls, ran over to me laughing and calling, "Madame, mon père est mort!" "Madame, my father is dead, my father is dead, he was shot!" I covered my ears with my hands, then snatched her up and silenced her. There were others ready to call the same thing, but the nurses stopped them.

The little ones went on with their romping while I passed inside to see the equipment for caring for them. In a good-sized, airy room were long rows of white cradles, one for each child, with his or her name and age written on a white card at the top. After their play and their dinner they were put to sleep in these fresh cradles.

Their mothers or friends brought them before seven in the morning, to be taken care of until seven at night. They were bathed, their clothing was changed to a sort of simple uniform, and then they were turned loose outside to play, or to be amused in various ways by the faithful nurses. They were weighed regularly, examined by a physician, and daily given the nourishing food provided by the relief committee. In fact, they had the splendid care common to the 1,900 crèches or children's shelters in Belgium. But this crèche was alone in its strange, tragic setting. In the midst of utter ruin are swung the white cradles. In front of them, under the guardianship of gay cocks and lions, golden-haired babies are laughing and romping. Further on more ruins, desolation, silence!

IV

"The Little Bees"

Madame has charge of a Canteen for Enfants Débiles (children below normal health) in one of the crowded quarters of Brussels. These canteens are dining-rooms where little ones come from the schools at eleven each morning for a nourishing meal. They form the chief department of the work of the "Little Bees," a society which is taking care of practically all the children, babies, and older ones, in this city, who are in one way or another victims of the war. And in July 1916, they numbered about 25,000.

The canteens have been opened in every section of the city, in a vacant shop, a cellar, a private home, a garage, a convent—in any available, usable place. But no matter how inconvenient the building, skilful women transform it at once into something clean and cheery. In the whole of Belgium I have never seen a run-down or dirty relief center. In some the kitchen is simply a screened-off corner of the dining-room, in others it is a separate and excellently equipped quarter. I visited one crowded canteen where every day the women had to carry up and down a narrow ladder stairway all the plates and food for over 470 children. But they have so long ago ceased to think in terms of "tiredness," that they are troubled by the question suggesting it. And these are the women who have been for over nine hundred days now—shoulder to shoulder with the men—ladling out one and one-quarter million pints of soup, and cooking for, and scrubbing for, and yearning over, hundreds of thousands of more helpless women and children, while caring always for their own families at home. If after a long walk to the canteen (they have neither motors nor bicycles) Madame finds there are not enough carrots for the stew, she cannot telephone—she must go to fetch whatever ingredient she wants! Each canteen has its own pantry or shop with its precious stores of rice, beans, sugar, macaroni, bacon and other foodstuffs of the C. R. B., and in addition the fresh vegetables, potatoes, eggs, and meat it solicits or buys with the money gathered from door to door, the gift of the suffering to the suffering.

The weekly menus are a triumph of ingenuity; they prove what variety can be had in apparent uniformity! They are all based on scientific analysis of food values, and follow strictly physicians' instructions. One day there are more grams of potatoes, another more grams of macaroni in the stew; one noon there is rice for dessert, the next phosphatine and now a hygienic biscuit—a thick, wholesome one—as big as our American cracker.

It was raining as I entered the large, modern tenement building which Madame had been fortunate enough to secure. I found on one side a group of mothers waiting for food to take home to their babies, and on the other the little office through which every child had to pass to have his ticket stamped before he could go upstairs to his dinner. This examining and stamping of cards by the thousand, day after day, is in itself a most arduous piece of work, but women accomplish it cheerfully.

Ready for the Children:

A "Little Bee" Canteen for Sub-Normal Children

On the second floor, between two large connecting rooms, I found Madame, in white, superintending the day's preparation of the tables for 1,662. That was the size of her family! Fourteen young women, with bees embroidered in the Belgian colors on their white caps, were flying to and fro from the kitchen to the long counters in the hallway piled with plates, then to the shelves against the walls of the dining-room, where they deposited their hundreds of slices of bread and saucers for dessert. Some were hurrying the soup plates and the 1,662 white bowls along the tables, while others poured milk or went on with the bread-cutting. Several women were perspiring in the kitchens and vegetable rooms. The potato-peeling machine, the last proud acquisition which was saving them untold labor, had turned out the day's kilos of potatoes, which were already cooked with meat, carrots, and green vegetables into a thick, savory stew. The big fifty-quart cans were being filled to be carried to the dining-room; the rice dessert was getting its final stirring. Madame was darting about, watching every detail, assisting in every department.

It was raining outside, but all was white, and clean, and inviting within. Suddenly there was a rush of feet in the courtyard below. I looked out the window: in the rain 1,662 children, between three and fourteen years, mothers often leading the smaller ones—not an umbrella or rubber among them—were lining up with their cards, eager to be passed by the sergeant. These kind-hearted, long-suffering sergeants kept this wavering line in place, as the children noisily climbed the long stairway—calling, pushing. One little girl stepped out to put fresh flowers before the bust of the Queen. Boys and girls under six crowded into the first of the large, airy rooms, older girls into the second, while the bigger boys climbed to the floor above. With much chattering and shuffling of sabots they slid along the low benches to their places at the long, narrow tables. The women hurried between the wiggling rows, ladling out the hot, thick soup. The air was filled with cries of "Beaucoup, Mademoiselle, beaucoup!" A few even said "Only a little, Mademoiselle." Everybody said something. One tiny, golden-haired thing pleaded: "You know I like the little pieces of meat best." In no time they discovered that I was new, and tried slyly to induce me to give them extra slices of bread, or bowls of milk.

In this multitude each was clamoring for individual attention, and for the most part getting it. Very little ones were being helped to feed themselves; second portions of soup were often given if asked for. Madame seemed to be everywhere at once, lifting one after another in her arms to get a better look at eyes or glands. Her husband, a physician of international reputation, was in the little clinic at the end of the hall, weighing and examining those whose turn it was to go to him that day. Later he came out and passed up and down the rows to get an impression of the general condition of this extraordinary family. When for a moment husband and wife stood together in the middle of the vast room, they seemed with infinite solicitude to be gathering all the 1,662 in their arms—their own boy is at the front. And all the time the 1,662 were rapidly devouring their bread and soup.

Then began the cries of "Dessert, Mademoiselle, dessert!" Tired arms carried the
1,662 soup plates to the kitchen, ladled out 1,662 portions of rice, and set them before eager rows. Such a final scraping of spoons, such fascinating play of voice and ges-
ture—then the last crumb eaten, they crowded up to offer sticky hands with "Merci,
Mademoiselle" and "Au revoir." The clatter of sabots and laughter died away through
the courtyard, and the hundreds started back to school.

The strong American physician, who had helped ladle the soup, tried to swing his
arm back into position. I looked at the women who had been doing this practically
every day for seven hundred days. Madame was apparently not thinking of resting—
only of the next day's ration. I discovered later that at four o'clock that afternoon she
had charge of a canteen for four hundred mothers and their new babies, and that after
that she visited the family of a little boy who was absent, according to the children,
because his shirt was being washed.

All attempts to express admiration of this beautiful devotion are interrupted by the
cry, "Oh, but it is you—it is America that is doing the astonishing thing—we must
give ourselves, but you need not. Your gift to us is the finest expression of sympathy
the world has known."

II

Before Madame was made director of the canteen for 1,662, she had charge of one
in a still poorer quarter of the city. I went to look for it on Assumption Day, the day
of the Ascent of the Blessed Virgin. I knew the street, and as usual, the waiting line of
children in front told the number. Scrubbed cheeks, occasional ribbon bows and cheap
embroidery flounces showed the attempt of even these very poor mothers to celebrate
their fête day. Throughout the city, those fortunate enough to be called Mary were
being presented with flowers, which since the war have been sold at extremely low
prices, for the flowers still grow for Belgium, who supplied the markets of Europe before she was besieged.

From early morning we had seen old and young carrying great sheaves of phlox and
roses, or pots of hortensia, to some favorite Mary. But these little ones had no flowers, yet they were gay, as Belgian children invariably are—always ready with the swiftest
smiles and outstretched hands, or, with a pretty song if one asks for it. Little tots of
three know any number of the interminable chansons familiar in France and Belgium.
They chattered and laughed, caught my hand as I went down the stairs—for this
dining-quarter is below the sidewalk, in rooms that are known as "caves." I was prepared for something dark and cheerless, instead I found the whitewashed walls gay
with nursery pictures and Belgian and American flags. The long tables were covered
with bright red-and-white checked oilcloth. The small windows opening just above
the sidewalk allowed sufficient light and air to keep everything fresh. The kitchen was
immaculate—shelves for shining vessels, others for the sacks of sugar, boxes of macaroni. On a table stood the inevitable scales—Thursday is weighing day, when one of
the best physicians of Brussels examines the children, recording the weights that form
the basis for judgment as to the success of the ration.

The 430 bowls of milk were already on the tables. Madame was hurrying about among her helpers—twelve faithful Belgian women. They had all been there since eight o'clock, for this was a *viande* day (there are three a week) and when there is meat that must be cut into little pieces for between four and five hundred children, it means an early start. Two women were still stirring (with long wooden spoons) the great tub full of savory macaroni and carrots—a test in itself for muscle and endurance. The meat was in separate kettles. The bread had been cut into over 400 portions. The phosphatine dessert (of which the children cannot get enough) was already served at a side table. The "Little Bees" originated this phosphatine dessert, which is a mixture of rice, wheat and maize flour, phosphate of lime and cocoa. They have a factory for making it, and up to August 1916, had turned out 638,000 kilos.

A gentleman in black frock suit and large hat came in to look about, and then went back to the lengthening line. Madame explained that he was the principal of the communal school of the quarter, and that he came every day to keep the children in order. I learned, too, that on every single day of the vacation, which had begun and was to continue until the middle of September, he and one of his teachers went to the school to distribute to all the school-children the little roll of white bread that they are allowed at eight-thirty each morning. Many of these have but little at home. This roll helps them out until the canteen meal at eleven thirty, which can be had only on a physician's authorization. From now on a larger meal is to be given in the schools—a joy not only to the pupils but also to their teachers, who everywhere are devoting themselves to this work of saving their children. Several of the younger women helping Madame had been working wearily all the year in the professional schools, but as soon as their vacations arrived, begged to be allowed to give their time to the canteens. They were all most attractive in their white aprons and caps—most serious in their attention to the individual wants of that hungry family.

A few minutes later the principal appeared again—all was ready now. Then the little ones began to march in. They came by way of an anteroom, where they had their hands washed, if they needed washing—and most of them did—and quite proudly held them up as they passed by us. They were of all sizes between three and fourteen. One pale little fellow was led in by his grandmother who was admitted (though no mothers or grandmothers are supposed to come inside), because he wailed the minute she left him. It was easy to see why mothers could not be allowed, though one was glad the rule could be broken, and that this sad, white-faced grandmother could feed her own charge. It was terrible, too, to realize what that plate of savory stew would have meant to her, and to see that she touched no morsel of it. Even if there had been an extra portion, the women could not have given it to her: the following day the street would have been filled with others, for whom there could not possibly be extra portions.

If a child is too ill to come for its dinner, a member of the family can carry it home. Practically all the canteens have a visiting nurse who investigates such cases, and keeps the number much lower than it would otherwise be.

When I asked Madame how she was able to give so much time (from about 8 A.M. till 1 or 2 P.M. every day of the year), she smiled and shrugged her shoulders: "But that is the least one can do, the very least! One never thinks of the work, it is of the children—and we know they love us—we see them being kept alive! Some of them are getting stronger—these weaklings. What more can we wish?"

V

Mrs. Whitlock's Visit

THE second time, I visited Madame's canteen with the wife of the American Minister, and I found what it meant to be the wife of the United States Minister in Belgium! From the corner above to the entrance of the court the street was lined with people. At the gateway a committee headed by the wife of the Bourgmestre of Brussels met us. Within the court were the hundreds of children—with many more mothers this time—all waiting expectantly, all specially scrubbed, though no amount of scrubbing could conceal their sad lack of shoes. There were smiles and greetings and little hands stretched out all along the line as we passed.

Inside there was no more than the usual cleanliness—for the canteens are scrupulously kept. Madame and her assistants had tiny American flags pinned to their white uniforms. In the corridors the American and Belgian flags hung together. A special permission had been obtained to take a photograph of their guest at the window.

The tables were laid, and the lines began moving. As the little girls filed in, one of them came forward, and with a pretty courtesy offered Mrs. Whitlock a large bouquet of red roses. The boys followed, and their representative, struggling with shyness, recited a poem as he gave his flowers. All the children were very much impressed with this simple ceremony, and under the two flags, as the quavering little voice gave thanks to "those who were bringing them their daily bread," there were no grown-ups without tears in their eyes.

American flags of one kind or another hang in all the canteens, along with pictures of President Wilson, mottos expressing thanks to America, C. R. B. flour-sacks elaborately embroidered—on all sides are attempts to express gratitude and affection. That morning, as the Legation car turned a corner, a little old Flemish lady in a white frilled cap stepped forward and clapped her hands as the American flag floated by. Men lifted their hats to it, and children salute it. In the shop windows one often sees it draping the pictures of the King and Queen!

This is not a tribute to the American flag alone, but also to the personality of the man who has so splendidly represented this flag and to the men who carried the American soul and its works into Belgium through the C. R. B. Belgium will never forget its immediate debt to Brand Whitlock and to these hundreds of Americans whose personal service to this country in its darkest hour is already a matter of history. Just as Mrs. Whitlock was leaving, Madame fortunately discovered a shabby little girl who still squeezed a bedraggled bunch of white roses—and made her happy by bringing her forward to present it.

These children, as I have said, are all in need of special nourishment; they are those who have fallen by the wayside in the march, brought down by the stern repression of the food supply. One of the most striking effects of the war has been the rapid increase in tuberculosis. Many of the thousands in the canteens are the victims of "glands" or some other dread form of this disease.

However, in some respects the children of the very poor are better off than they have ever been. For the first time they are receiving nourishing food at regular hours. And this ration, along with the training in hygiene and medical attention, is having its good effect. One hundred and twenty-five physicians are contributing their services to the "Little Bees" in Brussels alone, where, during the first six months of 1916, infant mortality had decreased 19 per cent. It would be difficult to estimate the time given by physicians throughout the whole country, but probably half of the 4,700 are contributing practically all their time, and almost all are doing something. It is a common sight in the late afternoon to see a physician who has had a full, hard day, rushing to a canteen to examine hundreds of children. Outside the zone of military preparation, 200,000 sub-normal children of from three to seventeen years, and over 53,000 babies under three months, are on their "relief" lists, besides a large number of adults.

Outside Brussels, the canteens are conducted in much the same way as those of the "Little Bees." Committees of women everywhere are devoting themselves to the children.

VI

The Bathtub

WAY over in the northeast, in Hasselt, a town of 17,000 inhabitants, there is an especially interesting canteen—only one of thousands in Belgium, mind you! A year ago, when a California professor was leaving San Francisco to become a C. R. B. representative, he was offered a farewell dinner—and in the hall his hostess placed a basket, with obvious intent! The money was not for the general fund, but to be spent by him personally for some child in need.

He was assigned to Hasselt, for the Province of Limbourg, and there he very soon decided that a splendid young Belgian woman who had been giving her whole time to nursing wounded soldiers would be the person to know which of their children was most in need of his little fund. When he proposed turning it over to her, she quite broke down at the opportunity it offered. She and her mother were living in a rather large house, but on a limited income. She would find the sick child and care for it in her own home. A few days later the professor called to see her "child"—and he found twelve! She had not been able to stop—most of them were children whose fathers were at the front. They were suffering from rickets, arrested development, paralysis, malnutrition. She was bathing them, feeding them, and following the instructions of a physician, whom she had already interested. Her fund was two hundred and fifty dollars, but in her hands it seemed inexhaustible. She added children, one after another. Then, finally, the Relief Committee came to the support of her splendid and necessary work with its usual monthly subsidy, with which the women buy the supplies most needed from the relief shops. She is now installed in the middle of the town— with a kitchen and dining-room downstairs, and a little clinic and bathroom upstairs. The forty-six centimes (less than ten cents) a day that she received per child, enabled her to furnish an excellent meal for each.

But she soon found that her children could not be built up on one meal, and she stretched her small subsidy to cover a breakfast at eight and a dinner at four to 100 children. She balances the ration, makes the daily milk tests, and looks after every detail personally. Upstairs in the prized tub devoted helpers bathe the children who need washing, care for their heads, and for all the various ailments of a family of 100 subnormal children. Because of the glycerin it contains, soap has been put on the "nonentry" list, which makes it so expensive that the very poor are entirely without it. The price has increased 300 per cent since the war. Incidentally, one of the reasons for the high price of butter is that it can be sold for making soap, at an extraordinary figure.

This particular tub is a tribute to the ingenuity of the present American representative—also a professor, but from farther East. Before the terrific problem of giving children enough bread and potatoes to keep them alive, bathrooms sometimes appear an unnecessary luxury. The relief committee could not furnish Mademoiselle a bathroom! But to those working with the sick and dirty children it seemed all-essential. Hasselt is not a rich town, everybody's resources had been drained—how should the money be found? Finally the C. R. B. delegate had an inspiration—there was a big swimming-tank in Hasselt. To the people, the American representative, though loved, is always a more or less surprising person. If it could be announced that by paying a small sum they could see the strange American swim, everybody who had the small sum would come—he would swim for the bathroom! It was announced, and they came, and that swimming fête will go down in the annals of the town! The canteen got its bathroom, and there was enough left over to buy a very necessary baby-scales.

Mademoiselle took us to the houses where we saw the misery of mothers left with seven, nine, eleven children, in one or two little rooms. There was no wage-earner— he was at the front; or there was no work. One woman was crying as we went in. She explained that her son, "a bad one," had just been trying to take his father's boots. She pulled out from behind the basket where the twins were sleeping under the day's washing, a battered pair of coarse, high boots. There were holes in the hob-nailed soles, there was practically no heel left. The heavy tops still testified to original stout leather, but never could one see a more miserable, run-down-at-the-heel, leaky, and useless pair of boots. Yet to that woman they represented a fortune—there is practically no leather left in the country, and if there were, how could her man, when he came back, have the money to buy another pair, and how could he work in the fields without his boots? There were eight children—eight had died.

And she wept bitterly because of the son who had tried to take his father's boots, as she hid them behind the twin's basket. I had heard of the sword as the symbol of the honor and power of the house; in bitter reality it is the father's one pair of boots!

VII

The Bread in the Hand

I SOON came to have the curious feeling about the silent stone fronts of the houses that if, I could but look through them I should see women sorting garments, women making patterns for lace, women ladling soup, painting toys, washing babies. Up and down the stairs of these inconvenient buildings they are running all day long, back and forth, day after day, seeking through a heroic cheerfulness, a courageous smile, to hold back tears.

And chiefly I was overwhelmed by the enormous quantities of food they are handling. The whole city seems turned into a kitchen—and there follows the inevitable question: "Where does it all come from?" The women who are doing the work connect directly with the local Belgian organizations, by the great system of decentralization, which is the keynote of the C. R. B. just these three magic letters spell the answer to the inevitable question.

At the C. R. B. bureau I had seen the charts lining the corridors. They seemed alive, changing every day, marking the ships on the ocean, the number of tons of rice, wheat, maize or sugar expected; and how these tons count up! In the two years that have passed, 1,000,000 tons each year, meaning practically one ship every weekday in the month; 90,000 tons at one time on the Atlantic! Other charts show the transit of goods already unloaded at Rotterdam. Over 200 lighters are in constant movement on their way down the canals to the various C. R. B. warehouses, which means about 50,000 tons afloat all the time. I had seen, too, the reports of the enormous quantities of clothing brought in 4,000,000 dollars worth, almost all of it the free gift of the United States.

In the director's room were other maps showing the territory in charge of each American. Back of every canteen and its power to work stands this American, the living guaranty to England that the Germans are not getting the food, the guaranty to Germany of an equal neutrality, and to the Belgians themselves the guaranty that the gifts of the world to her, and those of herself to her own people, would be brought in as wheat through the steel ring that had cut her off. One had only to think of the C. R. B. door in the steel ring as closed, to realize the position of this neutral commission. The total result of their daily and hourly coordination of all this organization inside Belgium, their solitude for each class of the population, their dull and dry calculations of protein, fat and carbohydrates, bills of lading, cars, canal boats, mills and what not, is the replenishing of the life stream of a nation's blood.

Thus, the food dispensed by the women is part of the constantly entering mass, and between its purchase, or its receipt as gift by the C. R. B., and its appearance as soup for adults, or pudding for children, is the whole intricate structure of the relief organization. The audible music of this creation is the clatter of hundreds of typewriters, the tooting of tugs and shrieks of locomotives, but the undertones are the harmonies of devotion.

Everybody who can pay for his food must do so—it is sold at a fair profit, and it is this profit, gained from those who still have money, that goes over to the women in charge of the canteens for the purchase of supplies for the destitute.

They often supplement this subsidy through a house-to-house appeal to the people. For instance, in Brussels, the "Little Bees" are untiring in their canvass. Basket on arm, continually they solicit an egg, a bunch of carrots, a bit of meat, or a money gift. They have been able to count on about 5,000 eggs and about 2,500 francs a week, besides various other things. Naturally, the people in the poorer sections can contribute but small amounts, but it is here that one finds the most touching examples of generosity—the old story of those who have suffered and understood. One woman who earns just a franc a day and on it has to support herself and her family, carefully wraps her weekly two-centime piece (two-fifths of a cent) and has it ready when one of the "Little Bees" calls for it.

Our American Young Men

A committee leader in the Hainaut, once said to me, "Madame, one of the big things Belgium will win in this war is a true appreciation of the character and capacity (quite aside from their idealism) of American young men.

"I'll confess," he continued, "that when that initial group of young Americans came rushing in with those first heaven-sent cargoes of wheat, we were not strongly reassured. We knew that for the moment we were saved, but it was difficult to see how these youths, however zealous and clear-eyed, were going to meet the disaster, as we knew it."

"We organized, as you know, our local committees, and headed them by our Belgians of widest experience; our lawyers of fifty or sixty, our bankers, our leaders of industry. We could set all the machinery, but nothing would work unless the Americans would stand with us. The instructions read: 'The American and your Belgian chairmen will jointly manage the relief."

"And who came to stand with us? Who came to stand with me, for instance? You see," and he pointed to splendid broad-shouldered C. ahead of us, "that lad—not a day over twenty-eight—just about the age of my boys in the trenches, and who, heaven knows, is now almost as dear to us as they!"

"But in the beginning I couldn't see it; I simply couldn't believe C. was going to be able to handle his end of our terrific problem. But day by day I watched this lad quietly getting a sense of the situation, then plunging into it, getting under it, developing an instinct for diplomacy along with his natural genius for directness and practicality that bewildered me. It has amazed us all." "We soon learned that we need not fear to trust ourselves to that type of character, to its adaptability and capacity, no matter how young it seemed."

Of course there have been older Americans who have brought to their Belgian co-workers equal years as well as experience, but one of the pictures I like best to remember is this of Monsieur _____, a Belgian of fifty-five or sixty, in counsel with his eager American délégué of twenty-eight. To the partnership, friendship, confidence, the Belgian added something paternal, and the American responded with a devotion one feels is lifelong.

Between the visits to mills and docks, and the grinding over accounts, orders of canal boats and warehouses, there are hours for other things. I remember one restful one spent at this same Monsieur's table—he is an excellent Latin scholar and a wise philosopher—when he and his young American friend for a time forgot the wheat and fat in their delight to get back to Virgil and Horace.

Young D., a Yale graduate, furnished another example of these qualities Monsieur stressed. If he had been a Westerner, his particular achievement would have been less surprising, but he came from the East.

He reached Belgium at the time of a milk crisis. We were attempting, and, in fact, had practically arranged, the plan to establish C. R. B. herds adjacent to towns, to insure a positive supply for tiny babies. The local committees went at it, but one after another came in with discouraging reports. Even their own people were often preventing success by fearing and sometimes by flatly refusing to turn their precious cows into a community herd. Then one day D., who, so far as I know, had never in his career been within speaking distance of a cow, put on something that looked like a sombrero and swung out across his province. We had hardly had time to speculate about what he might accomplish, before he returned to announce that he had rounded up a magnificent herd, and that his district was ready to guarantee so much pure milk from that time on!

"What had he done, where we had failed?" asked Monsieur. "He had called a meeting of farmers in each commune, and said: 'We, the Americans, want from this commune five or ten cows for the babies of your cities. We give ourselves to Belgium, you give your cows to us. We will give them back when the war is over—If they are alive!' And he got them!" They would have given this cheerful beggar anything—these stolid old Flemish peasants.

TOPICS FOR WRITTEN AND ORAL DISCUSSION

1.If you live near a military installation or a Veterans' Affairs Hospital, seek permission to go there and interview chaplains and talk with them about their methods for comforting the grieving survivors of soldiers. If you are so inclined, ask them if they could use your help because understanding and acting on that understanding should always be the goal of education.

2. Locate a relief agency in your area, or even nationally, and research their support mission and strategy. If you can, contact an individual member of that agency personally and have them get you in touch with other individuals who have gone to disaster areas where that agency has been called to serve. If it is also possible, contact someone who has been assisted by that agency and discover what his or her perspective is. Write a narrative based on these interviews.

3. Volunteer to work in a local soup kitchen that helps indigents receive their daily nutritional requirements. Get recipes for the soup they serve and make some for your class. Discuss the difficulties in having to live solely off of that soup. While you're at it, talk with the individuals who frequent the soup kitchen. Find out the narrative thread of their lives. Write a story about the people of the soup kitchen, about the war that they all fight against poverty and despair.

4. Write a personal essay about the most difficult loss you have faced in your life. In this essay, be sure to include those people or agencies that helped you get through this experience: members of your family, a teacher or counselor, a friend, or a religious organization. Finally, conclude your essay with thoughts about the lasting effects of this loss. Imagine, then, a time when just about everyone you knew was suffering from a similar loss, like it was during World War I. Imagine what that environment would have been like. Discuss this issue in class later.

5. Debate the topic of whether women have a legitimate role in combat. If so, where and how? If not, what is the proper role of women in war?

6. Organize a panel discussion on the role of memorial art. Discuss such works of memorial art as the Vietnam War Memorial or the World War II Memorial. Also, discuss the need for a World War I memorial—which, believe it or not, doesn't yet exist in the nation's capital.

7. Pretend that you had to evacuate your home because of an immediate emergency. You have only 15 minutes to pack your most valuable possessions. Because there is not nearly enough room in your car to take everything you value, make a list of 10 specific items that you will take. In class, compare and discuss students' lists.

8. Write a research paper on important contributions to the military that have been made by women throughout the years. You'll be surprised how many women there are to write about, so just choose one and write about her in detail. Read each essay in class and discuss.

NOTES

1.   Edith Wharton, *A Son at the Front* (DeKalb: Northern Illinois University Press, 1995 [1922]), 40. All subsequent citations are from this text and page numbers are indicated parenthetically.

2.   Leo Braudy, *From Chivalry to Terrorism: War and the Changing Nature of Masculinity* (New York: Knopf, 2003), xvi.

3.   Alan Price, *The End of the Age of Innocence: Edith Wharton and the First World War* (London: Palgrave Macmillan, 1996), ix–x.

4.   R.W.B. Lewis, *Edith Wharton: A Biography* (New York: Fromm, 1985), 370.

5.   Lewis, *Wharton,* 371.

6.   Hoover, Herbert, "Introduction," in *The Women of Belgium: Turning Tragedy to Triumph,* Charlotte Kellogg, http://www.lib.byu.edu/zrdu/wwi/memoir/ckellogg/wbelg1.htm.

7.   Stephen Pope and Elizabeth-Anne Wheal, *The Macmillan Dictionary of the First World War* (London: Macmillan, 1997), 115.

SUGGESTIONS FOR FURTHER READING

Braudy, Leo. *From Chivalry to Terrorism: War and the Changing Nature of Masculinity.* New York: Knopf, 2003.

Brittain, Vera. *Chronicle of Youth: Great War Diary, 1913–1917.* London: Phoenix, 2000.

Cather, Willa. *One of Ours.* New York: Scribner's, 1922.

Ephron, Amy. *A Cup of Tea.* New York: Ballantine, 1997.

Hansen, Arlen J. *Gentlemen Volunteers: The Story of the American Ambulance Drivers in the Great War, August 1914–September 1918.* New York: Arcade, 1996.

Harries, Meirion, and Susie Harries. *The Last Days of Innocence: America at War, 1917–1918.* New York: Vintage, 1997.

Wharton, Edith. *A Backward Glance.* New York: Scribner's, 1933.

3

War Poetry and Pat Barker's
Regeneration (1991)

LITERARY ANALYSIS

War has always been a brutish experience, but the soldiers who enlisted and marched off to that gathering storm in August 1914 soon found that modern technology, besides making the battlefield more lethal, had also made combat more alienating and inhumane. In *Technology and War: From 2000 B.C. to the Present,* van Creveld describes the revolutionary change in warfare that World War I brought to bear on the common soldier:

> Ultimately the net effect of the progress in weapons technology was to increase enormously the volume of fire that could be delivered, the range at which it could be delivered, and the accuracy with which that square by square meter by square meter, the battlefield became a more deadly place than ever before. Metal in the form of bullets from quick firing rifles and machine guns, as well as fragments from artillery shells, came hurtling through the air in quantities that would previously have appeared absolutely incredible. In the words of a book that acquired great fame after 1919, warfare entered a new medium and increasingly took place in a storm of steel... .
>
> The tactical significance of this was that, perhaps for the first time since the invention of organized warfare, infantry no longer fought standing erect on their feet and organized in formation. This was a truly revolutionary change, the impact of which would take several decades to work out.[1]

In *The Storm of Steel: From the Diary of a German Storm Trooper on the Western Front,* Ernst Juenger describes a scene that was typical of World War I soldiers during nighttime raiding parties: "We crawled on all-fours right up to the English wire and then took cover behind scattered clumps of grass. After a while several English appeared dragging a roll of wire. They stopped just in front of us and began cutting at the roll of wire with wire-clippers and talking in whispers. We crept nearer together in order to hold a muttered consultation."[2]

While the war began in an atmosphere of idealistic hopes and romantic delusion—yes, as a war to end all wars—it eventually became a conflict of desperate human deprivation. Modern war was dehumanizing. While great technological advancements had created horrible machines of enormous destructive capacities, the human "machine" had not evolved all that much since man first stood upright. These new machines of death and destruction not only exponentially increased the casualty rates, they increased the psychological harm to those who survived as well.

Advances in the understanding of human psychology, especially by the famous Viennese psychologist Sigmund Freud (1856–1939), made it evident to a few pioneering doctors that many soldiers were being psychologically incapacitated by their war trauma. One such doctor was Dr. William H. R. Rivers at Craiglockhart War Hospital near Edinburgh, Scotland; he treated many soldiers for a condition that was then known as shell shock (or neurasthenia), which is better known today as post-traumatic stress disorder. The analysis in this chapter examines the poetry of Siegfried Sassoon and Wilfred Owen and then analyzes Pat Barker's *Regeneration,* a novel about the work of Dr. Rivers at Craiglockhart. The theme of this chapter is primarily that the rapid technological advances in warfare created a dramatic sense of alienation, and the concomitant inability of the top military leadership to use these new technologies effectively and efficiently—humanely—forced a handful of combatants into an antiwar stance. However, it should be noted that this antiwar stance was not so much pacifistic as it was against the way the war was being waged.

Rupert Brooke was considered the exemplar poet of his generation during the first two years, but as the war continued and the casualties mounted, aesthetic considerations of the war shifted from that of noble support and martyrdom to that of criticizing the wastage of a whole generation. For example, the 1973 edition of *The Norton Anthology of Modern Poetry* includes the poetry of Siegfried Sassoon and Wilfred Owen, but not that of Rupert Brooke. Of course, it was largely the U.S. antiwar movement of the 1960s and 1970s that changed war literature into protest literature. As an example of how highly considered Brooke was during his time, F. Scott Fitzgerald—who was inducted and commissioned in the army but never fought in World War I—carried a copy of Brooke's poetry with him throughout his military service. Fitzgerald also entitled his first novel *This Side of Paradise* from Brooke's poetry.[3]

Brooke was born in Rugby, Warwickshire, England, on 3 August 1887 and was educated at King's College, Cambridge. After the war commenced, Brooke received a commission in the Royal Navy.[4] Brooke participated in the 1914 British defense of Antwerp and retreated back to England when that operation failed. Already weakened by a bout of dysentery, Brooke later died from blood poisoning when a mosquito bite turned septic. He was buried on the Aegean isle of Skyros, his own perpetual corner of England, where he had been training for the upcoming Gallipoli campaign. Brooke's most famous poem, "The Soldier," immortalized him as a romantic British war poet:

> If I should die, think only this of me:
>   That there's some corner of a foreign field
> That is forever England. There shall be
>   In that rich earth a richer dust concealed;
> A dust whom England bore, shaped, made aware,
>   Gave, once, her flowers to love, her ways to roam,
> A body of England's, breathing English air,
>   Washed by the rivers, blest by suns of home. [1914][5]

It is interesting to speculate whether Brooke's poetry would have eventually been affected by the horror of trench warfare. Samuel Hynes has a good idea: "He is a poet of his time, but his time was those few months of the First World War, when Englishmen still believed that it was sweet and proper to die for one's country, and when Brooke's war sonnets could be read without bitterness or irony."[6] Hynes goes on: "We think of Brooke as a War Poet. But quite inaccurately. In the first place, it would be more precise to call him an On-the-way-to-war Poet, for, with ironic appropriateness, he died of natural causes en route . . . and the emotions that his war sonnets express are not those of a combatant, but of a recruit. The *real* War Poets—Owen and Sassoon and Graves . . . came later, out of the trenches."[7] So the answer seems to be, yes.

Allyson Booth, in her excellent *Postcards from the Trenches: Negotiating the Space between Modernism and the First World War*, describes the stark reality of the war that Brooke was totally unaware of when he wrote his most famous poem:

Trench soldiers in the Great War inhabited worlds construed, literally, of corpses. Dead men at the front blended with the mud and duckboard landscapes, emerging through the surface of the ground and through the dirt floors of dugouts: "In the ground here there are several strata of dead, and in many places the delving of the shells has brought out the oldest and set them out in display on the top of the new ones" (Barbusse 278). Live soldiers found themselves buried in falling dirt while shells disinterred their dead companions from shallow graves. Casualty lists that wound around buildings or spilled into extra newspapers columns shocked a civilian population confronted with statistics documenting the erasure of a generation; the corps escapes of trench warfare embodied that erasure.[8]

In "The Soldier," which comes out of his volume of war poetry *1914,* Brooke uncritically and unironically celebrates soldierly sacrifice for England. The poem is a sentimental call to arms that inspired the English people as they entered the war. It not only portends Brooke's own death, but it also articulates a notion that was commonly held by his countryman at the time: that England exists wherever an English soldier is buried.

What happens, however, in a conflict where there are so many bodies that they often go unburied and without an appropriate sense of sacramental care? Ultimately, it is too easy to state that Brooke was too naive to portend the condition of modern warfare to come—very few had that insight[9]—but it does underscore a poignancy that is still evident today if you travel to the battlefield memorials. There are thousands of British lads, as well as the remains of all the other major combatants, buried over the European continent, far from home. Again, Booth describes the conditions at the time:

> In 1916, the British government decided that soldiers would be buried where they died; families would not have the right to demand the return of combatants' bodies for burial (Curl 319). Around the same time, the introduction of conscription changed the group that constituted military families. In its War Graves issue, the *Times* of London described how, suddenly, "British soldiers were men whose parents or wives had not accepted, as one of the conditions of a professional soldier's career, the possibility of an unknown grave in a foreign country; [and] their relatives poignantly and insistently demanded . . . the fullest information as to the location of the graves of those who fell."[10]

Booth goes on to describe that in the absence of a body, words provided the only sense of closure for the bereaved families. She writes that for

> The families of soldiers killed at the front . . . death was not a corpse at all but a series of verbal descriptions. Next of kin were informed of a casualty by a telegram, the terse language of which gave merely the date and location of death: "Regret to inform you Captain E. H. Brittain M. C. Killed in action Italy June 15th" (Brittain 438). The telegram was frequently followed by letters from

friends and/or commanding officers, who gave more precise details about the location and circumstances of death.[11]

In contrast, Siegfried Sassoon's late war poetry, precisely because it incorporates this modern reality, is completely devoid of the romantic notions that are rife in Brooke's work.

As such, Sassoon's war poetry is starkly realistic and ironic. In his 1917 poem, "Glory of Women," Sassoon writes that "You love us when we're heroes, home on leave, / Or wounded in a mentionable place." A mentionable place could have multiple meanings here. One meaning is that the soldier is wounded in a geographical place that is identifiable, mentionable only because it would not be censored by the authorities. The second meaning is that the soldier is wounded in a place on his body that could be mentioned to a proper lady, such as an arm or a leg. Either meaning involves one form of censorship or another for the soldier. This irony underscores the poem's overall sarcastic tone concerning the disparity between the front and home— between the soldier's horrific experience and the polite society the women live in. The old-fashioned women just do not understand the modern condition of war.

Siegfried Sassoon (1886–1967) was born into a well-to-do Jewish-English family and grew up in the English countryside of Kent, aspiring from an early age to be a poet. When the war began, Sassoon enlisted in the Sussex Yeomanry but soon received a commission in the Royal Welch Fusiliers (RWF), in May 1915. On 17 November 1915, Sassoon landed in France and joined the First Battalion RWF near Béthune in the Artois sector.[12] Sassoon lost his younger brother, who had been severely wounded at Gallipoli and buried at sea, on 1 November 1915. Another personal tragedy occurred on 18 March 1916, when a close friend was killed at the front. Paul Moeyes, in his critical study of Sassoon, observes that these personal losses did not yet affect his poetry:

> [T]here is as yet no trace in his [early war] poems that would suggest the bitter war-satires he was to write later on. At this stage Sassoon and his early war poems do not differ greatly from the poets and poems that are usually quoted to illustrate an initial war enthusiasm, Rupert Brooke's *1914* sonnets....Brooke, especially, caught the mood of many a soldier who had not yet had any front-line experience, and many of the war poets that are usually juxtaposed with Brooke shared his enthusiasm when still inexperienced.[13]

Sassoon's early war poetry was not all that different than many others in the Edwardian and Georgian period; it sought to create beauty—not to convey modern reality. In fact, Moeyes notes that Sassoon initially objected to his friend Robert Graves's war poetry as being too realistic, but at that time Graves had had vastly more frontline experience than his friend.[14]

But as Sassoon's experience in trench warfare increased, his idealistic notions of poetry finally succumbed to reality—as it had for Graves, too. Sassoon, who had been an avid sportsman in his prewar life, initially proved to be an aggressive warrior, and he felt at home in the hard-fighting RWF units. Furthermore, Sassoon proved to be a caring and dedicated leader of his troops. On 16 April 1917, Sassoon was wounded in the shoulder by a sniper and sent home to convalesce in England. It was during this return home that Sassoon began to articulate his feelings against the war effort. His social associations eventually led him to Bertrand Russell and members of the pacifist, antiwar movement in England, and they influenced him to write his "A Soldier's Declaration" on 15 June 1917. Instead of court-martialing Sassoon, the military authorities sent him to Craiglockhart Hospital to be treated as a shell-shocked officer. It was at Craiglockhart that he met fellow poet Wilfred Owen.

Similar to Sassoon's, Owen's war poetry is ironic and rife with realistic details of his own firsthand war experience. Owen, who had been wounded by an explosion while sleeping in a trench, had been sent to Craiglockhart to rehabilitate his emotional wounds. At Craiglockhart, Owen came under the spell of Sassoon's charm and literary talents, especially the older poet's fondness for Thomas Hardy, the father of the bitterly ironic. In particular, Hardy's bifurcated poetic vision, which could both look back to the Victorian period and look ahead to the modern is a perfect model of both men's poetic experience of the war.

Also like Sassoon's, Owen's early work belied the bitter vision of his later war poetry. For example, his 1909–1910 poem, "To Poesy," which is an ode to poetry itself, indicates a precious art-for-art's sake sensibility. For example, this poem ignores the brewing political and nationalistic realities going on around him that would eventually explode into war and condemn many of his generation to suffering and death, including Owen himself. Written in archaic diction, it belies his prewar poetic naiveté that would eventually be lost during the war. Other romantically derivative poems written by him during this period likewise reflect innocence; "Supposed Confessions of a Second-rate Mind in Dejection," "The Dread of Falling into Naught," "[Deep Under Turf Grass]," "Happiness," and "To Eros," are prime examples. Even the poems that he wrote when war first broke out, such as "1914," seem unaware of the amount of human suffering that was ahead, but, then again, the rest of the world was ignorant of it as well.

Besides Sassoon, Owen was also influenced by other war poets, such as Graves.. Miranda Seymour, in her biography of Graves, describes the occasion of the first meeting between the two men. Seymour writes:

On 12 October Graves left London to visit Sassoon at Craiglockhart. He was met at the station by a slight, handsome young man with a nervous stammer. On the way to the golf course where Sassoon was waiting to meet them, he introduced himself as Wilfred Owen, a poet and editor of the hospital magazine. His admiration for Sassoon was undisguised.

William Rivers, the doctor whom Graves had met on his first visit was away at this time; instead of discussing their symptoms with him, as they had planned to do, Sassoon and Graves talked about the war, poetry, and Owen. Before he left, Graves was given a copy of "Disabled." Wilfred Owen's most recent poem, and urged by Sassoon to offer friendly criticism.

Owen had become deeply attached to Sassoon as a friend and mentor after showing him some of his early work. In September, Sassoon praised and helped to revise "Anthem for Doomed Youth" but he was perhaps too close to Owen to realize that the poems were not simply admiring imitations of his own style. It was Graves, not Sassoon, who recognized "the real thing, a genuine new talent" as soon as he read "Disabled." ...

As for Sassoon, at Craiglockhart he was writing some of the finest poetry to come out of the war but Graves was not altogether sure that he liked it. ... "Don't send me any more corpse poems," he pleaded in an undated letter, before urging Sassoon to fix his hopes on a new postwar world which would be, admittedly, emptier but wiser "and happier than anything that has gone before."[15]

Sassoon's antiwar declaration had little impact on England's war effort during the war. Sassoon himself returned to the front and was subsequently wounded. However, his poetic antiwar stance has had an enormous impact on subsequent contemporary poets and intellectuals who view the condition of any war skeptically, especially those who opposed the Vietnam War in the 1960s and 1970s.

Pat Barker's first novel in her World War I trilogy, *Regeneration* (1991), is primarily set at Craiglockhart War Hospital and recreates the meeting of Sassoon and Owen when they both were being treated for shell shock. Besides Sassoon, the other major character in this novel is Dr. Rivers, another historical figure who pioneered the humane treatment of shell-shocked soldiers. Although it is a work of fiction, the novel is factually based. Sassoon, a patient of Rivers's, has entered the hospital soon after delivering his "A Soldier's Declaration." A military review board has declared that because Sassoon is "suffering from a severe mental breakdown," he would not have to face a court-martial but would be sent to Craiglockhart for recovery instead.[16] Sassoon, a reluctant patient because he does not believe he belongs in this psychiatric hospital, finally resolves to go back to the war. Although he does not suffer from pronounced shell shock, he certainly has been traumatized by the war. His spiritual wounds are evident indeed, and these are what Dr. Rivers attempts to heal in his sessions with the poet. In the novel's end, Rivers is worried about Sassoon's departure from Craiglockhart:

> How on earth was Siegfried going to manage in France? His opposition to the war had not changed. If anything it had hardened. And to go back to fight, believing as he did, would be to encounter internal divisions far deeper than anything he'd experienced before. Siegfried's "solution" was to tell himself that he was going back only to look after some men, but that formula would not survive the realities of France. However devoted to his men's welfare a platoon commander might be, in the end he is there to kill, and to train other people to kill. Poetry and pacifism were a strange preparation for that role. Though Siegfried had performed it before, and with conspicuous success. But then his hatred of the war had not been as fully fledged, as articulate, as it was now. (249)

The facts tell us that Rivers was correct in his concern about Sassoon, but he may have underestimated his patient's resolve and pluck. Sassoon did successfully return to the front again; this time he managed to avoid any more confrontations with his superiors. But he was subsequently wounded in combat for the last time and sent home for good. Owen, who like Sassoon had returned to the front, was killed on 4 November 1918. After the war, Sassoon was instrumental in getting poetry published posthumously. Only five of his friend Owen's poems had been previously published.

Rivers has other patients besides Sassoon and Owen, and their symptoms of war trauma are far more traumatic. There is a fictional Billy Prior, who was originally suffering from speechlessness after being traumatized in the trenches, and there is Willard, whose emotional trauma has caused him to be paralyzed; Anderson, who suffers from perpetual vomiting and nightmares; Lansdowne, a claustrophobic; Fletcher, a delusional paranoid; Broadbent, a pathological liar. And the list goes on and on. This is where Barker's talents as a fiction writer are best exemplified. The overall complexity and depth of the problem that Rivers faced as a doctor is probably too unfathomable for contemporary readers to comprehend, so Barker reduces the number of patients to a more manageable, but nonetheless intolerable, representative handful.

Underscoring the importance of words, Rivers's primary method of treatment is conversation, which involves concentration and empathy. Ultimately, Rivers is the novel's hero because he will personally absorb the psychological trauma of his patients' collective experience. In the end, Rivers is exhausted and suffers from his own emotional wounds: "That evening after dinner Rivers tried to work on a paper he was due to give to the Royal Society of Medicine in December. As he read through what he'd written, he became aware that he was being haunted by images" (234). Although haunted by the war, Rivers nevertheless perseveres. His professional philosophy is clear but complex: while Rivers believes it is his duty to return these men to the front, he also believes that humanity has an obligation to regenerate them back to life as well. Therefore, not only is regeneration the title of the novel, it is its major theme. The novel's overall tone is ironic: while the novel is clearly sympathetic to the plight of these soldiers, it remains aloof to the ultimate meaning of their sacrifice and pain. As such, Barker's novel, like the poetry of Sassoon and Owen, does not wallow in futile sentimentality and unrestrained hagiography of the war and its poetic heroes. Nothing denigrates the valor of great men than to lose their humanity in needless mythologizing. Let their own words speak for themselves.

HISTORICAL DOCUMENTS AND CONTEXT

Siegfried Sassoon's War Against the War

The inestimable war literature critic Paul Fussell, in *The Great War and Modern Memory*, observes that before the war

> Sassoon was healthy and unthinkingly patriotic, and he loved anything to do with horses. By the morning of August 5, 1914, he was in uniform as twenty-eight-year-old cavalry trooper. In a short time he transferred to the Royal Welch Fusiliers as a Second Lieutenant of Infantry, and before long he was in action on France. Initially enthusiastic, he was very soon appalled by what he saw there. But throughout he was an extremely brave and able officer, nicknamed "Mad Jack" by his men... .
>
> What [Alfred] Blunden call Sassoon's "splendid war on the war" took place initially in the pages of the *Cambridge Magazine* which published many of the anti-war—or better, anti-home-front—poems collected in the volume *The Old Huntsman* in May, 1917. Two months later he issued his notorious *non serviam,* "A Soldier's Declaration." He expected to be court-martialed for this, but his friend Robert Graves managed to arrange that he face a medical board instead. It found that he needed rest, and he was sent off to mental sanitarium instead....In June, 1918, he brought out his final blast against the war, *Counter-Attack and Other Poems.* In July he was wounded in the head and invalided home.
>
> By the time of the Armistice he was exhausted and trembly, sleepless and overwrought, fit for no literary work. He found peace and quite again in Kent, but nightmares kept intruding.[17]

By 1926, Sassoon began to finally recover his energy from the war and started his life's work by writing a series of six memoirs: *Memoirs of a Fox-Hunting Man* (1928), *Memoirs of an Infantry Officer* (1930), and *Sherston's Progress* (1936). This trilogy was later republished as *The Memoirs of George Sherston.* He later wrote *The Old Century and Seven More Years* (1938), *The Weald of Youth* (1942), and *Siegfried's Journey* (1945). He died in 1967 at the age of 80.[18]

FROM SIEGFRIED SASSOON'S "A SOLDIER'S DECLARATION" COUNTER-ATTACK

http://www.sassoonery.demon.co.uk/sassdefy.htm

I am making this statement as an act of willful defiance of military authority, because I believe that the War is being deliberately prolonged by those who have the power to end it. I am a soldier, convinced that I am acting on behalf of soldiers. I believe that this War, on which I entered as a war of defense and liberation, has now become a war of aggression and conquest. I believe that the purpose for which I and my fellow soldiers entered upon this war should have been so clearly stated as to have made it impossible to change them, and that, had this been done, the objects which actuated us would now be attainable by negotiation. I have seen and endured the sufferings of the troops, and I can no longer be a party to prolong these sufferings for ends that I believe to be evil and unjust. I am not protesting against the conduct of the war, but against the political errors and insincerities for which the fighting men are being sacrificed. On behalf of those who are suffering now I make this protest against the deception which is being practiced on them; also I believe that I may help to destroy the callous complacency with which the majority of those at home regard the contrivance of agonies which they do not, and which they have not sufficient imagination to realize.

The Hydra

As a way to keep some of the patients both busy and informed during their stay in Craiglockhart, the medical staff, particularly A. J. Brock, supported the publishing of a hospital magazine, *The Hydra,* from April to September 1917; a subsequent publication replaced *The Hydra* thereafter. *The Hydra,* which was published every two weeks, "is a unique record of life at Craiglockhart in 1917–18, reporting on lectures, meetings, expeditions, hobbies and entertainment; patients also contributed topical jokes about the hospital, as well as verse, stories and cartoons."[19] Starting with the 21 July 1917 issue, Wilfred Owen edited six editions and published his first two poems, "The Song of Songs" and "The Next War." As editor, Owen also published "Dreamers" and "Wirers," two poems by Siegfried Sassoon. The collaboration of these two distinctly different men is one of the rare accidents of this war that turned out for the collective good of humanity. In *The Great War and the Shaping of the 20th Century,* Jay Winter and Blaine Baggett express the event well: "Poetry was a concentrated way of expressing the tensions which in thousands of soldiers produced shell shock. Sassoon found one language for it: open protest. Owen found another: compassion. Their verse captured stress that soldiers faced, and the state of mind of those broken by it. But Sassoon was, after all, only one man, and his defiance quickly disappeared in the rush of events; his poetry has lasted longer."[20]

While a lot of the reported activity in *The Hydra* seems normal, upon further reflection it may appear almost too normal. One must imagine that performing these activities could have required extraordinary effort from many of these soldiers. Remember, treatment for shell shock ranged from electroconvulsive shock therapy to hypnosis and psychotherapy. Luckily, the majority of the treatments merely involved the recuperation of ordinary vocational skills, which is why there is so much coverage of these "ordinary" activities throughout *The Hydra*. Gardening and poultry keeping was a form of healing for some as much as writing was for Sassoon and Owen.

World War I transmogrified even the most ordinary experience in the collective lives of people into something extraordinary and surreal. As Winter and Baggett articulate it: "Shell-shocked men were imprisoned in their own worlds. Just reaching them was an Olympian task; for them to act together was impossible. That is why Owen and Sassoon spoke to them and for them in their poetry."[21] It is also why as time has progressed, as more and more of civilization begins to suffer from a form of shell shock, the poetry of these war-damaged men has also increasingly spoken to greater numbers of people at large.

FROM *THE HYDRA: THE MAGAZINE OF THE CRAIGLOCKHART WAR HOSPITAL,* NO.7, 21 JULY 1917

Napier University, http://www.nulis.napier.ac.uk/
SpecialCollections/CraigCon/warpoets/hydra/hyo07/hyo07con.htm

Notes and News

Gardening

The Poultry Keeping and Gardening Association has now taken over the supervision of all the hospital grounds, and hedge-cutting promises to become a favorite pastime. Major Bryce has been performing prodigies with a scythe, but the thought of neurasthenic enthusiasts endeavoring to emulate him makes us shudder. One can do much with a scythe. The vegetables are coming along fast, and when we look at the large tract under cultivation, we feel almost proud of our amateur gardeners.

Poultry Keeping

The poultry farm is beginning to take definite shape now, and demands a lot of attention. The chickens are beginning to get quite large, and while July is (we are told by Mr. Bird, who surely ought to know) a bad month for poultry, everything appears to be most satisfactory.

Billiards

Of billiards there is little to report. No fresh handicaps have so far been started, and the billiard tables are not, perhaps, as much in demand as formerly. We are able to contradict the report that the two officers, who spent the day potting each other, had their blankets moved into the billiard room. As they cannot decide which of them holds the record for flukes, we congratulate both equally on their endeavors.

Cricket

We are fortunate in having amongst our recent arrivals several very useful players for our eleven, and there is no reason why we should not be able to turn out quite a good team in future.

Unfortunately, Mr. Downes has left us, and has rather weakened our battling side, as he could generally be relied upon for at least a score of runs. He was also very useful as a change bowler, and his fielding was distinctly good.

It is, however, no use weeping over the loss of one good player, because this hospital should be able to put forward at least two dozen cricketers. We are afraid some are very reluctant to come forward. The hospital would like to put its best eleven into the field, but it is quite impossible to do this if patients will not let us know they are players, or will not let us see them at practice, and although we have now quite a number of players who show keenness, we should still like to see a little more enthusiasm.

On Wednesday, 4th July, we again met the Merchiston eleven on their own ground. The afternoon was dull, but we had no rain, and later in the afternoon the sun shone brilliantly. We won the toss, and runs soon began to pile up to the bats of Gilling and Kershaw. Before the first wicket fell the score had reached 68, and before the fourth 150. Up to this period we looked like making a large score, but things did not turn out as well as was expected, and the whole side was out for 176, Kershaw, Gilling, Lake and Downes all battling well.

Merchiston now had their turn, Major Bingham and Kershaw opening the bowling. Each secured two wickets in their first two overs, Merchiston thus losing four wickets for only 9 runs. Shortly after Kershaw came off, being very tired after his strenuous innings, Merchiston were all out for 128, leaving us with a margin of nearly 50.

. . . . .

Hospital Wedding

A large number of people, including many military and naval officers, attended West St Giles church, on Wednesday, the 11th July, to witness the marriage of Major S.J. Montgomery and Miss M. Crawford. Major Montgomery, who is on the General List, had a very long spell of active service, both as Brigade Major and Divisional Machine Gun Officer, before coming as a patient to Craiglockhart.

We offer them our heartiest congratulations, and wish them both a bright and prosperous future.

Golf

At the invitation of the Merchants of Edinburgh Golf Club, a medal match was played in aid of the Scottish Red Cross. We congratulate Mr. Scott on his brilliant round of 78, and Capt. Stevens on his 79.

On Thursday a match was played between the Craiglockhart Club and the Hospital, consisting of four singles and four foursomes. The match was lost (6–2), Mr. Scott and Mr. Cruikshank being the only winners on the Hospital side. Mr. Scott, after being five down, made a wonderful recovery and won by one hole, while Mr. Cruikshank was on top all the way, and won four up and two to play. We congratulate both of them. A return match is to be played on the 19th inst.

We have, at last, come to an arrangement with the course officials, and in future the charge will be 2s. per week or 6s. per month, instead of sixpence a day. Tickets must be obtained from the Greenkeeper.

The Golf Tournament was won by Mr. Scott, who beat Major Bingham by a hole.

Camera Club

There still continues unabated interest in photography, and the admission of new officers has added fresh and further enthusiasm in this side of the house, which is very encouraging.

It is very gratifying to see that the dark room rules are bearing fruit, and that care is being observed regarding flooding and water wastage.

Capt. Sampson, assisted by Mr. Rowse, are now taking charge of the Camera Club, as Capt. Buchanan is likely to be going to Bowhill shortly. It is proposed to institute a system of exchange of prints, and the opportunity is taken to express the hope that there will be a cordial and hearty co-operation.

"Bucolics"

The New Camera Club

The old photographic club has risen from its ashes, and the new Camera Club was inaugurated on Sunday evening, 15th July. There was really a record attendance.

A committee was formed, and the following officers were elected: Major G. Hunter, D.S.O., Chairman; Capt. C. Sampson, R.A.M.C., Secretary; and Capt. Buchanan, R.A.M.C., Lieut. E.J. Shuter, and Lieut. G.H. Baylis, members.

It was decided to place the club on a firm footing, and to make it interesting, entertaining, and instructive.

There will be a weekly meeting held in Lieut. Macintyre's room every Sunday evening at 9 p.m. when photographs and cameras will be exhibited, and everything done to enlist the co-operation of everybody interested in the art.

The first meeting will take place on Sunday next at 9 p.m., and everyone is requested to bring with him his camera, and any films and negatives that will be of mutual interest to others.

It is hoped that members will lend their utmost support by doing all they can to make the club go well and strong, and this is best brought about by soliciting the sympathies and interest of non-members.

Those who are just embarking on their first photographic enterprises will receive every help and advice from their brother members, and encouragement will be the chief object of the club.

Choice of camera, the price, where to buy it, and how to use it will be one of the benefits obtained by belonging to the club, and we can already promise the assistance, in every direction, of many experts whose experiences are great. We shall, by bringing along our duds or failures, find many good Samaritans, and learn from each other much that is good and of value.

Inquiries addressed to the secretary and placed in the letter-rack will receive prompt attention, and please don't hesitate to ask for any information you may require.

All photographic apparatus to be disposed of exchanged, or repaired can be dealt with through the club, and it is also hoped that good materials at reasonable prices will be procurable through the club for use by the members.

By the mutual interchange of negatives on loan, members will be able to procure lasting records of the war, and photographic souvenirs of intense interest.

So come one, come all. Bring your cameras and let us see what we can do. We intend to hold photographic competitions from time to time, and to leave no stone unturned to keep the meetings and general workings of the club lively and full of amusement.

The Secretary

Field Club

On the 13th inst. there was held an enthusiastic preliminary meeting, at which Mr. Chase gave a paper on "Mosses of the Craiglockhart District," illustrated by specimens, diagrams, and microscopic slides. At the close it was resolved that a field club should be definitely constituted, that there should be a meeting every Monday evening for a paper and discussion, and that, if possible, excursions should be arranged. The following office-bearers were elected: President, Capt. Brock; secretary, Mr. Chase. Recruits are wanted. Don't wait to be pushed. "The wind's on the heath." The club hopes to take in periodicals, and to co-operate as far as possible with other existing organizations in the Hospital—such as, obviously, the Camera Club. Our guide, philosopher, and friend, the Major, is down for the next paper. One who apparently came to last Friday's meeting in order to do penance for his sins, writes: "To most of us, the subject of moss smelt mouldy with fusty suggestiveness... Moss! The unkempt beard of senile ruins; the pall of dead paths that lead nowhere; the praying-stool of hermits. What attachment has it for the rolling stones that the war has made us all? Mr. Chase, with a microscope, drawings, and lively description, showed it to be one of the most beautifully interesting of living things. And just as the whole plant world sprang from mosses, and much humbler growths than mosses, so we hope that from this beginning will develop an important and varied system of natural work. One gentleman objected to our calling our club a Natural History Society, because natural history reminded him of school-marms and spectacles. We do not want all our excursions to be through the jungle of *hortus succes*.

"Our broodings over the face of the earth, and the firmament, and the waters under the earth, will be quite primitive—without form, but, we hope, not void."

TOPICS FOR WRITTEN AND ORAL DISCUSSION

1. Visit a local Veteran's Hospital or a mental health clinic and interview some of the doctors who treat patients for their emotional difficulties. Write a paper concerning some of the treatment techniques that they use to cure their patients.

2. Visit a local soup kitchen or homeless shelter and inquire how many of the people that they help served either in the Vietnam War or other wars. Interview some of these veterans and write an essay about their war experiences and the personal problems that they have experienced.

3. Research the antiwar movement during the American Civil War and the concomitant problem of desertion, and compare it with the antiwar movement during World War I. Write an essay about the similarities and differences.

4. Invite individuals who protested or objected to the Vietnam War to class and have them discuss the reasons for their differences with the war effort then. Interview them to establish a record of the event.

5. Invite to class individuals who participated in the Vietnam War effort and who did not object to America's policy then. Have them discuss the reasons for their support and why they participated in the war. Interview them to establish a record of the event.

6. Write a comparison and contrast essay using the two interviews above about these two types of experiences during the Vietnam War.

7. Organize a debate on whether the antiwar poets acted correctly in their poetic and political attitude toward the World War I effort.

8. Organize a debate on whether the antiwar effort in the United States against the Vietnam War was correct in its political and social attitude toward that war effort. Particularly debate the various methods of protest.

9. Research the antiwar effort in Germany during World War I. How was it similar and how was it different from those discussed above?

NOTES

1. Martin Van Creveld, *Technology and War: From 2000 B.C. to the Present* (New York: Free Press, 1991), 171.

2. Ernst Juenger, *The Storm of Steel: From the Diary of a German Storm-Trooper Officer on the Western Front* (New York: Howard Fertig, 1996), 71.

3. Andrew Turnbull, *Scott Fitzgerald: A Biography* (New York: Scribner, 1962), 119; also, from a letter from Fitzgerald to Maxwell Perkins, 16 August 1919, *F. Scott Fitzgerald: A Life in Letters,* ed. Matthew J. Bruccoli (New York: Scribners, 1994), 30.

4. *Merriam-Webster's Encyclopedia of Literature* (New York: Merriam-Webster, 1995), 176.

5. Rupert Brooke, "The Soldier," in *The Great War Reader,* ed. James Hannah (College Station: Texas A&M University Press), 359.

6. Samuel Hynes, *Edwardian Occasions Essays on English Writing in the Early Twentieth Century* (New York: Oxford University Press), 144.

7. Ibid.

8. Allyson Booth, *Postcards from the Trenches: Negotiating the Space between Modernism & the First World War* (New York: Oxford, 1996), 50. The reference in this citation is from Henri Barbusse's *Under Fire: The Story of a Squad,* trans. Fitzwater Wray (New York: Dutton, 1917).

9. Lord Kitchener did. He was a modern.

10. Booth, *Postcards,* 24. The citation in this quotation is from James Stevens Curl, *A Celebration of Death: An Introduction to Some of the Buildings, Monuments, and Settings of Funerary Architecture in the Western European Tradition* (New York: Scribner's, 1980).

11. Booth, *Postcards,* 25–26. The citation in this quotation is from Vera Brittain, *Testament of Youth: An Autobiography Study of the Years: 1900–1925* (New York: Macmillan, 1933).

12. Paul Moeyes, *Siegfried Sassoon: Scorched Glory: A Critical Study* (New York: St Martin's Press, 1997), 29.

13. Moeyes, *Siegfried Sassoon,* 30.

14. Moeyes, *Siegfried Sassoon,* 32.

15. Miranda Seymour, *Robert Graves: Life on the Edge* (New York: Henry Holt, 1995), 69–70.

16. Pat Barker, *Regeneration* (New York: Plume, 1993 [1991]), 4. All subsequent citations are from this text and page numbers are indicated parenthetically.

17. Paul Fussell, *The Great War and Modern Memory* (New York: Oxford University Press, 1975), 91.

18. Fussell, *The Great War and Modern Memory,* 90–92.

19. Dominic Hibberd, "The War Poets Collection" (Edinburgh: Napier University), http://www.nulis.napier.ac.uk/specialcollections/craigcon/warpoets/hydra.htm.

20. Jay Winter and Blaine Baggett, *The Great War and Shaping of the Twentieth Century* (New York: Penguin, 1996), 226.

21. Winter and Baggett, *Great War,* 226.

SUGGESTIONS FOR FURTHER READING

Falls, Cyril. *The Nature of Modern Warfare.* New York: Oxford, 1941.

Leed, Eric. *No Man's Land: Combat and Identity in World War I.* Cambridge: Cambridge University Press, 1979.

Ross, Robert H. *The Georgian Revolt: Rise and Fall of a Poetic Ideal, 1910–1922.* London: Faber, 1967.

Russell, Bertrand. *Portraits from Memory.* London, 1958.

Sassoon, Siegfried. *The Complete Memoirs of George Sherston.* London: Faber, 1972.

———. *Diaries: 1920–1922.* Edited and introduced by Rupert Hart-Davies. London: Faber, 1981.

Silkin, Jon. *Out of Battle: The Poetry of the Great War.* London: Oxford University Press, 1972.

Swinnerton, Frank. *The Georgian Literary Scene, 1910–1935: A Panorama.* London: Hutchinson, 1950.

Winter, Jay. *Sites of Memory, Sites of Mourning.* Cambridge: Cambridge University Press, 1995.

4

The Strategic Technology of Modern Warfare:
Propaganda and Civilian Bombing

HISTORICAL DOCUMENTS AND CONTEXT

The technology of modern war not only tormented the combatants on a tactical level at the front, but it also affected the citizens on a strategic level at home. This chapter not only discusses the use of the airplane's distant cousin, the dirigible, or zeppelin, which was used as a long-range bomber for the first time in war, but also the uses of mass media propaganda by governments to shape public opinion—two dramatic examples of strategic technologies used in World War I. Although long-range, strategic bombing would not become a major force until World War II, propaganda (especially against the Germans) had as much impact on determining the eventual outcome of World War I as any other singular aspect of the conflict.

What is propaganda? In *From Chivalry to Terrorism: War and the Changing Nature of Masculinity,* Leo Braudy states that propaganda quite simply links "personal honor to national interest."[1] In "Of Fraud and Force Fast Woven: Domestic Propaganda during the First World War," Aaron Delwiche defines propaganda as activities that manipulate the attitudes of a particular group to act in a prescribed way.[2] For example, in America, propaganda was essential in getting its people ready to fight a war. Delwiche writes: "It is one of history's great ironies that Woodrow Wilson, who was re-elected as a peace candidate in 1916, led America into the First World War. With the help of a propaganda apparatus that was unparalleled in world history, Wilson forged a nation of immigrants into a fighting whole. An examination of public opinion before the war, propaganda efforts during the war, and the endurance of propaganda in peacetime raise significant questions about the viability of democracy as a governing principle."[3] The primary problem is with so much propaganda in use, no one could ever be certain of the truth again. They did not know whom to believe.

In *The Pity of War*, Niall Ferguson correctly observes that the "First World War was the first media war."[4] Just as it not only changed the modern battlefield, technology (in the form of mass media) also allowed governments to direct their citizenry at home against the enemy. The war was thus fought not only on the battlefield but in the words that were being used both at home and abroad. Besides the domestic poster campaigns to recruit soldiers and rally public support for the war, particularly in Great Britain and the United States, the first major effort at propaganda was the newspaper reporting of the German violation of Belgium neutrality and the acts of atrocities against the Belgian citizens who resisted German aggression. Ferguson describes this activity:

> Notoriously, Entente propaganda exaggerated the "atrocities" inflicted on the Belgian by the advancing German armies. After the war, the Liberal pacifist Arthur Ponsonby gave a celebrated (but in fact bogus) illustration of how a report in the *Kolnische Zeitung*–"When the fall of Antwerp became known, the church bells were rung"—was supposedly transmuted via successive Entente papers into: "The barbaric conquerors of Antwerp punished the unfortunate Belgian priest for their heroic refusal to ring the church bells by hanging them as living clappers to the bells with their heads down."...The *Sunday Chronicle* was one of many British papers which alleged that the Germans had cut off the hands of Belgian children, while the former scaremonger William le Queux related with ill-disguised relish "the wild orgies of blood and debauchery" in which the Germans allegedly indulged, including "the ruthless violation and killing of defenseless women, girls and children of tender age."...The bayoneted baby was another favored image.[5]

These exaggerations, and others like them, greatly affected public opinion. For one thing, the circulations of the major international papers swelled. Ferguson notes that the number of subscribers of the *Daily Mail* grew from 946,000 before the war to just under 1.5 million in the first month of the war and stayed that high for about two years.[6] The short-term effect of this propaganda was to get the public behind the war effort and to have enough men enlisted in the military. The long-term effect of propaganda is that citizens lose confidence in governments and national institutions, and, therefore, become more distrustful and alienated from culture and society.

PROPAGANDA

The following are two examples of propaganda posters used during the war.

FROM PROPAGANDA POSTERS

U.S. propaganda poster. Courtesy of Defense Visual
Information Center and the National Archives and Records
Administration.

http://www.worldwar1.com/post005.htm

U.S. propaganda poster. Courtesy of Defense
Visual Information Center and the National Archives
and Records Administration.

http://www.worldwar1.com/post007.htm

The Propaganda Leaflet

Propaganda leaflets are attempts by opposing armies to try and break the morale of the enemy's soldiers. Although this type of propaganda was never proven to be all that effective, the themes and issues that it attempts to exploit nonetheless are illuminating, reflecting national prejudices and propagandistic strategies.

FROM PROPAGANDA LEAFLETS

World War I Document Archive,
http://www.lib.byu.edu/~rdh/wwi/1915/propleaf.html

French Propaganda Leaflet

Pass this along!
German War Comrades!
Think about this:

1. Only greedy rulers want war. The people want peace, and work, and bread.

2. Only the German Kaiser with his militarists, Junkers, and arms manufacturers wanted war, prepared for it and brought it on. No one wanted to fight Germany, no one opposed her desires for a "place in the sun."

3. If a murderer shoots a revolver on the street, it is the duty of every peace-loving, dutiful citizen to hurry to the aid of the fallen. For that reason Italy, Rumania, and the United States went to war against Germany; to free Belgium, Serbia, and France from the clutches of the murderer.... .

10. Stop fighting! Turn your cannons around! Come over to us. Shoot anyone who wants to hinder you from coming.

YOUR DEMOCRATIC COMRADES
IN FRENCH PRISONS

British Leaflet

FOR WHAT ARE YOU FIGHTING, MICHEL?
They tell you that you are fighting for the Fatherland. Have you ever thought why you are fighting?

You are fighting to glorify Hindenburg, to enrich Krupp. You are struggling for the Kaiser, the Junkers, and the militarists....

They promise you victory and peace. You poor fools! It was promised your comrades for more than three years. They have indeed found peace, deep in the grave, but victory did not come!...

It is for the Fatherland....But what is your Fatherland? Is it the Crown Prince who offered up 600,000 men at Verdun? Is it Hindenburg, who with Ludendorff is many kilometers behind the front lines making more plans to give the English more cannon fodder? Is it Krupp for whom each year of war means millions of marks? Is it the Prussian Junkers who still cry over your dead bodies for more annexations?

No, none of these is the Fatherland. You are the Fatherland....The whole power of the Western world stands behind England and France and America! An army of ten million is being prepared; soon it will come into the battle. Have you thought of that, Michel?

Russian Proclamation to the German Soldiers:

The Provisional Government has fallen. The power is now in the hands of the Russian people, and the new government considers the immediate conclusion of peace as its foremost duty . . . .

We charge you soldiers to stand by us in the fight for peace and socialism, for socialism alone can give the proletariat a lasting peace . . . .

Brothers, if you support us, the cause of freedom is assured success . . . .

Our soldiers have laid down their arms. It is now for you to follow this standard of peace.

May peace triumph! May the Socialistic and International Revolution live!

For the Council of People's Commissars.

LENIN, TROTSKY

December 5, 1917

American Leaflet from the Friends of German Democracy

BROTHERS!

The world is in great need. You and you alone can end this need rapidly. We are American citizens of German descent. We know you and trust you. We beg you to trust us.

The great German nation is the barbarian and the breaker of trust in the eyes of the world. You can recover your good reputation only if you overthrow this government, which has made German intelligence and German industry a danger to the world. Take the determination of your destiny into your own hands . . . .

If you will do this the world war will end. In the name of America we give you our word that the new Germany will be taken up as an honorable member of the society of nations. Your intelligence and industry will once again be a blessing to humanity, instead of a curse. . . . Arise for a struggle for a free Germany!

In the name of Americans of German descent.

UNION OF FRIENDS OF

GERMAN DEMOCRACY

New York, March 1918

The Zeppelin Attacks on Great Britain

Although the Germans had the technological capability to bomb London at the start of the war, Wilhelm's fond memories of his childhood visits to England made him initially reluctant to use them. However, after the war got bloodier, his reluctance soon disappeared. The first Zeppelin raid against the English homeland occurred on 19 January 1915, killing two people and injuring 16 others.[7] Ari Unikoski writes, in " *The War in the Air—Bombers: German Zeppelins,*" that the "most successful Zeppelin raid on London in the entire war was on the 8th of September 1915. This raid caused more than half a million pounds of damage, almost all of it from the one Zeppelin, the L13, which managed to bomb central London. This single raid caused more than half the material damage caused by all the raids against Britain in 1915."[8] On 21 March 1915, Zeppelins also attacked Paris, killing 23 Frenchmen and injuring 30. The Allies quickly devised defenses against the Zeppelin airships: barrage balloons to block passage and incendiary and explosive bullets proved to be most effective. While it is estimated that only 10 percent of the bombs dropped ever hit their target, Zeppelins proved to be a huge psychological weapon in the war:

> The Zeppelin attacks had a profound psychological impact on the Allies. The Germans were ordered, under the Treaty of Versailles, to hand over all their airships, but their crews preferred to destroy as many of them as they could. The need to tie up numerous squadrons in home defense can be marked as the Zeppelin's greatest achievement, for as a weapon of war they proved themselves unsatisfactory. Of the 115 Zeppelins employed by the Germans, 53 were destroyed and a further 24 were too damaged to be operational....The cost of constructing those 115 Zeppelins was approximately five times the cost of the damage they inflicted.[9]

FROM THE GREAT ZEPPELIN RAID, 31 JANUARY 1916

World War I Document Archive,
http://www.lib.byu.edu/~rdh/wwi/memoir/zeppelin.html

January 31st./February 1st., 1996
Tom Morgan: Personal research, records of conversations with witnesses.

This article was begun on January 31st, 1996, at just before 9.00 p.m. At around that time and on that date eighty years before, two German airships were flying South over Shropshire, and although they didn't know it, they would soon bomb my town, and almost kill my great grandfather, my grandmother and her sister.

On January 31st, 1916, nine airships left their bases at Friedrichshaven and Lowenthal, an unusually large number. This time they would not creep across the North Sea under cover of darkness to haphazardly bomb the South coast of England and slink back home. This time their orders were to fly across the entire breadth of England and bomb Liverpool which, until then, had been considered well beyond the range of the raiders. The unprecedented scale and audacity of this raid would show the British a thing or two. It would make them realize that nowhere was safe from aerial attack. No longer could anyone say they were out of reach. Even distant Liverpool had become, to use a phrase which would become commonplace in later wars, a legitimate target.

. . . . .

At 9.00 p.m. on 31st January, 1916, the people of Liverpool who were out and about—and there must have been many on that Monday evening, heard no droning engines to make them look upwards. Any who did look up anyway, saw no threatening, silvery cigar-shaped airship about to bomb them. In the streets of Liverpool that night, no fat, frock-coated, top-hatted merchants trod women and children underfoot as they rushed to save themselves, as German posters had depicted. There was no fear. There was no panic. There was no danger. Above all, there was no Zeppelin. L21 was nowhere near Liverpool.

·····

It was Derby which passed below the misty panes of the observation-window. When he [the German captain of the Zeppelin] thought he had crossed the coast and passed on over the Irish Sea, he had been wrong. He had been flying over the sparsely-populated and unlit areas of North Shropshire and Eastern Wales. When he thought he had flown over Liverpool and Birkenhead and the Mersey, he had been wrong....Bombs fell on Tipton and Bradley and then the first bombs fell on Wednesbury. They landed in the King Street area, near to a large factory. A woman, Mrs. Smith, of 14, King Street, left her house to see what the noise was. A little way down the street she saw fires and presumed an explosion at the factory. She walked towards the fires but bombs began to fall behind her. She turned and hurried home, to find her house demolished and all her family killed—her husband Joseph, daughter Nellie aged 13, son Thomas, 11. Three bodies were quickly located. The youngest girl Ina, just a seven, was lying dead on the roof of the factory. Her body would not be found until the morning. The first Wednesbury deaths had occurred.

·····

"The War Must be Brought Home"

Before the United States entered the war, James W. Gerard served as the American ambassador to Germany from 1913 to 1917. His disdain for the German people, both in their homeland and in America, was well known. He openly worried about a German-American revolt the moment U.S. military forces engaged the German army. "His solution was startling simple: to hang German-Americans from lamp posts.[10]

Gerard published *Face to Face with Kaiserism* in 1918. The tone of his arguments about Germany and the prosecution of the war are bombastic and propagandistic—hardly the attitude of a diplomat. One of the most revealing statements he makes about retaliatory bombings against Germany is: "Who is not sorry for the poor people who may suffer, but the war must be brought home to them." It not only shows how effective propaganda had been in dehumanizing the enemy but also how far the political leadership of all nations wanted to take the psychological pain and suffering to the people.

FROM *FACE TO FACE WITH KAISERISM*,
JAMES W. GERARD, 1918

Chapter 24, *When Germany Will Break Down*

http://www.lib.byu.edu/~rdh/wwi/memoir/Gerard2/Kaiserism8.htm

I remember a picture exhibited in the Academy at London, some years ago, representing a custom of the wars of the Middle Ages.

A great fortress besieged, frowns down on the plain under the cold moonlight. From its towering walls the useless mouths are thrust forth—if refused food by the enemy, to die—the children, the maimed, the old, the halt, the blind, all those who cannot help in the defense, who consume food needed to strengthen the weakened garrison.

Every country of the world today is in a state of siege, is conserving food and materials, but not yet has Germany sent forth her useless mouths, to Holland, to Scandinavia and to Switzerland, a sign that not yet is the pinch of hunger in the Empire imperative.

Since I arrived in America in March, 1917, I have been like Cassandra, the prophetess fated to be right, but never believed. I said then Germany would never break because of starvation, or fail because of revolution, and that her man-power was great.

· · · · ·

There is nothing in the war for the German who is not a noble or a junker, an officer or an official. German victory will only bend the collar of caste and servitude, low wages and militarism tighter on the German neck. Sooner or later the deceived German will discover this; revolution will not come during the war, but after it, unless it closes with a German peace, or unless in anticipation of revolt, rights are granted to the people.

We cannot stop, we cannot bear the burden of the debts of this war and at the same time burden ourselves with future military preparation to meet a confident conquering Germany ready to carry the sword into South America. Whatever the sacrifice, we must go on.

And—for each country and—for the Allies as a whole there is one word, Unity.

· · · · ·

The Allies must guard against any move which can add to the man power of the Central Powers, and this reason alone is sufficient reason never to permit the Arabs and Syrians, who have been so oppressed by the Turks, to suffer again under the rule of the Young Turks.

The world must not be disturbed again by Prussian dreams of world conquest, nor must Jerusalem and the Holy Land, towards which the eyes of all Christians have turned for twenty centuries, be voluntarily given back to the Turks.

To allow the Germans access to Baghdad is to invite trouble—a second attempt of the Kaiser to don the turban and proclaim a Holy War in the interest of the fat merchants of Hamburg and Frankfort.

If this were an old time war, when sly diplomats sat at a green table, exchanging territories and peoples like poker chips, we might consent to the partition and destruction of Russia as most natural. But this war is between two systems, and wars either will be continued or cease hereafter. We who hope for the end of war cannot permit Germany to add to her man power any part of the rapidly multiplying population of that great territory which we now call Russia.

It is probable that Russia will go through the stages of the great French Revolution. We have had already the revolution made by the whole nation, Dumas, army, and the control of the respectable moderate Republicans. The period of the Jacobins, the extremists, has come, too, and we must in the end expect the appearance of the military leader, a strong man who will bring order. That is what will happen, for Russia cannot remain a nation under the control of any government which cheerfully consents to dismemberment of her territory. Perhaps Trotzky will be clever enough to transform himself into a patriotic militant leader, if not, then he will not long remain at the head. All these movements of lesser so-called nationalities are fostered by Prussian propagandists.

. . . . .

Every one sympathizes with the Poles and hopes for the establishment of a really free and independent Poland, and not a Poland under the rule or protection of either Austria or Germany. It will be a great experiment, because in the past the great state of Poland, one of the greatest in Europe, was broken because of the incapacity of the Poles to rule themselves. Their armies showed great bravery, the Polish cavalry, winged like angels, terrified enemy cavalry horses and charged often to victory; but the Polish aristocrats, camped with thousands of retainers at the place where the King was elected, sat patiently waiting for the highest bidder before giving their votes.

. . . . .

But a new, real Poland would not be governed by its aristocracy, and under a democratic government the splendid Polish race could be trusted to work out successfully their political salvation.

Should the strong man fail to appear in Russia and the Bolsheviks continue to rule, then the confusion of Russia may not prove an immediate help to Germany.

In the first place, no one now works in Russia; the population will be in want of food and will not have any great surplus to export; and it will be a long time before Germany can draw any material help from the Steppes of incompetency. Had Russia immediately settled down to a new form of government, the case might have been different, but now Germany or some power in Russia must first organize that vast country for production under new conditions before Germany can begin to profit from the withdrawal of Russia from the war except, perhaps, in that important factor— the release of German troops from the Eastern frontier. But as time passes the Germans may use food from Russia to bribe northern neutral nations into an alliance with the Central Empires.

Revolutions are contagious. In 1848, the movement started in France spread all over Europe. The burdened horse on the road evinces a tendency to get out of hand at the mere sight of another horse cavorting about a pasture. The Germans are in blinders and driven by heavy hand, but forgotten as liberty is in Germany, the German

Michael, the peasant chained to the soil, the hard-driven, poorly paid worker of the cities, at least, will exhibit a spirit of uneasiness, when across the line he sees Ivan, the Russian moujik, capering about, free from restraint and running things at his own sweet will. The yoke fits tight to Michael's neck, the German Kaiser drives hard from his All Highest Place; but no Emperor seemed more secure than the head of the Romanoffs, and the very fact that the chains of the yoke seem so strong may make the driven cattle all the more ready to toss the yoke aside when knowledge of power comes to the lower castes of Germany and Austria.

On the question of war Prussia is a civilization as different from that of France, Great Britain and America as is China.

Ministers of the Gospel, professors, poets, writers, teach war; the necessity, the glory, the nobility of war. Long before Nietzsche wrote and Treitschke taught war as a part of the Prussian creed the teachings of these mad philosophers expressed an indigenous feeling in Germany. It is not some abstract belief to be studied. It is a vital, burning, ever-present question which affects deeply, intimately, every man in this world. For until the Prussians are made weary of this belief and converted to a milder life, there is no woman in any corner of the earth, however remote, who may not have to see her son or husband go out to die in the fight against Prussian aggression, who may not, if this fight fails, be dragged away with her daughters to become slaves or endure that which is far worse than slavery.

If the Prussian people themselves cling to their Gods of War, if Kaiser and Crown Prince fulfil their ideals, if the Prussian leave the reins in the hands of these warlike task masters and refuse to join the other peoples in stamping out the devil of war, then the conflict must go on, go on until the Germans get their stomachs full of war, until they forget their easy victories of the last century, until their leaders learn that war as a national industry does not pay, until their wealth and their trade has disappeared, until their sons are maimed and killed and their land laid waste, until the blinders fall from their eyes and they sicken of Emperor and Crown Prince, of the almost countless Kings and Grand Dukes and Princes, Generals and Admirals, Court Marshals and Chamberlains and Majors and Adjutants, Captains and Lieutenants, who now, like fat, green, distended flies, feed on the blood of Germany. What is there in war for any one but those men of froth at the top? It is this infernal king business that is responsible; so much of the king tradition is bound up with war that a king with power feels that he is untrue to the traditions of his ancestors if he fails at some period of his career to give the court painters and the court poets and the court historians a chance to portray him as a successful warrior.

The British air minister recently announced that reprisal raids were to be made on German towns. Who is not sorry for the poor people who may suffer, but the war must be brought home to them. They have made no protest while Zeppelins killed babies and women and children in the "fortress" of London. The "fortress" of London, indeed! First the Germans attack an open town, contrary to every rule, and then, when guns are mounted to ward off future attacks, the Germans christen the town a "fortress" and claim the right to continue this slaughter of non-combatants.

Postcards were sold and eagerly bought all over Germany showing the Zeppelins bombing towns. When some German father sits by the hospital bed of his dying daughter, who sobs out her life torn with a fatal wound, let him tack one of these postcards over the bed and in looking on it remember that "he who lives by the sword shall perish by the sword," that it was at the command of the Kaiser and the Crown Prince when they thought only the German Zeppelins could make a successful air raid that these massacres were ordered and that the German people at the time yelled their approval of deliberate dastardly murder.

"Te Deum" has been always the favorite psalm sung in cathedrals for all Christian conquerors, but neither psalms nor the paid pastor's praises of the Emperor will satisfy the German people, who have made awful sacrifices for intangible victories.

TOPICS FOR WRITTEN AND ORAL DISCUSSION

1. Select a controversial international story and find as many different kinds of news coverage of this story as you can. Using sources from the Internet will enhance your ability to find international sources. Write an essay describing the different spins the various sources use in developing the story.

2. What are the most important advances in technology today that would dominate the contemporary battlefield? Write an essay speculating how this technology would work in an imaginary war scenario.

3. Research the use of technology during both Persian Gulf Wars. Write an essay describing how U.S. technology totally outgunned the limited technology of the Iraqi government during both conflicts.

4. Despite the rapid advances in technology, battlefield casualties have decreased since the end of World War I. Although World War II had more casualties overall, the death rate of the individual soldier compared to the total number under arms decreased. Since World War II, the chances of dying on the battlefield have notably decreased among the North American and European armies. Research and write an essay about this decrease.

NOTES

1. Leo Braudy, *From Chivalry to Terrorism: War and the Changing Nature of Masculinity* (New York: Knopf, 2003).
2. Aaron Delwiche, "Of Fraud and Forces Woven: Domestic Propaganda during the First World War," FirstWorldWar.com (accessed 11 August 2001).
3. Ibid.
4. Niall Ferguson, *The Pity of War* (New York: Basic Books, 1998), 212.
5. Ferguson, *The Pity*, 232.
6. Ferguson, *The Pity*, 241.
7. FirstWorldWar.com, http://www.firstworldwar.com/airwar/bombers_zeppelins. htm.
8. Ibid.
9. Ibid.
10. FirstWorldWar.com, http://www.firstworldwar.com/bio/watson.htm.

SUGGESTIONS FOR FURTHER READING

Buitenhuis, Peter. *The Great War of Words: British, American, and Canadian Propaganda and Fiction, 1914–1933.* Vancouver: University of British Columbia Press, 1987.
Faulkner, Peter. *Modernism.* London: Methuen, 1977.
Winter, Jay. *The Great War and the British People.* London: Macmillan, 1985.
———. *The Experience of World War I.* London: Macmillan, 1988.

5

Aftermath:

An Analysis of F. Scott Fitzgerald's *Tender Is the Night* (1935), Virginia Woolf's *Mrs. Dalloway* (1925), and Paul West's *Love's Mansion* (1992)

LITERARY ANALYSIS

What are the lingering effects of this horrendous 1914–1918 catastrophe? How much has it cost us? Calculating these costs could almost be a never-ending endeavor. Imagine for a moment that in 1914 the European powers had avoided the bloodshed; there is a good chance that the remainder of the twentieth century would have avoided subsequent bloodshed as well. Europe could have eventually exploded for other reasons, but if World War I had not happened at all, not only would 9 or 10 million soldiers not have died, countless others would have also avoided being wounded, and others would have never experienced shell shock and the other assorted psychological traumas that the war caused. Had World War I not occurred, the Bolsheviks could never have hijacked Russia, so the Cold War would never have warmed up; the great influenza epidemic of 1918–1919 would not have been as severe; Hitler would not have had any reason to stir up postwar resentments because the German economy would never have risen to such high inflationary levels. The imagined possibilities could just go on and on.

However, that war did happen, and we have had to pay a huge price for what just a handful of men were not able to accomplish—to avoid a war that fundamentally changed Western civilization forever. The war to end all wars became the war without end.

Tender Is the Night (1935)

While Fitzgerald drew from several men to create his protagonist Richard Diver, the most significant model was the author himself. Like the man who created him, Diver seems spiritually out of step with the modern world. More than any other aspect, Diver longs for emotional and spiritual connectivity with other human beings; he craves for both a sense of the past and an attachment with the world that is never readily available to him. More than anything else, he possesses an old-fashioned, Romantic (with a capital R) view of the world. Yet World War I was to modernism as humanism was to the Renaissance; it was the engine that fueled dramatic changes in the first 25 years of the twentieth century and demolished romanticism (in all senses of the word) with it. The war, as a by-product of advanced technology and regressive culture, accelerated a sense of disjointedness in the modern world. Primarily, the intense competition for superior military weapons and their indiscriminate use during the war had accelerated cultural changes faster than human beings could psychologically assimilate: a clear manifestation is the number of shell-shocked victims during the war. These psychological effects not only lingered long after the conflict was over, but the psychological damage also spread across various facets of society—affecting combatants and noncombatants alike.

Diver is a psychological barometer for these troubled times. And for Diver it is the speed of change that he finds most confounding in the postwar world. Therefore, time and place become primary issues in the novel. For example, in a famous passage from *Tender Is the Night*, Diver and a group of his friends are visiting the Somme battlefield. That is a matter of fiction. Nine years before this imaginary visit took place, on 1 July 1916, the world literally blew up there, at Beaumont-Hamel, two small villages in the Picardy region of northern France. That is a matter of history. That place, on that date, was a scene of carnage, the Somme's bloody first day, and the world has not been the same since.

On that day, at that place, the 1st Newfoundland Regiment in particular took many casualties. The British plan was for the offensive to start precisely at 0720 hours with a large mine explosion under the German lines, and 10 minutes later, the main assault would go over the top. Why the 10-minute delay in the attack, however? No one today knows for certain, but the results were catastrophic for those who had to face the murderous German machine gun fire. During those 10 minutes after the initial mine explosion, the Germans were able to regroup and pour deadly fire on the advancing Newfoundlanders, resulting in the deaths of hundreds of men in an area no longer than a mile and no wider than the length of two football fields.

In comparison to the 30,000 total British casualties on the Somme that day, it may not seem all that much, but within the span of 30 minutes the 1st Newfoundland Regiment (and there was only one) suffered 90 percent casualties. In his guide to the Beaumont-Hamel sector of the Somme battlefield, Nigel Cave further conceptualizes the butcher's bill:

> The Newfoundland Regiment had suffered horrendously high losses. Every officer that went over the top became a causality—fourteen officers were killed, as were two hundred and nineteen other ranks; twelve officers and three hundred and seventy four other ranks were wounded....On top of these casualties was the ninety-one other ranks who were missing; only sixty eight who had been in the attacking force were unwounded when it came to the roll call. Well over ninety percent that went into the action became casualties.[1]

The population of Newfoundland at the time was only about 250,000 people, and by war's end they had supplied the 1st Newfoundland Regiment with 6,000 troops.[2] No matter how one calculates it, these losses were significant to these people.

In the novel, Diver surveys this same field where so many men had died and suffered and ruminates about the loss. A student of the war, Diver understands precisely what happened on that small field on 1 July 1916, nine years earlier. He knows the human and cultural costs:

> "This land here cost twenty lives a foot that summer," he said to Rosemary. She looked out obediently at the rather bare green plain with it low trees of six years' growth... .
>
> "See that little stream—we could walk to it in two minutes. It took the British a month to walk to it—a whole empire walking very slowly, dying in front and pushing forward behind. And another empire walked very slowly backward a few inches a day, leaving the dead like a million bloody rugs. No Europeans will ever do that again in this generation.
>
> " ...This western front business couldn't be done again, not for a long time. The young men think they could do it but they couldn't. They could fight the first Marne again but not this. This took religion and years of plenty and tremendous sureties and the exact relation that existed between the classes. The Russians and Italians weren't any good on this front. You had to have a whole-souled sentimental equipment going back further than you could remember. You had to remember Christmas, and postcards of the Crown Prince and his fiancée, and little cafés in Valence and beer gardens in Unter den Linden and weddings at the maire, and going to the Derby, and your grandfather's whiskers... .
>
> "All my beautiful lovely safe world blew itself up here with a great gust of high explosive love," Dick mourned persistently.[3]

Diver's elegy about these battlefield losses is full of philosophical regret. As Diver points out, it is events like this that led to such a dramatic and rapid change in cultural history—in the way writers and thinkers viewed the past. In that he has to live in a postwar world at odds with his own sensibilities, Diver's sense of loss is real enough, representing the feelings of the "lost generation"—the group of men and women who survived the war and inherited the tragic cultural aftermath of World War I. Many members of this lost generation not only questioned the values of the past but openly despaired of the future as well. Emotionally and, in many cases, physically bankrupt, the lost generation seemed only to have one philosophy to live by—live hard and die young.

Diver's perspective culminates several years of reading and reflection on the historical catastrophe that World War I had created. At the heart of his despair is that the modern perspective of loss itself profoundly changed after World War I. What Diver is mourning is the loss of a traditional meaning of loss. Whereas before the war, it took centuries for time to bring about the complete ruination of castles, villages, and groups of people, high explosive artillery shells in a matter of minutes could now destroy such things.[4] It is this rapid acceleration of time that has become the spiritual enemy of mankind, which is why time is a major preoccupation of the modern literary and artistic sensibility. The loss of whole villages that had hitherto been unimaginable had become all too commonplace, which not only altered the psychology of a whole generation of people, but also bequeathed cynicism and despair as the birthright of subsequent generations to come.

As was stated in the beginning of this analysis, Diver significantly resembles Fitzgerald. Like Diver, Fitzgerald never faced combat, although he did serve in the U.S. Army during the last years of the war. Also like Diver, Fitzgerald maintained a keen intellectual interest in the war throughout his life; so much so that one of the main regrets of his life was that he did not get over to France. It seemed to have haunted him. Finally, like Diver, Fitzgerald visited the Somme battlefield in the fall of 1925.[5] Looking back, it is fascinating how Fitzgerald's singular, brief visit to this scene of carnage remained such an intense experience for him. In the rich imagination of someone like Fitzgerald, this visit, which probably lasted no more than 30 minutes—the same amount of time it took to lose so many men of the 1st Newfoundland Regiment—would grow into one of the most important passages about the devastations of modern war.

Mrs. Dalloway (1925)

Mrs. Dalloway is set during the summer of 1923, when Clarissa Dalloway decides to go out and "buy the flowers herself" for a dinner party. While this activity seems safe enough, the experiences she encounters along the way are ominously indicative of the lasting effects of the war. Although Clarissa is not capable of interpreting what they mean or even understanding that the war will never really be over, she does, nevertheless, sense the war's troubling residue around her. Woolf writes:

> The War was over, except for some one like Mrs. Foxcroft at the Embassy last night eating her heart out because that nice boy was killed and now the old Manor House must go to a cousin; or Lady Bexborough who opened a bazaar, they said, with the telegram in her hand, John, her favorite killed; but it was over; thank Heaven—over.[6]

What Clarissa does not understand is that while the actual hostilities may be over, the war's effect obviously is not. She is not capable of knowing that the battlefield has shifted to the home front, where the survivors are fighting personal, spiritual, and physical battles against the invisible enemy of despair.

To a weary citizenry, the sights and noise of postwar London resemble a battlefield. The locus of suffering has shifted to a different time and place—away from the battlefield and out of the war—into the time of peace and home. The sounds of war are everywhere. For example, there is the sound and sight of an airplane spelling out the name of a popular candy, an airplane and pilot that would have recently been in aerial combat. There is also the backfire of an automobile, a noise described in the novel as a "pistol shot," which frightens Mrs. Dalloway. It also startles Septimus Warren Smith, a veteran suffering from shattered war nerves. Neither of them initially thinks that the noise is from an automobile; they think it is from a weapon. It may seem like a minor issue, but it is important to recognize that on this particular London street Woolf has the sound of an automobile's backfire unite the consciousness of Mrs. Dalloway and Septimus, the man whose suicide later becomes the talk of Clarissa's party. Although they never personally meet, the point is that their individual and distinctly different experiences of the war have forever united them, without them even knowing it. They are primarily frightened by the same thing—the modern world.

Even someone as conventional, as un-intellectual, yes, as obtuse, as Mrs. Dalloway could sense that the postwar world she lived in was radically different from the one before. The war—more than any other single event—changed social conventions and filled the minds of everyone with images of death, destruction, and pain. More than any other aspect of the novel, Woolf demonstrates that human consciousness fundamentally changed after the war.

Love's Mansion (1992)

While British society obviously suffered during and after the war—the grief for loved ones, significant and lasting—nothing, however, could ever compare to what the soldiers actually experienced. In Paul West's *Love's Mansion,* it is Hilly, Harry's future wife, who knew that Harry had been wounded even before he came home. She felt it, but then again, she had a lot of feelings about things:

> From that stuporous war, Hilly knew he would come home coarsened: war to her was not so much a bloodbath as a degrader, returning men to the habits of their ancestors, lowering their standards of behavior, shifting them from Bach to Sousa. So she expected Harry to come back spitting into the gutter, wiping his nose on his sleeve, cutting potatoes with his fork, holding his cup with both hands, walking on the wrong side of her.[7]

But such suspicions, even as close to the truth as they were, tell more about Hilly, and the social expectations of the times, than anything else:

> This was her mother in her, of course, the ultimate argument against Church Row, where he came from, and never mind how skillful his father was in the mending of bell-ropes, how delicate and crumbly his mother's pastry emerged from her damp, inert hands. After the militarizing of Harry would come his pacifying, the gradual new-honing of his manners, the detoxification of his mind, which Hilly would attempt with coaxing, music, and a diet short on beef. It never occurred to her that, in the extreme convulsions of war, he might have discovered in himself a register of gentleness by which to live ever after. (79)

The narrator of this story is the son of Harry and Hilly (who, like West, is also a novelist). As these observations indicate, the son is very perceptive in that he exposes the essential differences in both his parents' war experiences—the combatant's versus the noncombatant's.

Whereas the changes that Hilly experienced during the war would be more normal, Harry, on the other hand, would undergo a dramatic transformation of personality—all before he turned 20 years of age. Yes, the same Harry may have come home outwardly (although he would be blind in one eye) and while he may be coarsened by his active service, he also returned inwardly softened by his life-and-death exploits. One may not necessarily see the change, but it was there nevertheless. Later, Harry's son would know that there was a difference, but Hilly seemingly could not, would not more likely, recognize the differences. Although she never understood why, Harry's life would always be shaped by an existential disregard for normalcy. It would at times drive his wife to distraction. Harry's novelist son tries to explain: "How could the dogs of war convert him into a peaceable puppy? He would never forget how to site and fire the Vickers gun, but he had learned how to make his brain lie down and sleep. In fact, after the trenches, he would become (and remain) a compulsive washer, but he would also become a little more a Caliban, wild" (79). Here lies the basis of a domestic conflict that would shape the rest of their lives. She would try to force him into social propriety, to soften him without realizing that he had been softened far too much already. Hilly, like so many others like her, could never fully comprehend her veteran husband because she did not know the worst that he knew deep in his shattered bones and mangled eye, indeed, deep in his very soul. After the war, it was a domestic situation played out all over the world.

While none of these novels are necessarily political in approach, each narrative clearly demonstrates how the war changed the psychology of a generation of people and how that led to dramatic changes in all facets of modern life. More than anything else, the anxieties of modern people, reflected in these novels, demanded immediate and often radical change in society, laws, and culture. The poet Ezra Pound's adage to "make it new" not only became the mantra of modernist literature but all of Western civilization as well.

HISTORICAL DOCUMENTS AND CONTEXT

While a complete description of all the personal, social, intellectual, or historical changes that World War I set into motion would be impractical for the scale of this casebook, a representative sample of the most dramatic ones would not. The origins of the communist Soviet Union, the emergence of American idealism on the world stage, the failed creation of the League of Nations, and the origination of the State of Israel were significant developments in the early twentieth century, and World War I initiated them all.

The End of the Russian Romanov Dynasty and the Beginning of Soviet Totalitarianism

At the beginning of hostilities, Russia, with a standing army of 1.4 million men, was considered a formidable military force, in fact, the largest in Europe. Twenty-five percent of the country's national budget went toward military spending. While Russia never seemed to have enough resources to go around, it did have plenty of manpower, but that, too, was not without its unique problems. As Hew Strachan points out:

> Low levels of educational achievement meant that manpower in quantity did not necessarily translate into manpower in quality. Although having an exceptionally low ration of officers to men (1:27, as against 1:21 in Germany), the Russian army was over 4,000 officers below establishment in 1909. The Germany army could keep its officer corps small by dint of its excellent NCOs, mostly drawn from the wealthier peasantry or the lower middle class, and reflecting high levels of national education. In Russia such men were commissioned. Consequently, the Russian army was as short of NCOs as it was of officers....Russian backwardness, therefore, demanded that more resources be devoted to military education, but also dictated that, because so much attention had to be given to basics, the overall level of professional competence would nonetheless remain low. The scale of these structural problems meant that, despite the high levels of military expenditure, Russia was constantly trading off manpower against equipment, or one of them against training; in the desire to improve the first two, the third suffered.[8]

In order for the massive Russian army to succeed, it had to mobilize and transport the army westward very rapidly. Yet Russian infrastructure was anything but modernized. Primarily hindering transportation of the army was the lack of sufficient railway lines. At the time, Russia had the lowest number of railway track per area of land than any other European country and had been forced to reduce investment on railroad construction due to the dramatic increase in military spending.[9] Here is yet another example that modern warfare was more about economics than anything else, and, regrettably, the battlefield was where the great reckoning always occurred.

The war went poorly for Imperial Russia almost from the very beginning. Russia experienced a series of military disasters in 1914. In separate battles at Masurian Lakes and Tannenberg, the Russian army lost 1 million men. Then, in the 1915 Brusilov Offensives, they lost another 2 million.[10] These devastating military defeats destabilized the central Russian government and started the process that would topple the Romanov monarchy. Social unrest and political chaos, as well as corruption in the court—best symbolized by the prominence of the notorious Rasputin—finally forced the abdication of Nicholas on 15 March 1917. When his brother also refused to reign, the Romanov dynasty came to a sudden and unceremonious end.[11] Even before the war had started, Russia was politically unstable, teeming with revolutionaries who wanted to overthrow the czar and eliminate the powerful aristocracy. There had even been an unsuccessful revolution against the czar in 1905.

In the immediate aftermath of the abdication, several contending political affiliations attempted to regain a semblance of governmental order, but working against them all were the Bolsheviks, who wanted complete worker control over the government and the confiscation of all private property, as well as the immediate end of the Russian involvement in the war. Their leader was Vladimir Ilyich Lenin (1870–1924), who had had been in Swiss exile since the 1905 revolution.[12] German operatives helped return Lenin to Russia in the spring of 1917, which marked the beginning of the end not only for the Russian monarchy but for any other form of government except a Soviet one. Lenin and his political ally in the Soviet movement, Leon Trotsky, eventually gained control over the Russian provisional central government, which had been led by Alexander Kerensky, a Moscow lawyer who had been named the prime minister of the Provisional Government.

Kerensky had made the fateful decision for Russia to stay in the war, despite having inherited a government in utter crisis and a war effort in tatters. When Kerensky ordered a new offensive against the Germans, the army revolted in large numbers, which eventually led to the overthrow of the Provisional Government in October 1917 by the Bolshevik Party. Immediately after the overthrow, Lenin and Trotsky began peace negotiations with Germany and the other Central Powers. Trotsky himself went to Brest-Litovsk, the capital city of the Ukraine, "to turn ceasefire into peace."[13] Yet Trotsky would soon learn that the Germans wanted complete control over western Russia, which at the time seemed too high a price for him to accept, so he walked away from the peace talks. Trotsky, however, had no choice but to return. Finally facing the stark realities about the condition of the Russian army, he ultimately had to accept even harsher terms because in the meantime the German army had begun annexing the same territory through military conquest.

The Treaty of Brest-Litovsk was finally signed on 3 March 1918, which officially ended hostilities between these previously warring nations, ceding to Germany about 30 percent of the population that had once been under Russian rule.[14] Despite their success, this treaty actually did little to help the Germans in the long run; their allies soon resented them, and their enemies, the Bolsheviks, never upheld the treaty. In the short term, however, the cessation of warfare on the Eastern Front allowed much-needed troops to be sent to the Western Front, where they reinforced the German army for Operation Michael, their massive and initially successful spring 1918 offensive.

Looking back, the longer-term ramifications of this treaty have far outweighed any other implications. While the negotiating and signing of a separate treaty not only broke Russia away from the Allies, it more importantly marked a dramatic Russian political retreat from the Western world until the end of the century. In essence, despite the harsh terms the Bolsheviks had to swallow, the Treaty of Brest-Litovsk nevertheless legitimized a Soviet form of government.

Despite all of the pomp and circumstance that marked their lives, the end of the Romanovs was anything but ceremonial. On 17 July 1918, members of the Ekaterinburg, Ural, Communist Party murdered the Romanovs. During the middle of the night, 16 July 1917, the Romanov family was awakened and herded into the basement of a house that for several months had been their prison. A group of soldiers came into the room and shot the whole family dead. The Romanovs' bodies were taken to an open pit, dismembered, incinerated, and doused with acid.[15]

Jay Winter and Blaine Baggett, in *The Great War and the Shaping of the Twentieth Century*, describe what happened to them after that:

> Later the remains were buried in a nearby forest. On July 25, 1918 the Czechs took Ekaterinburg, and monarchist officers raced to free the Tsars. But no one found the family or even their bodies. The house itself remained standing, scarred by bullet marks and a destination for pilgrims. In 1977 Boris Yeltsin, First Secretary of the region, ordered the house to be destroyed. The remains of the imperial family were found later and positively identified only in 1994.[16]

Remarkably, neither the German Empire nor the Soviet Union exists today, but the Peace Treaty of Brest-Litovsk, in that it represents much of what was wrong about twentieth-century politics, is an important historical document nonetheless. For example, in only the second article, right after the cessation-of-war clause, the treaty outlaws the use of propaganda against the warring countries, an indication of propaganda's perceived power. Second, and more importantly, unelected representatives of nondemocratic governments cynically decided the fate of millions of people. Boundaries were set, people were divided, and nations were dissolved without any humane consideration whatsoever. This seemingly incautious statement in Article III, "the territories lying to the west of the line agreed upon by the contracting parties which formerly belonged to Russia, will no longer be subject to Russian sovereignty; the line agreed upon is traced on the map submitted as an essential part of this treaty of peace," set a precedent whereby maps perpetually had to be changed, and not because of any reformation of natural geography, but only because of the ambition of a few ruthless men.

FROM PEACE TREATY OF BREST-LITOVSK, 3 MARCH 1918

World War I Document Archive,
http://www.lib.byu.edu/~rdh/wwi/1918/brestlitovsk.html

Article I. Germany, Austria-Hungary, Bulgaria, and Turkey, for the one part, and Russia, for the other part, declare that the state of war between them has ceased. They are resolved to live henceforth in peace and amity with one another.

Article II. The contracting parties will refrain from any agitation or propaganda against the Government or the public and military institutions of the other party. In so far as this obligation devolves upon Russia, it holds good also for the territories occupied by the Powers of the Quadruple Alliance.

Article III. The territories lying to the west of the line agreed upon by the contracting parties which formerly belonged to Russia, will no longer be subject to Russian sovereignty; the line agreed upon is traced on the map submitted as an essential part of this treaty of peace. A Russo-German commission will establish the exact fixation of the line.

No obligations whatever toward Russia shall devolve upon the territories referred to, arising from the fact that they formerly belonged to Russia.

Russia refrains from all interference in the internal relations of these territories. Germany and Austria-Hungary purpose to determine the future status of these territories in agreement with their population.

Article IV. As soon as a general peace is concluded and Russian demobilization is carried out completely Germany will evacuate the territory lying to the east of the line designated in paragraph 1 of Article III, in so far as Article IV does not determine otherwise.

Russia will do all within her power to insure the immediate evacuation of the provinces of eastern Anatolia and their lawful return to Turkey.

. . . . .

Article V. Russia will, without delay, carry out the full demobilization of her army inclusive of those units recently organized by the present Government. Furthermore, Russia will either bring her warships into Russian ports and there detain them until the day of the conclusion of a general peace, or disarm them forthwith. Warships of the States that continue in the state of war with the Powers of the Quadruple Alliance, in so far as they are within Russian sovereignty, will be treated as Russian warships.

. . . . .

Article VI. Russia obligates herself to conclude peace at once with the Ukrainian People's Republic and to recognize the treaty of peace between that State and the Powers of the Quadruple Alliance. The Ukrainian territory will, without delay, be cleared of Russian troops and the Russian Red Guard. Russia is to put an end to all agitation or propaganda against the Government or the public institutions of the Ukrainian People's Republic.

Estonia and Livonia will likewise, without delay, be cleared of Russian troops and the Russian Red Guard. The eastern boundary of Estonia runs, in general along the river Narwa. The eastern boundary of Livonia crosses, in general, lakes Peipus and Pskow, to the southwestern corner of the latter, then across Lake Luban in the direction of Livenhof on the Dvina. Estonia and Livonia will be occupied by a German police force until proper national institutions insure security and until public order has been established. Russia will liberate at once all arrested or deported inhabitants of Estonia and Livonia, and insures the safe return of all deported Estonians and Livonians.

Finland and the Aaland Islands will immediately be cleared of Russian troops and the Russian Red Guard, and the Finnish ports of the Russian fleet and of the Russian naval forces. So long as the ice prevents the transfer of warships into Russian ports, only limited forces will remain on board the warships. Russia is to put an end to all agitation or propaganda against the Government or the public institutions of Finland.

. . . . .

Article VII. In view of the fact that Persia and Afghanistan are free and independent States, the contracting parties obligate themselves to respect the political and economic independence and the territorial integrity of these states.

. . . . .

Article IX. The contracting parties mutually renounce compensation for their war expenses, i.e., of the public expenditures for the conduct of the war, as well as compensation for war losses, i.e., such losses as were caused [by] them and their nationals within the war zones by military measures, inclusive of all requisitions effected in enemy country.

. . . . .

Article XIII. In the interpretation of this treaty, the German and Russian texts are authoritative for the relations between Germany and Russia; the German, the Hungarian, and Russian texts for the relations between Austria-Hungry and Russia; the Bulgarian and Russian texts for the relations between Bulgaria and Russia; and the Turkish and Russian texts for the relations between Turkey and Russia.

. . . . .

In testimony where of the Plenipotentiaries have signed this treaty with their own hand.

Executed in quintuplicate at Brest-Litovsk, March 3, 1918.

The German Empire Falls and the 11 November 1918 Armistice

The political negotiations leading up to the 1918 Armistice were almost as intriguing as those during the opening of the 1914 hostilities. On 25 October 1918, Allied Commander Marshal Foch gathered his three top generals—Pétain, Haig, and Pershing—to his headquarters in Senlis, France, and solicited recommendations about how to advise the civilian Supreme War Council, the Allied political leadership—England's Lloyd George, Italy's Orlando, and France's Clemenceau. Foch was eager to hear what his fellow generals had to say about negotiating an armistice with the Germans.[17]

In her interpretation of these events, Margaret MacMillan writes:

> The Great War had begun with a series of mistakes and it ended in confusion. The Allies (and let us include their Associate the United States in the term) were not expecting victory when it came. Austria-Hungary was visibly collapsing in the summer of 1918, but Germany still looked strong. Allied leaders planned for at least another year of war....The armistice with Germany, the most important and ultimately the most controversial of all, was made in a three-cornered negotiation between the new German government in Berlin, the Allied Supreme War Council in Paris and Wilson in Washington.[18]

The following list of demands by the Allied military and political leadership not only determined what was essential in accepting a permanent cease-fire with Germany, but also set the stage for future negotiations in 1919. Despite what may be interpreted otherwise, Germany's acceptance of these terms was definitely the same as accepting defeat.

During this time, Germany was not only surrendering its military, but surrendering its monarch as well. The end of the Hapsburg monarchy came very quickly in the fall of 1918. With social conditions in Germany deteriorating by the day and their army collapsing almost to the border, Wilhelm had no choice but to abdicate his throne on 9 November 1918, and to seek exile in the Netherlands.[19] It was reported at the time that Emperor Wilhelm II, the last monarchy in Germany, surrendered his sword to a Dutch border guard—not to the king of England or another member of royalty, one of God's appointed representatives on earth—but to a petty bureaucrat. World War I not only forced modern realities on the ordinary citizens of Europe, modernity was thus forced upon their former rulers as well.

FROM THE ARMISTICE DEMANDS, 11 NOVEMBER 1918

World War I Document Archive,
http://www.lib.byu.edu/~rdh/wwi/1918/prearmistice.html

Official release by the German Government, published in the *Kreuz-Zeitung,* November 11, 1918.

The following terms were set by the Allied powers for the Armistice.

1. Effective six hours after signing.

2. Immediate clearing of Belgium, France, Alsace-Lorraine, to be concluded within 14 days. Any troops remaining in these areas to be interned or taken as prisoners of war.

3. Surrender 5000 cannon (chiefly heavy), 30,000 machine guns, 3000 trench mortars, 2000 planes.

4. Evacuation of the left bank of the Rhine, Mayence, Coblence, Cologne, occupied by the enemy to a radius of 30 kilometers deep.

5. On the right bank of the Rhine a neutral zone from 30 to 40 kilometers deep, evacuation within 11 days.

6. Nothing to be removed from the territory on the left bank of the Rhine, all factories, railroads, etc. to be left intact.

7. Surrender of 5000 locomotives, 150,000 railway coaches, 10,000 trucks.

8. Maintenance of enemy occupation troops through Germany.

9. In the East all troops to withdraw behind the boundaries of August 1, 1914, fixed time not given.

10. Renunciation of the Treaties of Brest-Litovsk and Bucharest.

11. Unconditional surrender of East Africa.

12. Return of the property of the Belgian Bank, Russian and Rumanian gold.

13. Return of prisoners of war without reciprocity.

14. Surrender of 160 U-boats, 8 light cruisers, 6 Dreadnoughts; the rest of the fleet to be disarmed and controlled by the Allies in neutral or Allied harbors.

15. Assurance of free trade through the Cattegat Sound; clearance of mine fields and occupation of all forts and batteries, through which transit could be hindered.

16. The blockade remains in effect. All German ships to be captured.

17. All limitations by Germany on neutral shipping to be removed.

18. Armistice lasts 30 days.

Woodrow Wilson's Fourteen Points and the Rise of American Idealism

Many different characteristics have been attributed to Woodrow Wilson over the years, but there is one particular aspect of his character that everyone seems to agree upon, and that was his idealism. Despite the fact that German submarines sank American ships—and many more American lives were lost on ships of other nationalities, such as the *Lusitania*—and that through the Zimmerman telegraph, Germany had tried to coax Mexico to declare war against the United States, Wilson still needed an *ideal* for American boys to fight in the war. On 8 January 1918, Wilson, confident that American intervention would turn the tide, conveyed his principals for the peace that he knew would come. In one year, he would be in Paris personally negotiating the Peace Treaty of Versailles.

In this speech, Wilson's main theme is that the world should be "made safe for every peace-loving nation." It is precisely his tone of fairness and openness in these Fourteen Points—the voice of a reasonable man—that may have caused the most problems with the Allies. The mere fact that it is not about punishing Germany brought consternation to the Allies. While Wilson's lack of anger against Germany—despite the atrocities—disturbed his friends, it brought hope to his enemies. Some would call it New World naiveté; others would call it American idealism, but more would call it hubris.

FROM PRESIDENT WOODROW WILSON'S FOURTEEN POINTS, 8 JANUARY 1918

http://www.lib.byu.edu/~rdh/wwi/1918/14points.html

It will be our wish and purpose that the processes of peace, when they are begun, shall be absolutely open and that they shall involve and permit henceforth no secret understandings of any kind. The day of conquest and aggrandizement is gone by; so is also the day of secret covenants entered into in the interest of particular governments and likely at some unlooked-for moment to upset the peace of the world. It is this happy fact, now clear to the view of every public man whose thoughts do not still linger in an age that is dead and gone, which makes it possible for every nation whose purposes are consistent with justice and the peace of the world to avow nor or at any other time the objects it has in view.

We entered this war because violations of right had occurred which touched us to the quick and made the life of our own people impossible unless they were corrected and the world secure once for all against their recurrence. What we demand in this war, therefore, is nothing peculiar to ourselves. It is that the world be made fit and safe to live in; and particularly that it be made safe for every peace-loving nation which, like our own, wishes to live its own life, determine its own institutions, be assured of justice and fair dealing by the other peoples of the world as against force and selfish aggression. All the peoples of the world are in effect partners in this interest, and for our own part we see very clearly that unless justice be done to others it will not be done to us. The program of the world's peace, therefore, is our program; and that program, the only possible program, as we see it, is this:

I.   Open covenants of peace, openly arrived at, after which there shall be no private international understandings of any kind but diplomacy shall proceed always frankly and in the public view.

II.   Absolute freedom of navigation upon the seas, outside territorial waters, alike in peace and in war, except as the seas may be closed in whole or in part by international action for the enforcement of international covenants.

. . . . .

IV.   Adequate guarantees given and taken that national armaments will be reduced to the lowest point consistent with domestic safety.

V.   A free, open-minded, and absolutely impartial adjustment of all colonial claims, based upon a strict observance of the principle that in determining all such questions of sovereignty the interests of the populations concerned must have equal weight with the equitable claims of the government whose title is to be determined.

VI.   The evacuation of all Russian territory and such a settlement of all questions affecting Russia as will secure the best and freest cooperation of the other nations of the world in obtaining for her an unhampered and unembarrassed opportunity for the independent determination of her own political development and national policy and assure her of a sincere welcome into the society of free nations under institutions of her own choosing; and, more than a welcome, assistance also of every kind that she may need and may herself desire. The treatment accorded Russia by her sister nations in the months to come will be the acid test of their good will, of their comprehension of her needs as distinguished from their own interests, and of their intelligent and unselfish sympathy.

VII.   Belgium, the whole world will agree, must be evacuated and restored, without any attempt to limit the sovereignty, which she enjoys in common with all other free nations. No other single act will serve as this will serve to restore confidence among the nations in the laws which they have themselves set and determined for the government of their relations with one another. Without this healing act the whole structure and validity of international law is forever impaired.

VIII.   All French territory should be freed and the invaded portions restored, and the wrong done to France by Prussia in 1871 in the matter of Alsace-Lorraine, which has unsettled the peace of the world for nearly fifty years, should be righted, in order that peace may once more be made secure in the interest of all.

IX.   A readjustment of the frontiers of Italy should be effected along clearly recognizable lines of nationality.

X.   The peoples of Austria-Hungary, whose place among the nations we wish to see safeguarded and assured, should be accorded the freest opportunity to autonomous development.

XI.   Rumania, Serbia, and Montenegro should be evacuated; occupied territories restored; Serbia accorded free and secure access to the sea; and the relations of the several Balkan states to one another determined by friendly counsel along historically established lines of allegiance and nationality; and international guarantees of the political and economic independence and territorial integrity of the several Balkan states should be entered into.

XII.   The Turkish portion of the present Ottoman Empire should be assured a secure sovereignty, but the other nationalities which are now under Turkish rule should be assured an undoubted security of life and an absolutely unmolested opportunity of autonomous develop-

The Big Four—Lloyd George of Great Britain, Orlando of Italy, Clemenceau of France, Wilson of the United States—at the Paris Peace Conference, 1919. Courtesy of Defense Visual Information Center and the National Archives and Records Administration.

ment, and the Dardanelles should be permanently opened as a free passage to the ships and commerce of all nations under international guarantees.

XIII.   An independent Polish state should be erected which should include the territories inhabited by indisputably Polish populations, which should be assured a free and secure access to the sea, and whose political and economic independence and territorial integrity should be guaranteed by international covenant.

XIV.   A general association of nations must be formed under specific covenants for the purpose of affording mutual guarantees of political independence and territorial integrity to great and small states alike.

· · · · ·

The Treaty of Versailles and the Reality of Modern Politics

Just as the new weapons of war shocked and disoriented the sensibilities of modern soldiers, the realities of twentieth-century politics were similarly discombobulating to the citizens of the world, especially for Germans, who not only lost the war but subsequently lost the peace as well. The great Prussian military philosopher Clauswitz once stated that war is "nothing but a continuation of politics with the admixture of other means."[20] However, in the immediate postwar period, politics became nothing but a continuation of war—thus, a means of destruction unto itself. Whereas the Allies were not able to annihilate the Germans militarily during the war, they (especially England, France, and Italy) were going to do their best to destroy their old enemy after it.

No one document in the last century better exemplifies this concept of political warfare than the Peace Treaty of Versailles. In *1919: The Year Our World Began,* William Klingaman summarizes the situation:

> The world broke in two in 1919. Like a ghost that lingered past the appointed hour, the nineteenth century—with its essential orderliness, its self-confidence, and its faith in human progress—had tarried until August 1914, when the major European powers suffered a collective attack of muddleheadedness that led directly to the senseless slaughter of millions of the best young men of a generation. Four and a half years later, as the world tried to pick up the pieces after the wrenching cataclysm of the Great War, it became apparent to many (but by no means all) contemporary observers that the last remaining vestiges of the old order had been swept away, and that mankind had entered a new age that was considerably less rational and less forgiving of human imperfections.[21]

From 18 January 1919, to the signing of the Peace Treaty of Versailles on 28 June 1919, the great political powers of the world convened in Paris to negotiate a lasting peace with Germany. Woodrow Wilson himself attended the Paris conference and personally negotiated for the United States. He was primarily interested in the formation of a League of Nations.

If Wilson's Fourteen Points would have remained the guiding principle of the Treaty of Versailles—especially concerning the establishment of the Covenant of the League of Nations—then the treaty would have been anything but about "realpolitiks." Wilson essentially wanted to change the course of history by establishing a group of nations that would work out their differences civilly—without having to resort to warfare. Such a league could reasonably work out any problems. As such, the influence of American idealism is evident from the very beginning of this treaty. Of course, the very first social covenant or compact among a group of equal people occurred on the *Mayflower,* in a document the Puritans wrote before landing on their Promised Land. In essence, this documents asserts that with God's help the world can be redeemed. A portion of the "Mayflower Compact" states that:

> Having undertaken for the Glory of God, and Advancement of the Christian Faith, and the Honor of our King and Country, a voyage to plant the first colony in the northern parts of Virginia; do by these presents, solemnly and mutually in

the Presence of God and one of another, covenant and combine ourselves together into a civil Body Politick, for our better Ordering and Preservation, and Furtherance of the Ends aforesaid; And by Virtue hereof to enact, constitute, and frame, such just and equal Laws, Ordinances, Acts, Constitutions and Offices, from time to time, as shall be thought most meet and convenient for the General good of the Colony; unto which we promise all due submission and obedience.[22]

The idea of a covenant is, thus, rooted in the New World, and the end of World War I offered America the opportunity to reform the Old World not only by its vast economic resources but by America's political vision and history as well, which is in the very heart of the first 30 articles of the treaty.

Margaret MacMillan describes Wilson's adamant desire to establish the League of Nations: "In Paris, Wilson insisted on chairing the League commission, because for him the League of Nations was the centerpiece of the peace settlement.... It was a pledge that humanity was making to itself, a covenant."[23] However, before the Treaty was finally negotiated, the 410 other articles in the treaty eviscerated the first 30. MacMillan writes that ultimately the League of Nations was such a disastrous failure, the "United States never managed to join at all. So great was the taint of failure that when the powers contemplated a permanent association of nations during the Second World War, they decided to set up a completely new United Nations. The League was officially pronounced dead in 1946. It had ceased to count at all in 1939."[24]

FROM PEACE TREATY OF VERSAILLES, ARTICLES 1–30 AND ANNEX OF THE COVENANT OF THE LEAGUE OF NATIONS, 28 JUNE 1919

THE HIGH CONTRACTING PARTIES, In order to promote international cooperation and to achieve international peace and security by the acceptance of obligations not to resort to war by the prescription of open, just and honorable relations between nations by the firm establishment of the understandings of international law as the actual rule of conduct among Governments, and by the maintenance of justice and a scrupulous respect for all treaty obligations in the dealings of organized peoples with one another Agree to this Covenant of the League of Nations.

Article 1.

The original Members of the League of Nations shall be those of the Signatories which are named in the Annex to this Covenant and also such of those other States named in the Annex as shall accede without reservation to this Covenant. Such accession shall be effected by a Declaration deposited with the Secretariat within two months of the coming into force of the Covenant Notice thereof shall be sent to all other Members of the League. Any fully self-governing State, Dominion, or Colony not named in the Annex may become a Member of the League if its admission is agreed to by two-thirds of the Assembly provided that it shall give effective guarantees of its sincere intention to observe its international obligations, and shall accept such regulations as may be prescribed by the League in regard to its military, naval, and air forces and armaments. Any Member of the League may, after two years' notice of its intention so to do, withdraw from the League, provided that all its international obligations and all its obligations under this Covenant shall have been fulfilled at the time of its withdrawal.

. . . . .

Article 3.

The Assembly shall consist of Representatives of the Members of the League. The Assembly shall meet at stated intervals and from time to time as occasion may require at the Seat of the League or at such other place as may be decided upon. The Assembly may deal at its meetings with any matter within the sphere of action of the League or affecting the peace of the world. At meetings of the Assembly each Member of the League shall have one vote, and may not have more than three Representatives.

Article 4.

The Council shall consist of Representatives of the Principal Allied and Associated Powers, together with Representatives of four other Members of the League. These four Members of the League shall be selected by the Assembly from time to time in its discretion. Until the appointment of the Representatives of the four Members of the League first selected by the Assembly, Representatives of Belgium, Brazil, Spain, and Greece shall be members of the Council. With the approval of the majority of the Assembly, the Council may name additional Members of the League whose Representatives shall always be members of the Council; the Council with like approval may increase the number of Members of the League to be selected by the Assembly for representation on the Council. The Council shall meet from time to time as occasion may require, and at least once a year, at the Seat of the League, or at such other place as may be decided upon. The Council may deal at its meetings with any matter within the sphere of action of the League or affecting the peace of the world. Any Member of the League not represented on the Council shall be invited to send a Representative to sit as a member at any meeting of the Council during the consideration of matters specially affecting the interests of that Member of the League. At meetings of the Council, each Member of the League represented on the Council shall have one vote, and may have not more than one Representative.

. . . . .

Article 6.

The permanent Secretariat shall be established at the Seat of the League. The Secretariat shall comprise a Secretary General and such secretaries and staff as may be required. The first Secretary General shall be the person named in the Annex; thereafter the Secretary General shall be appointed by the Council with the approval of the majority of the Assembly. The secretaries and staff of the Secretariat shall be appointed by the Secretary General with the approval of the Council. The Secretary General shall act in that capacity at all meetings of the Assembly and of the Council. The expenses of the Secretariat shall be borne by the Members of the League in accordance with the apportionment of the expenses of the International Bureau of the Universal Postal Union.

. . . . .

Article 8.

The Members of the League recognize that the maintenance of peace requires the reduction of national armaments to the lowest point consistent with national safety and the enforcement by common action of international obligations. The Council, taking account of the geographical situation and circumstances of each State, shall formulate plans for such reduction for the consideration and action of the several Governments. Such plans shall be subject to reconsideration and revision at least every ten years. After these plans shall have been adopted by the several Governments, the limits of armaments therein fixed shall not be exceeded without the concurrence of the Council. The Members of the League agree that the manufacture by private enterprise of munitions and implements of war is open to grave objections. The Council shall advise how the evil effects attendant upon such manufacture can be prevented, due regard being had to the necessities of those Members of the League which are not able to manufacture the munitions and implements of war necessary for their safety. The Members of the League undertake to interchange full and frank information as to the scale of their armaments, their military, naval, and air programmers and the condition of such of their industries as are adaptable to war-like purposes.

. . . . .

Article 10.

The Members of the League undertake to respect and preserve as against external aggression the territorial integrity and existing political independence of all Members of the League. In case of any such aggression or in case of any threat or danger of such aggression the Council shall advise upon the means by which this obligation shall be fulfilled.

Article 11.

Any war or threat of war, whether immediately affecting any of the Members of the League or not, is hereby declared a matter of concern to the whole League, and the League shall take any action that may be deemed wise and effectual to safeguard the peace of nations. In case any such emergency should arise the Secretary

General shall on the request of any Member of the League forthwith summon a meeting of the Council. It is also declared to be the friendly right of each Member of the League to bring to the attention of the Assembly or of the Council any circumstance whatever affecting international relations which threatens to disturb international peace or the good understanding between nations upon which peace depends.

Article 12.

The Members of the League agree that if there should arise between them any dispute likely to lead to a rupture, they will submit the matter either to arbitration or to inquiry by the Council, and they agree in no case to resort to war until three months after the award by the arbitrators or the report by the Council. In any case under this Article the award of the arbitrators shall be made within a reasonable time, and the report of the Council shall be made within six months after the submission of the dispute.

Article 13.

The Members of the League agree that whenever any dispute shall arise between them which they recognize to be suitable for submission to arbitration and which cannot be satisfactorily settled by diplomacy, they will submit the whole subject-matter to arbitration. Disputes as to the interpretation of a treaty, as to any question of international law, as to the existence of any fact which if established would constitute a breach of any international obligation, or as to the extent and nature of the reparation to be made or any such breach, are declared to be among those which are generally suitable for submission to arbitration. For the consideration of any such dispute the court of arbitration to which the case is referred shall be the Court agreed on by the parties to the dispute or stipulated in any convention existing between them. The Members of the League agree that they will carry out in full good faith any award that may be rendered, and that they will not resort to war against a Member of the League which complies therewith. In the event of any failure to carry out such an award, the Council shall propose what steps should be taken to give effect thereto.

. . . . .

Article 16.

Should any Member of the League resort to war in disregard of its covenants under Articles 12, 13, or 15, it shall ipso facto be deemed to have committed an act of war against all other Members of the League, which hereby undertake immediately to subject it to the severance of all trade or financial relations, the prohibition of all intercourse between their nationals and the nationals of the covenant-breaking State, and the prevention of all financial, commercial, or personal intercourse between the nationals of the covenant-breaking State and the nationals of any other State, whether a

Member of the League or not. It shall be the duty of the Council in such case to recommend to the several Governments concerned what effective military, naval, or air force the Members of the League shall severally contribute to the armed forces to be used to protect the covenants of the League. The Members of the League agree, further, that they will mutually support one another in the financial and economic measures which are taken under this Article, in order to minimize the loss and inconvenience resulting from the above measures, and that they will mutually support one another in resisting any special measures aimed at one of their number by the covenant breaking State, and that they will take the necessary steps to afford passage through their territory to the forces of any of the Members of the League which are co-operating to protect the covenants of the League. Any Member of the League, which has violated any covenant of the League, may be declared to be no longer a Member of the League by a vote of the Council concurred in by the Representatives of all the other Members of the League represented thereon.

. . . . .

Article 18.

Every treaty or international engagement entered into hereafter by any Member of the League shall be forthwith registered with the Secretariat and shall as soon as possible be published by it. No such treaty or international engagement shall be binding until so registered.

Article 19.

The Assembly may from time to time advise the reconsideration by Members of the League of treaties which have become inapplicable and the consideration of international conditions whose continuance might endanger the peace of the world.

Article 20.

The Members of the League severally agree that this Covenant is accepted as abrogating all obligations or understandings inter se which are inconsistent with the terms thereof, and solemnly undertake that they will not hereafter enter into any engagements inconsistent with the terms thereof. In case any Member of the League shall, before becoming a Member of the League, have undertaken any obligations inconsistent with the terms of this Covenant, it shall be the duty of such Member to take immediate steps to procure its release from such obligations.

Article 21.

Nothing in this Covenant shall be deemed to affect the validity of international engagements, such as treaties of arbitration or regional understandings like the Monroe doctrine, for securing the maintenance of peace.

. . . . .

Article 23.

Subject to and in accordance with the provisions of international conventions existing or hereafter to be agreed upon, the Members of the League: (a) will endeavor to secure and maintain fair and humane conditions of labor for men, women, and children, both in their own countries and in all countries to which their commercial and industrial relations extend, and for that purpose will establish and maintain the necessary international organizations; (b) undertake to secure just treatment of the native inhabitants of territories under their control; (c) will entrust the League with the general supervision over the execution of agreements with regard to the traffic in women and children, and the traffic in opium and other dangerous drugs; (d) will entrust the League with the general supervision of the trade in arms and ammunition with the countries in which the control of this traffic is necessary in the common interest; (e) will make provision to secure and maintain freedom of communications and of transit and equitable treatment for the commerce of all Members of the League. In this connection, the special necessities of the regions devastated during the war of 1914–1918 shall be borne in mind; (f) will endeavor to take steps in matters of international concern for the prevention and control of disease.

. . . . .

Article 25.

The Members of the League agree to encourage and promote the establishment and co-operation of duly authorized voluntary national Red Cross organizations having as purposes the improvement of health, the prevention of disease, and the mitigation of suffering throughout the world.

Article 26.

Amendments to this Covenant will take effect when ratified by the Members of the League whose representatives compose the Council and by a majority of the Members of the League whose Representatives compose the Assembly. No such amendment shall bind any Member of the League which signifies its dissent there from, but in that case it shall cease to be a Member of the League.

Annex.

I. ORIGINAL MEMBERS OF THE LEAGUE OF NATIONS SIGNATORIES OF THE TREATY OF PEACE.

UNITED STATES OF AMERICA, BELGIUM, BOLIVIA, BRAZIL, BRITISH EMPIRE, CANADA, AUSTRALIA, SOUTH AFRICA, NEW ZEALAND, INDIA, CHINA, CUBA, ECUADOR, FRANCE, GREECE, GUATEMALA, HAITI, HEDJAZ, HONDURAS, ITALY, JAPAN, LIBERIA, NICARAGUA, PANAMA, PERU, POLAND, PORTUGAL, ROUMANIA, SERB-CROAT-SLOVENE STATE, SIAM, CZECHO-SLOVAKIA, URUGUAY STATES INVITED TO ACCEDE TO THE COVENANT.

ARGENTINE REPUBLIC, CHILE, COLOMBIA, DENMARK, NETHER-LANDS, NORWAY, PARAGUAY, PERSIA, SALVADOR, SPAIN, SWEDEN, SWITZERLAND, VENEZUELA.
II. FIRST SECRETARY GENERAL OF THE LEAGUE OF NATIONS.
The Honorable Sir James Eric Drummond, K.C.M.G., C.B.

. . . . .

Article 30.

In the case of boundaries which are defined by a waterway, the terms "course" and "channel" used in the present Treaty signify: in the case of non-navigable rivers, the median line of the waterway or of its principal arm, and, in the case of navigable rivers, the median line of the principal channel of navigation It will rest with the Boundary Commissions provided by the present Treaty to specify in each case whether the frontier line shall follow any changes of the course or channel which may take place or whether it shall be definitely fixed by the position of the course or channel at the time when the present Treaty comes into force.

Lord Balfour's Declaration of Jewish Statehood

Although Israel did not become a nation until 1948, political considerations for such a formation largely began during World War I. Arthur James Lord Balfour, a Conservative member of Parliament, who served as First Lord of the Admiralty and British Foreign Secretary during the war, was the first government official of any nation to publicly call for the formation of a Jewish nation state.[25] While serving as British Foreign Secretary, he wrote his now famous declaration in a letter to Lord Rothschild, a prominent Jewish leader of the Zionist movement. Throughout the war, British policy formulated the idea of a Jewish state in Palestine as a means to encourage Jews in both Russia and the United States to support the Allied efforts against Germany.[26] This letter was the first public indication that the British government had even formulated such an idea, which proved to be influential when forming a Jewish state gathered international support after World War II. Tragically, it took the 6 million Jews who lost their lives in the Holocaust to make the idea a reality.

FROM THE BALFOUR DECLARATION, 1917

http://www.yale.edu/lawweb/avalon/mideast/balfour.htm

November 2nd, 1917
    Dear Lord Rothschild,
    I have much pleasure in conveying to you, on behalf of His Majesty's Government, the following declaration of sympathy with Jewish Zionist aspirations that has been submitted to, and approved by, the Cabinet.

Aisne-Marne American Cemetery at Bellau Wood, France. Courtesy of Defense Visual Information Center and the National Archives and Records Administration.

"His Majesty's Government view with favor the establishment in Palestine of a national home for the Jewish people, and will use their best endeavors to facilitate the achievement of this object, it being clearly understood that nothing shall be done which may prejudice the civil and religious rights of existing non-Jewish communities in Palestine, or the rights and political status enjoyed by Jews in any other country."

I should be grateful if you would bring this declaration to the knowledge of the Zionist Federation.

Yours sincerely,

Arthur James Balfour

Honoring the Dead

During the decade following World War I, the need to memorialize the dead, the missing, and the unknown became a pressing social issue, primarily because for the first time in history casualty figures reached 9 to 10 million people dead. Almost half of these bodies were never found and properly buried.

As an indication of just how many memorials have been created, the Imperial War Museum recently started a 10-year process to count the number of war memorials in the United Kingdom. So far, they estimate that there are as many as 54,000 different war memorials in total, in which the majority of them commemorate World Wars I and II.[27] Concerning World War I alone, there are several representative memorials throughout the world: Newfoundland Memorial Park, at Beaumont Hamel, France; the Cenotaph, on London's Whitehall; the Menin Gate, in Ypres, Belgium; the Theipval Memorial to the Missing, on the Somme battlefield in France; the Verdun Memorial Battlefield, in particular the Douaumont Ossuary, where resides the remains of 120,000 unknown French and German soldiers who died at Verdun; and the Liberty Memorial, in Kansas City, Missouri.

To honor its dead and missing, the U.S. Congress established the American Battle Monuments Commission in March 1923 at the urging of General John J. Pershing, who was named its first commissioner by President Warren G. Harding. General Pershing was subsequently elected chairman of the commissioners, a position that he faithfully held until his death in 1948. Public Law 389 of the 66th Congress provided legislation for final dispositions of individual American World War I remains.[28] There are 30,921 American soldiers of World War I buried on foreign soil, in eight different cemeteries scattered throughout Western Europe. The American Battle Monuments Commission is solely responsible for the upkeep of these graves.

It is important for the living to know their brave soldiers will rest in peace forever.

TOPICS FOR WRITTEN AND ORAL DISCUSSION

1. "Over the top" is one phrase that came from the war, but there are many more that have common usage in today's vocabulary. Make a list of more and discuss their various usages today.

2. Locate several different maps from the last several decades and trace the changing boundaries of Europe since the beginning of World War I. List them and choose a specific area for further research. Find out about their culture and history and discuss in it class.

3. Debate this issue: The establishment of the United Nations has helped maintain peace in the world.

4. Debate this issue: whether Woodrow Wilson was a great advocate of American idealism and world peace or he was a cynical politician, a failed president with a large ego.

5. Get an appointment and visit the psychological clinic in a veteran's hospital in your area and discuss with them some of the mental problems that they see in their patients. Determine how much of it is due to their combat experiences. Are there common manifestations of their problems? Can noncombatants show signs of these problems as well? Calculate the costs of their treatment.

6. Visit a nearby military cemetery. Randomly identify the units of some of the soldiers that are buried there and research the history of that unit and the battles and wars that they fought in. If you have the opportunity, research the records of those soldiers and their units in the National Archives. Write a report on what you have discovered. Also, do charcoal rubbings on some of the grave makers. Display them in your classroom. Think about what they sacrificed and why. Discuss it in class.

NOTES

1. Nigel Cave, *Somme: Beaumont Hamel: Newfoundland Park* (London: Leo Cooper, 1994), 71.

2. Cave, *Somme*, 57.

3. F. Scott Fitzgerald, *Tender Is the Night* (New York: Charles Scribner's Sons, 1934), 56–57.

4. For a fuller explanation of Fitzgerald's vision of the post–World War I modern landscape and what it means, see James H. Meredith, "Fitzgerald and War," in *A Historical Guide to F. Scott Fitzgerald,* ed. Kirk Curnutt (Oxford: University of Oxford Press, 2004).

5. Matthew Bruccoli, *Some Sort of Epic Grandeur: The Life of F. Scott Fitzgerald* (New York: Carroll & Graf, 1993), 284.

6. Virginia Woolf, *Mrs. Dalloway,* edited by Stella McNichol and introduction and notes by Elaine Showalter (London: Penguin Classics, 2000), 4–5.

7. Paul West, *Love's Mansion* (New York: Random House, 1992), 79. All subsequent citations are from this text and page numbers are indicated parenthetically.

8. Hew Strachan, *The First World War: To Arms,* vol. 1 (Oxford: Oxford University Press, 2001), 299.

9. Strachan, *The First World War,* 298.

10. Stephen Pope and Elizabeth-Anne Wheal, *The Macmillan Dictionary of the First World War* (London: Macmillan, 1997), 406.

11. Pope and Wheal, *Dictionary,* 408.

12. Pope and Wheal, *Dictionary,* 284.

13. Jay Winter and Blaine Baggett, *The Great War and the Shaping of the 20th Century* (New York: Penguin, 1996), 273.

14. Pope and Wheal, *Dictionary,* 82–83.

15. Winter and Baggett, *Great War,* 324.

16. Ibid.

17. John S. D. Eisenhower, *Yanks: The Epic Story of the American Army in World War I* (New York: Free Press, 2001), 274.

18. Margaret MacMillan, *Paris 1919: Six Months that Changed the World* (New York: Random House, 2001), 19.

19. FirstWorldWar.com, "Who's Who: Kaiser Wilhelm II," http://www.firstworldwar.com/bio/wilhelmii.htm.

20. David G. Chandler, "The Art of War on Land," *RALPH: The Review of Arts, Literature, Philosophy and the Humanities,* 25(2) (Spring 2001), http://www.ralphmag.org/AP/land-war.html.

21. William Klingaman, *1919: The Six Months that Changed the World* (New York: St. Martin's, 1987).

22. The University of Oklahoma Law Center, "The Mayflower Compact," http://www.law.ou.edu/hist/mayflow.html.

23. MacMillan, *Paris 1919,* 85.

24. MacMillan, *Paris 1919,* 83.

25. FirstWorldWar.com, "Who's Who: Arthur Balfour," http://www.firstworldwar.com/bio/balfour.htm.

26. Ibid.

27. "History of Memorialisation." Imperial War Museum, http://www.iwm.org.uk/collections/niwm/history_memorials.pdf.

28. These facts were provided by *American Memorials and Overseas Military Cemeteries,* a publication of the American Battle Monuments Commission, Court House Plaza II, Suite 500, 2300 Clarendon Boulevard, Arlington, VA 22201.

SUGGESTIONS FOR FURTHER READING

Holt, Tonie, and Valmai Holt. *Major and Mrs. Holt's Battlefield Guide to the Somme.* London: Leo Cooper, 1998.

Klingaman, William. *1919: The Year Our World Began.* New York: St. Martin's Press, 1987.

Levenback, Karen L. *Virginia Woolf and the Great War.* Syracuse, N.Y.: Syracuse University Press, 1999.

Tate, Trudi. *Modernism, History, and the First World War.* Manchester, England: Manchester University Press, 1998.

Winter, Jay. *Sites of Memory, Sites of Mourning: The Great War in European Cultural History.* Cambridge: Cambridge University Press, 1998.

Index

About the Author

JAMES H. MEREDITH is a former Lieutenant Colonel and professor of English at the United States Air Force Academy. He has served on several Literary Society boards, and frequently writes on such literary figures as Fitzgerald, Hemingway, Stephen Crane, and Joseph Heller. He also writes on such historic figures and topics as Theodore Roosevelt, the American Civil War, and World War II. He is the author of *Understanding the Literature of World War II* (Greenwood, 1999).